OP 87/8

Santa Clara
County
Free Library

REFERENCE

SPANISH AND MEXICAN LAND GRANTS
IN THE CHIHUAHUAN ACQUISITION

NUMERO 16.

EL ciudadano José Joaquin Calvo, Gobernador y Comandante General del Estado de Chihuahua, á todos sus habitantes sabed: que el
Congreso del Estado há decretado lo que sigue.

El Congreso Constitucional del Estado de Chihuahua há tenido á bien ratificar y confirmar la
consesion hecha por el Alcalde Constitucional
de Presidio del Norte, el dia 25 del mes de Ene-
ro de 1832, mercenándole al Señor Don José Ygnacio Ronquillo Teniente Coronel del Ejército
activo, ciertas tierras, pastos y minerales situa-
dos al lado isquierdo del Rio Bravo del Norte,
al frente dé Presidio del Norte.

Lo tendrá entendido el Gobernador del Estado
y dispondrá se imprima, publique, circule y que
tengá su debido cuplimiento.—*Jose de Jesus Mu-
ñoz.*—Diputado Presidente.—*Juan Maria Ponce
de Leon.*—Diputado Secretario.—*Juan Jose Es-
carcega.*—Diputado Secretario.

Por tanto, mando se imprima, publique, circule y se cumpla en todas sus partes.

Palacio del Gobierno del Estado, Chihuahua
Septiembre 24 de 1834,

José J. Calvo,   *Luis Zuloaga.*
                                   Oficial mayor.

The Santa Barbara Decree   [See page 203]

Spanish and Mexican
Land Grants
in the
Chihuahuan Acquisition

BY

J. J. BOWDEN

~

289329

TEXAS WESTERN PRESS

THE UNIVERSITY OF TEXAS AT EL PASO

——————— *1971* ———————

Dust Jacket Illustration by

José Cisneros

Library of Congress Catalog Card No. 76-170985

ISBN NO. 0-87404-031-0

To

Dr. John L. Waller

who first sparked my interest in the history of the Spanish and Mexican Land Grants, and my family and friends, who have encouraged and have sustained me in this long endeavor.

C O N T E N T S

MAPS

[x]

PREFACE

● THE WRITTEN HISTORY OF MANKIND, nations and institutions generally reflects economic, social, political, geographical and environmental conditions, or a combination thereof, but few studies have seriously considered a fundamental element required in the development of an orderly society — the direct or indirect influence of land.

Land has played an important role in man's life since the inception of written records, and will continue to play such a role as long as man lives on and from the earth. the "Public Domain," in one sense, is like any natural resource in that once appropriated, it is forever depleted; however, land history continues, and can never be finally written. The history of land is not only the story of its ownership, but is also the record of the rise and decline of individuals and sovereigns having jurisdiction.

The records of land ownership, being of prime importance to society, have been carefully and painstakingly preserved in archives throughout the world. In these repositories lies a fertile field of primary historical data. These records contain the names, dates, and events that should be relied upon in the gathering of data for the history books of the future.

Many manuscripts, newspaper articles and books have been written on the history of far West Texas and New Mexico. These, however, have only scratched the surface. The cream of easily obtained facts has been skimmed off and compiled in these generally known works. Tedious scientific historical digging must now begin. The stories of the founding of Jamestown and Plymouth have been fully and scientifically told, but their Southwestern counterparts of Santa Fe and El Paso del Norte are still far from complete. While much early history of the Southwest, and particularly the area around El Paso, Texas, has been lost by the passage of time, a great deal remains to be learned from various state archives and official records.

In this atomic age, specialists in land matters (surveyors, attorneys and petroleum landmen) are generally too pressed for time to write the histories of the lands with which they are so intimately familiar, and those who have the interest and time have not been encouraged to do so by historians. Many of these land specialists feel that no one is particularly interested in the facts that they have tediously assembled in their work. Ordinarily, they are right, for local histories have no widespread general demand, and certainly these specialists could not be adequately compensated monetarily by publication of their knowledge pertaining to specific lands. Likewise, the amateur historian who is interested in a certain aspect of local history usually does not have the training to work in depositories of original land records and to assemble and analyze the facts obtainable therefrom. Therefore, for the historical data contained in these depositories to be brought forth and incorporated in this proper niche in the over-all history, the "labor of love" usually falls upon those few who have the time and courage to do the thankless job.

The history of the twenty-six private land claims located within the Chihuahuan Acquisition affords an excellent insight into how the United States and Texas have met their obligations to grantees holding valid pre-existing grants within an area obtained from a foreign sovereign. Although Texas probably acquired its portion of the Chihuahuan Acquisition un-encumbered by express treaty obligations, it consistently followed the principle of international law requiring a successor sovereign to recognize valid land titles. However, the uncertainties already experienced by those citizens holding inchoate Mexican grants in Texas caused Mexico to insist on the insertion of two provisions in the Treaty of Guadalupe Hidalgo.

Article VIII granted all Mexicans residing in the ceded territory the right to retain their Mexican citizenship. Mexican citizens could either remain in the ceded area or emigrate at any time to Mexico. The property rights of Mexicans not established in the ceded area were to be "inviolably respected," while the property rights of Mexicans who remained in the affected area, whether or not they elected to retain their Mexican citizen-ship, were to be protected to the same extent as those of citizens of the United States. Article X was designed to protect a number of inchoate grants located within the ceded area and Texas. These grants had been made by Mexico in due course, but, as a result of the outbreak of either the Texas Revolution or the Mexican War, the grantees had been prevented from timely performing the conditions precedent to which they had been made. This article required recognition of such grants to the same extent as if the territory within which they were located had remained in Mexico. It also provided that the time for the performance of such conditions should commence on the date of the exchange of ratifications of the treaty.

The United States Senate, by a vote of 38 to 14, ratified the treaty on March 10, 1848, with a minimum of changes. One was the deletion of Article X in its entirety, an act which naturally aroused the suspicions of the Mexican government. Notwithstanding its desperate situation, of being exhausted by war and having a foreign and hostile flag flying over its capital, Mexico insisted on solemn assurances from the American commis-sioners that vested private land claims of her citizens in the ceded territory would be recognized and protected by the United States. As a result of this firm stand, a supplemental document called a *protocol* was made be-tween the two countries on July 26, 1848, which, for all interests and pur-poses became a part of the treaty. The United States Commissioners agreed that "these grants, notwithstanding the suppressions of the Article of the treaty, preserve the legal value which they may possess, and the grantees may cause their legitimate titles to be acknowledged before the American tribunals." To transfer additional territory and permanently solve the boundary dispute which had arisen as a result of the ambiguities contained in the description of the land ceded by the Treaty of Guadalupe Hidalgo, the United States and Mexico entered into the Gadsden Treaty on December 30, 1853. Article VI of the Gadsden Treaty touched on the question of private land claims in the ceded area:

No grants of land within the territory ceded by the first article of this treaty, bearing date subsequent to the twenty-fifth day of September, when the minister and subscriber of this treaty on the part of the United States proposed to the government of Mexico to terminate the question of boundary, will be considered valid, or be recognized by the United States, nor will any grant made previously be respected, or be considered as obligatory, which have not been located and duly recorded in the archives of Mexico.

After the Treaty of Guadalupe Hidalgo and the Gadsden Purchase, the United States and Texas were confronted with the serious problem of determining and recognizing the validity of land claims located in the areas obtained from Mexico. From the outset it was recognized that three distinct types of grants had been made by Spain and Mexico — those made to colonies or settlements, those made to individuals, and those made to empresarios. Intricate questions of fact and complicated questions of law naturally arose in connection with authority to issue these grants, and the procedures followed in acquiring land under the Spanish and Mexican land systems.

This work does not answer all the questions, nor does it cover every detail in the land history of the area embraced. Its scope is limited to a study of the private land claims in existence at the time of the transfer of jurisdiction to Texas or the United States. Because so little has been written on this subject, the author hopes this book will serve as a model or a stepping stone for others which may follow.

J. J. Bowden

SPANISH AND MEXICAN LAND GRANTS
IN THE CHIHUAHUAN ACQUISITION

PART I

The Chihuahuan Acquisition

● THE GROUP OF TERRITORIAL ACQUISITIONS, covering approximately 23.2 million acres of land and hereinafter collectively referred to as the Chihuahuan Acquisition, embraces practically all of the Trans-Pecos portion of West Texas and a major portion of the southern tier of counties of New Mexico. These lands were severed from the Mexican state of Chihuahua at various times between 1836 and 1853, and embraced twenty-six Spanish or Mexican Grants.

Without going into the controversies over the boundaries of Chihuahua before and after the creation of the Republic of Mexico on October 4, 1824, the first date significant to this study is May 25, 1825, when Chihuahua passed an act[1] regulating the colonization of its public domain. This law complied with the provisions of the National Colonization Law of August 18, 1824,[2] which directed the states to enact local legislation governing colonization of the public domain within their respective jurisdictions. The Chihuahuan Colonization Law of 1825 indicates that the northern boundary of the State of Chihuahua was located just south of the Jornada del Muerto, near the present town of Las Cruces, New Mexico. Between 1823 and 1848 Chihuahua asserted jurisdiction over the area between El Paso del Norte and the Jornada del Muerto by permitting the Ayuntamiento of El Paso del Norte to issue grants in the Mesilla Valley and to regulate their development.

According to the Texas cases, Mexico lost *de jure* jurisdiction over the eastern portion of the Chihuahuan Acquisition when Texas won its Independence and passed the Boundary Act[3] of December 19, 1836. As a result of the Compromise of 1850,[4] an area consisting of 4,774,000 acres of the eastern portion — 20% of the Chihuahuan Acquisition — was added to New Mexico. This tract was located east of the Rio Grande between 32° and 32° 57' 43" north latitude and contained three grants made by Mexico. Since only two of these claims, covering a total of 50,207.09 acres, were recognized, approximately 4.7 million acres were added to the unappropriated public domain of the United States. The balance of the eastern portion still belongs to Texas and embraces an area of approximately 13,445,000 acres or 58% of the Chihuahuan Acquisition. Texas has recognized seven of the fourteen grants made by Mexico in this area. They

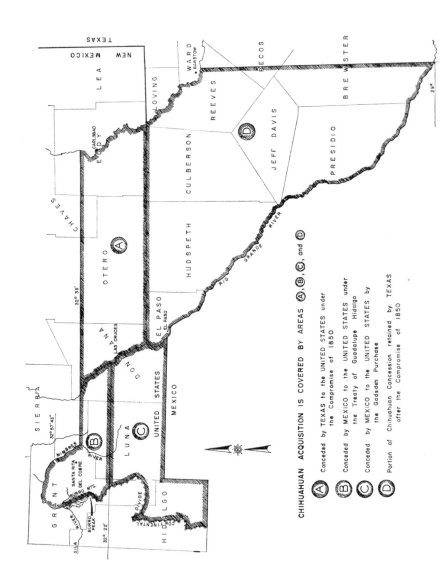

CHIHUAHUAN ACQUISITION IS COVERED BY AREAS Ⓐ, Ⓑ, Ⓒ, and Ⓓ

Ⓐ Conceded by TEXAS to the UNITED STATES under the Compromise of 1850

Ⓑ Conceded by MEXICO to the UNITED STATES under the Treaty of Guadalupe Hidalgo

Ⓒ Conceded by MEXICO to the UNITED STATES by the Gadsden Purchase

Ⓓ Portion of Chihuahuan Concession retained by TEXAS after the Compromise of 1850

contain a total of 66,519.98 acres. Except for the land covered by these recognized grants, title to all of the Texas portion of the Chihuahuan Acquisition vested in Texas.

The Treaty of Guadalupe Hidalgo,[5] which concluded the Mexican War, validated the Texas claim to the area north and east of the Rio Grande and ceded to the United States approximately one-third of Mexico's domain, of which 1,757,000 acres, or 8%, was embraced in the Chihuahuan Acquisition. This portion of the Chihuahuan Acquisition was also annexed to New Mexico and is situated west of the Rio Grande between the 1825 northern boundary of Chihuahua and the line established by the Bartlett-García Conde Compromise.[6] There is one rejected private land claim in this area.

The controversy which arose over the Bartlett-García Conde Compromise was settled by the signing of the Gadsden Treaty on December 30, 1853.[7] This treaty ceded to the United States an additional 3,219,000 acres of the Chihuahuan Acquisition — 14% of the total. This final segment of the acquisition was located west of the Rio Grande between the Bartlett-García Conde line and the present International Boundary. It likewise was annexed to New Mexico. Of the eight private land claims in the area, only five were totally or partially recognized.

Universally accepted principles of International Law, as well as specific provisions in both the Treaties of Guadalupe Hidalgo and the Gadsden Treaty, required the recognition by the United States of valid private land grants made by Spain and Mexico prior to these changes in sovereignty. From the outset, it was recognized that Spanish or Mexican grants fell into three distinct categories — community, individual, and empresario. However, serious problems arose over the establishment of forums to pass on their validity.

Intricate questions of fact and complicated legal issues naturally arose in connection with authority to issue valid concessions and the procedures to be followed in acquiring land under the Spanish and Mexican land system. Resulting delays tended to create hardship upon proprietors, friction between claimants and squatters, depressed land values and retarded development.

The history of the twenty-six recognized and unrecognized private land claims situated within the Chihuahuan Acquisition, strategically located at the cross roads of the north-south Latin and the east-west Anglo cultures and embracing multiple facets in America's territorial expansion, afford an excellent insight into the southwestern land grant validation problem — a problem which has not been fully and satisfactorily settled even at this late date.

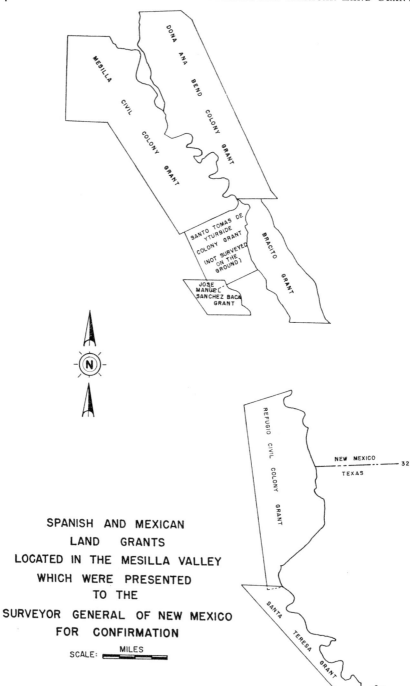

SPANISH AND MEXICAN
LAND   GRANTS
LOCATED IN THE MESILLA VALLEY
WHICH WERE PRESENTED
TO THE
SURVEYOR GENERAL OF NEW MEXICO
FOR CONFIRMATION

SCALE: ▬▬▬ MILES

REFERENCES

1 Matthew G. Reynolds, *Spanish and Mexican Land Laws* (St. Louis, 1895), 132-136.

2 Francisco F. de La Maza, *Código de Colonización y Terrenos Baldíos* (México, 1893), 191-193.

3 H. P. N. Gammel, *The Laws of Texas* (10 Vols., Austin, 1898), I, 1193-1194.

4 *United States Statutes at Large*, IX, 446-458, 462, 465, and 467-468 (1850).

5 Hunter Miller, *Treaties and Other International Acts of the United States of America* (6 Vols., Washington, D.C., 1937), V, 207-236.

6 *Senate Executive Documents*, 32nd Cong., 1st Sess., Doc. No. 119, 406 (1852).

7 Hunter Miller, *Treaties and Other International Acts of the United States of America* (6 Vols., Washington, D.C., 1942), VI, 293-437.

Part II

The Grants

~~~~~~

CHAPTER 1

The Guadalupe Miranda Grant ঽ৶

● DEEP LOYALTY AND PATRIOTISM for his native country influenced Guadalupe Miranda[1] to remain in Mexico after the signing of the Treaty of Guadalupe Hidalgo, despite the realization that he would have to sacrifice his vast land holdings in New Mexico. After the close of the Mexican War, Miranda invested heavily in the Santa Fe and San Antonio overland trade. In order to obtain an adequate pasturage for his teams, he petitioned the Governor of the State of Chihuahua, on February 19, 1851, for a grant of one *sitio* and three *caballerías* of grazing land, in accordance with the Act of October 22, 1833. The lands requested were located on the west side of the river, just north of the suburbs of the town of El Paso del Norte. The lands embraced the hills and river bends called *Muleros,* upon which Miranda's ranch was located. After due procedure before the Governor and the Director of the Geographical and Topographical Corps, the Governor of the State of Chihuahua allegedly granted to Miranda the lands which had been requested by a Decree dated July 13, 1851. On November 20, 1851, Guadalupe Miranda requested José María Maese, Second Judge of the First Instance of District of Bravos, to survey the grant and place him in lawful possession of the lands which had been given to him. Judge Maese gave public notice on November 21, 1851, that he intended to comply with Miranda's request on December 3, 1851. On the prescribed date, Judge Maese officially surveyed the grant and gave Guadalupe Miranda full and legal possession of the following described lands:

Beginning at the mouth of an arroyo called Peñasquito where it connects with the Rio Grande, said arroyo having its source in the hills called Muleros; thence up the west bank of said river 5,000 varas to a Tornillo; thence west 5,000 varas, crossing the main road to Mesilla, to a small sand hill; thence south 5,000 varas terminating in the hills on one side of Poleo Hill; thence east 5,000 varas, crossing a part of the Poleo Hill, to the place of Beginning; thence south 3,312 varas along the west bank of the Rio Grande to a place where the hills connect with said river; thence west 552 varas to the hills; thence north 3,312 varas; and thence east 552 varas to said point of Beginning.

A copy of each of the instruments pertaining to the grant was given to Guadalupe Miranda to serve as his muniment of title, and the original copy of the proceedings was allegedly filed in Judge Maese's office.[2]

Miranda lost his copy of his petition to the Governor dated February 19, 1851, and the Governor's decree of July 13, 1851. He attempted to secure a certified copy of these two instruments from the custodian of the Property Registry of the District of Bravos, but was advised that the books containing land *protocols* for the years 1848 through 1855 had been lost or destroyed.[3] Miranda apparently did not believe that he could secure the recognition of the grant without these documents; therefore he did not present his claim to the Surveyor General for confirmation.

After the Southern Pacific Railway Company had completed its main line across the grant, Josiah F. Crosby recognized the speculative value of the claim, and purchased it from Guadalupe Miranda, on January 18, 1888, for five dollars.[4]

Miranda gave Crosby all of the title papers he had in his possession, which consisted of a copy of his petition addressed to Judge Maese dated November 20, 1851, requesting the grant be surveyed and possession delivered to him; a copy of the Citation issued on November 21, 1851; and a copy of Judge Maese's Decree of December 3, 1851. Armed with this meager evidence, Crosby filed suit against the United States in the Court of Private Land Claims on February 28, 1893, seeking recognition and confirmation of the approximately 2,442 acres of land covered by the Guadalupe Miranda Grant, which were located north of the International Boundary Line.[5]

In his petition, Crosby alleged that the Governor of the State of Chihuahua had issued the grant to Miranda on July 13, 1851; that the grant had been duly made in accordance with the provisions of the Act of October 22, 1833; that the grant had been surveyed and possession delivered to Miranda by Judge José María Maese; and that all the grant papers had been filed in the Archives of Mexico. The government filed an answer in the case on December 29, 1896, putting into issue all of the allegations contained in Crosby's petition. The case was set for trial on July 5, 1898.

Meanwhile, Crosby's attorney, S. B. Newcomb, apparently realized that there was a material defect in Crosby's title. The Act of October 22, 1833, under which the grant allegedly was made provided that an individual could petition the Director of the Geographical and Topographical Corps of the State of Chihuahua for a grant covering a specifically described tract of vacant public domain. If the tract covered vacant public lands, the Director would approve the request and order the *jefe político* of the district in which the land was located to give public notice of the application for two consecutive weeks. If no one objected to the application, the Director would then survey the land and give public notice of the result of his survey for a period of nine days. If no one protested, the Director would forward the original file to the Assessor General of the State for an appraisal of the lands and assessment of costs incurred in connection with the proceedings. The Assessor General would then transmit the file to the Governor for his approval. If the proceedings were approved by the Governor and all costs had been paid, the Governor, together with the Director and Secretary of the Geographical and Topographical Corps, would execute a final report, which, with the other papers pertaining to the grant, would constitute a *protocol*.[6] It was clearly evident that the documents upon which Crosby's claim was based did not constitute a complete *protocol*. Newcomb recognized that a report by the Governor and the Director and Secretary of the Geographical and Topographical Corps was an essential element in the issuance of a valid and complete grant under the Act of October 22, 1833.

When the case came up for trial on July 5, 1898, Newcomb advised the court that Crosby did not wish to further prosecute the case. Based on this announcement, the court found that the plaintiff had not satisfactorily proved that a valid grant of land had been issued to Guadalupe Miranda. The court, therefore, dismissed the petition and rejected the claim.[7]

It is possible that a complete *protocol* might have been located in the Executive Archives or the Archives of the Geographical and Topographical Corps in 1898. Many of the Archives of the State of Chihuahua were destroyed during the 1916 Revolution. If Crosby could have found and presented a complete *protocol*, the court would probably have recognized that portion of the grant located in Doña Ana County, New Mexico.

R E F E R E N C E S

[1] Guadalupe Miranda was born in El Paso del Norte, Mexico in 1810. In 1825 his family sent him to Ciudad Chihuahua, where he received an excellent education under the tutelage of the Dominican and Franciscan fathers. After completing his education, Miranda moved to Santa Fe, New Mexico, in 1829, where he opened a private school. In 1832 he was appointed Superintendent of the Public Schools in Santa Fe by the Territorial Deputation. Miranda moved to El Paso del Norte in 1833. He returned to Santa Fe in 1838. When Manuel Armijo was appointed Governor of New Mexico by President Santa Anna, Miranda became his private secretary. He also served as Secretary of the Department of New Mexico, and Collector of Customs from April 9, 1839 to October, 1843. It was during this period that Governor Armijo granted Miranda and Charles Beaubien the tract of land which later became known as the Maxwell Grant. Miranda moved from Santa Fe to El Paso del Norte in December, 1843, where he was appointed Alcalde in 1845. Due to his interest in the welfare of the loyal Mexican citizens located in the area ceded to the United States under the Treaty of Guadalupe Hidalgo, he was appointed Commissioner of Emigration by the Mexican government in

1853 to supervise the repatriation of the persons who had elected to return to their native land. Some time after the year 1874, Miranda moved to Chihuahua, Mexico, where he died in about the year 1890. H. Bailey Carroll and J. Villasana Haggard, *Three New Mexico Chronicles*, (Albuquerque, 1942), 188; and *Deposition of Guadalupe Miranda in Magoffin v. Campbell* (Mss., Records of the United States Circuit Court for the Western District of Texas, Austin, Texas), Cause No. 1290-1/2.

2 Crosby v. United States, (Mss., Court of Private Land Claims, Records of the Bureau of Land Management, Santa Fe, New Mexico), No. 139.

3 *Ibid.*

4 *Deed Records* (Mss., Records of the Doña Ana County Clerk's Office, Las Cruces, New Mexico), XVII, 300.

5 Crosby v. United States (Mss., Court of Private Land Claims, Records of the Bureau of Land Management, Santa Fe, New Mexico), No. 139.

6 *Act of October 22, 1833* (Mss., Records of the Oficina de Correspondencia y Archivo, Gobierno del Estado de Chihuahua, Ciudad Chihuahua, Chihuahua, México).

7 *Journal* (Mss., Court of Private Land Claims, Records of the Bureau of Land Management, Santa Fe, New Mexico), IV, 10.

CHAPTER 2

The Barela Grant ৡ

● IN 1853 ROMULO BARELA, an influential citizen of El Paso del Norte, petitioned Commissioner of Emigration Guadalupe Miranda for a league of land lying west of the Rio Grande, between the Miranda and Santa Teresa Grants. Barela stated that he desired to plant an orchard on such lands. Commissioner Miranda found that the lands requested by Barela consisted only of sand hills and marshes, and that they were not suitable for colonization. He further found that occupation of such land by Barela would be in the interest of the general public welfare. Therefore, on June 26, 1853, Commissioner Miranda granted Romulo Barela the following described tract of land, which was located on the west bank of the Rio Grande, about five miles northwest of El Paso del Norte:

Beginning at a point a little above the ford or crossing on the Rio Grande known as Muleros ford; thence north along the west bank of the river 5,000 varas to Piedras Paradas; thence west 5,000 varas to a mound on the top of a sand hill; thence south 5,000 varas to the lands of Guadalupe Miranda; thence east 5,000 varas along the north line of the Guadalupe Miranda Grant to the place of Beginning.

The concession to Barela was purportedly made in conformity with the third article of the State Colonization Law of January 15, 1849, and article eighteen of the State Colonization Regulations of May 22, 1851.

Immediately after the grant was issued, Romulo Barela attempted to plant some fruit trees on the grant, but the enterprise failed. Thereafter he occasionally used the land as a pasture for livestock and irregularly cut and gathered fire wood off the land. Romulo Barela died in 1870 and was survived by his son, Romulo E. Barela, and Guadalupe Bermúdez, Juan M. Bermúdez and Ygnacia Bermúdez, the children and heirs of Guadalupe Barela de Bermúdez, deceased, who was the daughter of Romulo Barela. Some time after Romulo Barela's death, his son found a copy of the grant among his father's papers; later, the lands were used by Romulo E. Barela's tenants, Maria Ruidos and Jose Marujo. They pastured a small herd of cattle on the land until 1876. Apparently no further use was made of the grant by the claimants after 1876.

On April 1, 1902, Romulo E. Barela and his co-heirs filed suit in the Court of Private Land Claims for the confirmation of their claim.[1]

A representative of the government, upon making an on-the-ground examination of the premises covered by the Barela Grant, found that there were a number of persons asserting adverse claims to a portion of the lands covered by the Barela Grant. The government filed a motion, requesting that all interested parties be brought into the case. On May 14, 1902 the Court issued an order, requiring the claimants to bring all such adverse claims into the case as parties defendant.

The case was set for hearing on June 24, 1903. At the trial, the plaintiffs offered into evidence their muniments of title, together with oral testimony and certain depositions taken in El Paso, Texas on May 16, 1903. Such testimony and depositions were offered in support of the allegations contained in the plaintiff's petion. In its cross-examination of the witnesses, the government brought out the fact that Romulo Barela was not a member of any colony, but was in fact actually a resident of El Paso del Norte on the date the grant was issued to him. The government was also able to prove that the lands embraced within the grant had never been permanently occupied or improved.

The Court issued its decision in the case on June 26, 1903, the same day it decided the Sánchez case. The issues involved in the Barela and Sánchez cases were practically identical. The Court held that it was apparent from the title papers in the case that the Barela grant was not within the boundaries of any civil colony, that it was not made as a distribution of colony land, but that it was an individual grant made wholly independent of the founding or administration of any colony. The Court, therefore, found that Commissioner Miranda had no authority to make such an individual grant. Based on its decision in the Sánchez case, the Court ordered rejection of the grant and dismissal of the claimant's petition.[2]

Although the claimants gave notice of their intention of appealing the decision to the United States Supreme Court, they did not perfect such an appeal. By failing to appeal the decision, their claim was finally rejected and the lands covered by the Barela Grant were returned to the vacant public domain.

The Barela case was the last case tried before the Court of Private Land Claims. The Court continued in existence for almost a year after the decision in the Barela case, but it only conducted routine business and approved grant surveys.

R E F E R E N C E S

1 Barela v. United States (Mss., Court of Private Land Claims, Records of the Bureau of Land Management, Santa Fe, New Mexico), No. 281.

2 Journal (Mss., Court of Private Land Claims, Records of the Bureau of Land Management, Santa Fe, New Mexico), IV, 343-344.

CHAPTER 3

The Santa Teresa Grant ❧

• THE EARLIEST and perhaps most interesting of all of the private land claims located in the Mesilla Valley is the Santa Teresa Grant. It is the only Spanish grant situated in that valley. Before its title was confirmed and boundaries finally designated, it had been investigated by the Surveyor General of New Mexico, the Congress of the United States, the Court of Private Land Claims, and the United States Supreme Court.

Sometime prior to 1790, a four-league tract of land situated on the west bank of the Rio Grande, the southeast corner of which was located about seven miles northwest of El Paso del Norte, Mexico, was granted to Francisco García, the military commandant of El Paso del Norte, by the Lieutenant Governor of Nueva Viscaya. The tract became known as "Rancho de Santa Teresa." Francisco García used the tract primarily as a pasturage for his extensive herds of cattle and sheep from the time he acquired it until the summer of 1822. Zebulon Pike states that in 1807, Francisco García had twenty thousand sheep and a thousand cows in the vicinity of El Paso del Norte.[1]

During the summer of 1822, García was forced temporarily to abandon the grant when Apache war parties commenced crossing the Rio Grande at Muleros Ford. From 1822 until the time of his death in 1840, García pastured livestock on the grant whenever the Indian disturbances subsided. Under the Mexican Community Property Laws, García's undivided one-half interest in the Santa Teresa Grant passed to his five children. The other one-half interest in the grant was owned by Francisco García's widow, Josefa Hocasitas García.

José María García, eldest son of Francisco García, permanently re-occupied the Santa Teresa Grant in 1840. He repaired the ruined buildings and corrals on the ranch and stocked it with cattle, sheep, goats and horses. A portion of the grant was also placed under cultivation.

After the Battle of Bracito, the victorious American forces, under Colonel Alexander W. Doniphan, were quartered in the public buildings and certain private homes in the City of El Paso del Norte. A portion of Doniphan's troops occupied José María García's home, and after their departure, it was discovered that García's copy of the title papers to the Santa Teresa Grant were missing. The original copy of the *testimonio* to the Santa Teresa Grant, which had been filed in the Archives of the Ayuntamiento of El Paso del Norte, was also missing after the invading forces left the city. It is a notorious fact that the soldiers quartered in the Municipal Building destroyed a large portion of the public records by using them to kindle fires and to light candles. It was, therefore, presumed that both copies of the Santa Teresa Grant papers were either stolen or destroyed by the American occupation forces.[2]

Doña Josefa Horcasitas García died about 1848. Due to the loss or destruction of all of the copies of the title papers pertaining to the grant, it became necessary for the heirs of Francisco and Josefa Horcasitas García to institute a judicial inquiry under the provisions of the Act of the Republic of Mexico dated May 23, 1837, to perpetuate the testimony of certain witnesses which would tend to prove the validity of the Santa Teresa Grant and define its boundaries. José María García, as one of the executors of his mother's estate, instituted such an *ex parte* proceeding on January 7, 1853. Ventura López, Second Judge of the First Instance of the Canton of El Paso del Norte, after investigating the validity of the Santa Teresa Grant, issued a decree on January 16, 1853, which reaffirmed the title to the grant in José María García, Francisco Noriega y García, Rafael García, Pedro García, Guadalupe García Albo, and Jesús García, the heirs of Francisco García and Josefa Horcasitas García. The Court reestablished and defined the boundaries of the grant as follows:

Beginning at a cottonwood tree on the west bank of the river in the bend of Piedras Paradas; thence north along the west bank of the river 20,000 varas to a cottonwood tree on the west bank of the river in the bend of the Cobrena; thence west 5,000 varas to a monument of stone above the brow of the hills; thence south 20,000 varas to a monument of stone in a depression in the hills; thence east 5,000 varas to the point of Beginning.[3]

The Gadsden Treaty of December 30, 1853 solved the boundary controversy arising from the Treaty of Guadalupe Hidalgo by moving the International Boundary south to 31° 47′ north latitude, but it presented a new problem for the claimants of the Santa Teresa Grant. Since a major portion of the grant was located within the area ceded to the United States, the claimants would have to secure recognition of the grant by the United States. The dangers incident to a trip to Santa Fe, which required the crossing of the dreaded Jornada del Muerto, caused the owners of the grant to postpone their petitioning the Surveyor General for the confirmation of their title until June 4, 1877.[4]

Meanwhile, the executors of the estate of Josefa Horcasitas García had conveyed the southern one-half of the grant to Pablo Miranda on August 8, 1872. This conveyance was made in consideration of legal services rendered by Miranda in connection with the Mexican Judicial Inquiry of 1853.[5] Pablo Miranda sold his interest in the grant to Jesús María Escobar for $800.00.[6] Thereafter, Jesús María Escobar and his brother, Jesús Escobar y Armendaris, purchased the greater portion of the north half of the grant from a majority of the heirs of Francisco and Josefa García.[7]

Surveyor General Henry M. Atkinson, on December 11, 1878, held that the grant was valid and recommended the claim be confirmed by Congress into the heirs and assigns of Francisco García according to the boundaries set forth in the Mexican Decree of January 16, 1853. The Surveyor General stated that, in addition to the documentary evidence and peaceful occupation of the lands since 1790, which alone were sufficient to establish the validity of the grant, that the genuineness of the grant was corroborated by the fact that the southern boundary of the Refugio Civil Colony Grant was stated to be the lands of José María García, or the lands covered by the claim under investigation.[8]

The grant was surveyed in April, 1883, by John Shaw, a United States Deputy Surveyor, under Contract Number 184. This official survey disclosed that the grant straddled the International Boundary between the United States and Mexico. The portion of the grant located in the United States contained 9,681.29 acres of land. Surveyor General Atkinson approved the Shaw survey on November 28, 1883.[9]

No further action was taken on the petition for confirmation of the grant during the balance of Surveyor General Atkinson's term or during the term of his successor, Clarence Pullen. George W. Julian was appointed to the office on July 22, 1885. After reviewing the evidence pertinent to the Santa Teresa Grant, Julian reported on October 16, 1886, that the evidence supporting the grant established a strong equitable claim, if not a legal one, but that he could not recommend the approval of the claim, because the title papers of the grant were not then located in the Archives of Mexico, as required by Article Six of the Gadsden Treaty of December 30, 1853.[10]

Jesús Escobar, through M. Romero, Minister of the Mexican Legation in Washington, D.C., protested the acceptance of Surveyor General Julian's opinion on October 20, 1887. He stated that the claimants had offered

creditable evidence establishing the fact that the original Spanish muniments of title had been duly recorded in the Archives of El Paso del Norte,
but that they had been lost or destroyed by the agents of the United States.
He further stated that validity of the grant was based not so much upon
the original Spanish grant, which was valid and completed, as upon the
duly archived title created by virtue of the confirmation and recognition
of title to the grant by the Government of Mexico through a court of
competent jurisdiction in January, 1853. Escobar concluded that the Surveyor General's rejection of the grant on the grounds that it was not recorded in the Archives of Mexico was unfounded, and the requirement
should not prevent confirmation of the title by Congress. Escobar also
objected to the Shaw survey, and requested the grant be re-surveyed in
order to include four leagues of the lands, instead of merely 9,681.29 acres.
The protest concluded by pointing out that, despite the passage of thirty-
four years since the United States had assumed the obligation of inviolably
respecting the property rights of Mexican citizens and the lifetime efforts
by the claimants of the grant to secure confirmation of their claim, the
government had not discharged its solemn obligation.[11]

In response to Escobar's protest, S. M. Stockslager, acting Commissioner
of the General Land Office, replied that no further action could be taken
by the Executive Department to expedite Congressional action on the
Santa Teresa Grant, and if the grant was eventually approved by an Act
of Congress, the grant would be re-surveyed in order to conform with the
boundaries designated in such an Act. Romero wrote the Secretary of
Interior, T. H. Bayard, on July 13, 1888, and called the Secretary's attention
to the provisions contained in the Treaties of Guadalupe Hidalgo and
Mesilla, whereby the United States had agreed inviolably to respect vested
property rights. Romero stated that in the case of the Santa Teresa Grant,
it had been clearly established that the original grant had been legally
given, that it had been subsequently confirmed by the proper Mexican
authorities, and that evidence thereof had been duly recorded in the Public
Archives of El Paso del Norte. Romero advised the Secretary that if the
Department of Interior would not expedite the settlement of Escobar's
claim, then, as the Mexican Minister to the United States, he would have
no alternative but to present the claim through the Department of State.
He then proceeded to review the deplorable history of the United States'
efforts to settle the Spanish and Mexican Land Claims in New Mexico. He
called the Secretary's attention to the fact that during the twenty-six years
that had elapsed since the enactment of the Act of July 22, 1854, which
established the only procedure to be followed in proving the validity of
Spanish and Mexican Land Claims in New Mexico, that over one thousand
private land claims had been filed in the Surveyor General's office, that the
various Surveyors General had transmitted one hundred and fifty of such

claims to Congress, but that only seventy-five claims — or seven percent of the total number filed — had been acted upon by that body. Romero surmised that, based upon its previous progress, that it would take Congress several centuries to settle the land claims which had already been filed in the Surveyor General's office. As a result of Minister Romero's letter, Secretary Bayard requested President Benjamin Harrison to present the chaotic land grant problem to Congress, with his recommendation that an effective and competent court be established to determine the validity of Spanish and Mexican Land Claims in the Southwest.[12]

On July 1, 1890 President Harrison sent a special message to Congress, calling its attention to the urgent need of legislation for adjustment of New Mexico's private land grant problems. Awakened to the fact that special legislation was needed to provide a practical method for adjudicating private land claims, Congress passed an Act creating the Court of Private Land Claims on March 3, 1891.[13]

The tenacious owners of the Santa Teresa Grant persistently prosecuted their claim to the lands which they and their predecessors had occupied for more than a century by filing suit in the Court of Private Land Claims against the United States on March 2, 1893.[14] They alleged that they were owners of the Santa Teresa Grant by inheritance and purchase from the original grantee; that title to the grant was complete and perfect on the date the United States acquired sovereignty over the land in question; and that they and their predecessors had held peaceful, uninterrupted possession of the grant since the date of its conception. Their petition closed with a plea that the grant be confirmed in accordance with the boundaries set forth in the Mexican Court Decree of January 16, 1853.[15] M. R. Pendell, on December 24, 1894, acquired the interests in the Santa Teresa Grant which had formerly been owned by Jesús María Escobar and Jesús Escobar y Armendaris.[16] Pendell took their place in the suit. The case was tried before the court on the 29th and 30th of August, 1899. At the trial, Pendell produced a substantial amount of testimony and documentary evidence, tending to prove that the grant had originally been made by a duly authorized representative of the King of Spain, but the archives containing the original title documents had been sacked by the invading American forces during the Mexican War. The plaintiffs asserted that the grant had been duly reaffirmed in 1853, and, in support of this contention, attempted to introduce into evidence a certified copy of the Mexican Court proceedings.

The government objected to the admission of the Mexican Court proceedings on the grounds they merely perpetuated certain testimony, and therefore did not constitute a confirmation of the grant. The government pointed out that the Mexican proceedings failed to disclose the authority under which the grant was issued, the name of the granting authority, the date of the grant, or any of the other details connected with the alleged concession which were required to be set forth and proven under Section 6 of the Act of March 3, 1891. The government next asserted that a grant issued by a Lieutenant Governor of Nueva Viscaya about the close of the 18th century would be invalid, because the lands in question were then situated in the Province of New Mexico.[17] Continuing this line of reasoning, the government argued that if the original grant was invalid, the Mexican court proceedings, which were held in order to perpetuate the evidence of such a grant, could not cure this fatal defect in the plaintiffs' title. The court overruled the government's objections, and accepted introduction of the Mexican court proceedings into evidence.

Oral testimony presented by the plaintiffs tended to show that Francisco García and those holding under him had held peaceful possession of the grant for many years prior to the date of signing of the Treaty of 1853. On cross-examination, it was developed by the government that the plaintiff's possession had not been exclusive, for the inhabitants of El Paso del Norte had used the premises as a common pasture ground. There was also a large amount of testimony presented by both parties bearing on the boundaries of the grant. The plaintiffs contended that the southern boundary of the grant was located near the International Boundary Line. The government's contention, on the other hand, was that the grant's southern boundary was located at Piedras Paradas, as stated in the Mexican Court Decree. The Piedras Paradas were a group of well known rocks which were located some distance north of the Southern Pacific Railroad bridge across the Rio Grande. Evidence was also introduced by the defendants showing that the Guadalupe Miranda and Barela Grants were located between the Santa Teresa Grant and the International Boundary Line. The government also urged that even if all of the plaintiff's evidence concerning title and possession were true, the claim was still not entitled to confirmation, because they had failed to prove that a copy of the original grant papers was located and recorded in the Mexican Archives, as required by the Sixth Article of the Gadsden Treaty.

On May 4, 1900 the court, through Justice Henry C. Sluss, announced its majority opinion confirming the grant on the grounds that the long, peaceful possession of the land by Francisco García and his successors was sufficient, under the Doctrine of Presumption of Title announced in United States v. Chaves,[18] to establish the presumption that the Santa Teresa Grant was valid. A majority of the court was of the opinion that the Doctrine of Presumption also bound the court to assume that all necessary steps had been taken to vest absolute title to the grant in the plaintiffs, notwithstanding the Treaty requirements that the grant be located and duly recorded in the Archives of Mexico.[19] Justices William H. Murray and Thomas C. Fuller dissented. They stated it could not be presumed that title to the grant had been duly recorded in the Archives of Mexico. They noted that, under the laws of Mexico, failure to record the grant papers would not affect the validity of the grant. Therefore, they felt that the location of the grant papers in the Archives of Mexico was a prerequisite to recognition of any concession located within the area covered by the Gadsden Purchase. They reasoned that if the Treaty prohibited recognition of a perfect grant because it was not located and recorded in the Archives of Mexico, then the government was under no obligation to recognize a presumed grant.[20]

The Court of Private Land Claims, in its decree[21] of August 16, 1900, confirmed title to the following described land located in Doña Ana County, New Mexico, to the heirs and assigns of Francisco García:

The tract of land known as the "Santa Teresa": Bounded on the north by that bend known as 'Cobrena'; on the south by the bend of the Piedras Paradas, the same being somewhat to the north of the present location of the Southern Pacific Railroad bridge, where the same crosses the Rio Grande del Norte; on the east the old bed of the said Rio Grande del Norte, as the same ran and existed in the year 1853; and on the west the brow of the ridge running parallel with the said river.

In his report to the Attorney General, Matt G. Reynolds, the government's attorney, stated that he was of the opinion that the record did not justify confirmation of the grant.[22]

Acting upon Reynolds' recommendation, the government appealed the decision to the United States Supreme Court. That court, in affirming the judgment of the lower court on April 21, 1902, held the evidence of long uninterrupted possession of the lands in question, coupled with testimony showing that the United States occupational forces had partially destroyed the Public Archives of El Paso del Norte, was sufficient not only to presume the existence of the grant, but also to presume that the grant papers had been duly recorded in the Archives of Mexico, as required by the Gadsden Treaty.[23]

Wendell V. Hall, United States Deputy Surveyor, surveyed the Santa Teresa Grant on December 23, 1903, under, under Contract Number 362. The survey purportedly conformed with the boundary calls set out in the Decree of the Court of Private Land Claims, and showed the grant contained an area of 8,478.51 acres.[24]

Notice of the filing of the Hall Survey of the grant was given in accordance with Article 10 of the Act of March 3, 1891. This notice gave all persons claiming an interest in the lands covered by the survey ninety days in which to file their objections to the survey. George Zimpleman, Joseph W. Magoffin and Josephine Crosby protested the approval of the Hall Survey on the grounds it extended into the State of Texas and conflicted with the Canutillo Grant. They alleged that they owned and had occupied a portion of the lands in conflict ever since title to the Canutillo Grant had been confirmed by a Special Relinquishment Act of the Texas Legislature on February 11, 1858.

The Court of Private Land Claims overruled the Texas complainants' objections to the survey on the grounds that they had not offered any evidence tending to prove that Hall's survey had not correctly located the bed of the river as it existed in 1853. The Court held that the boundary between Texas and New Mexico was not a shifting and changing boundary, but was a fixed line located in the center of the bed of the Rio Grande as it ran on the date of signing of the Gadsden Treaty. The Court of Private Land Claims, therefore, approved the Hall survey of the Santa Teresa Grant on June 16, 1904.[25]

Realizing that the confirmation would greatly increase the value of the choice lands embraced in the Santa Teresa Grant, Pendell filed a quiet title suit against the unknown heirs of Francisco and Josefa García in the Third Judicial District Court of New Mexico, in order to remove any cloud cast on his title by the outstanding interest owned by such persons. The Court issued a Decree on August 1, 1907, which recognized and established Pendell's title to all of the Santa Teresa Grant against any and all adverse claims.[26]

After Pendell had cleared the cloud from his title, he reimbursed the government for one-half the cost of surveying the grant and demanded that a Patent be issued for such lands. Upon learning that the government intended to patent the Santa Teresa Grant, the State of Texas protested such action and requested that a hearing be held in order to permit it to show that Hall's survey embraced lands located within the jurisdiction of the State of Texas. Texas' protest was overruled by the Secretary of the Interior, and a Patent was issued on August 16, 1909 to Francisco García, his heirs and assigns, for the 8,478.51 acres of land designated in the Hall Survey.[27]

The Patent for the Santa Teresa Grant conflicted with 2,704 acres of land which had previously been patented by the State of Texas.[28] A patent issued by the United States to lands which formed a part of the public domain of the State of Texas would be absolutely void.

In order to settle the confusion and uncertainty which resulted from the Santa Teresa-Canutillo boundary dispute, New Mexico, following its admission into the Union, filed suit on January 31, 1913, in the United States Supreme Court, against Texas, in order to determine the exact location of its boundary along the Rio Grande between 32° and 31° 47' north latitude.[29] New Mexico alleged, in its Bill of Complaint, that the boundary was located in the channel of the Rio Grande as it ran on September 9, 1850, and on that date the river ran in an almost straight line down the extreme side of the Mesilla Valley from 32° to 31° 47'. This would have placed approximately 20,000 acres of land which had been patented by the State of Texas under the jurisdiction of New Mexico.

Texas filed an answer and cross bill on April 21, 1913, agreeing that the boundary was located in the middle of the channel of the river as it ran on September 9, 1850, but alleged that on that date the river was located near the center of the valley.

Both Texas and New Mexico admitted that the true boundary line between the two states was a fixed line located in the middle of the channel of the Rio Grande as it ran on September 9, 1850. The sole issued to be determined by the Court in the case was the actual location of the river on September 9, 1850.

It is a curious historical accident that the location of the river as it ran on September 9, 1850 had never been determined by an officially recognized survey. It was conceded that the river had not changed its course between 1848 and 1853. During this six-year period the river had separated two nations. The river had also divided two major political subdivisions of the United States for more than three-quarters of a century. Because it had not generally been accepted that the boundary between Texas and New Mexico was subject to the doctrine of accretion and avulsion, Texas had continuously claimed and exercised jurisdiction over the lands located east of the river, and had issued patents to nearly all of the land bordering the east bank of the river of 1850 located between 32° and 31° 47' north latitude.

Testimony pertaining to the true location of the river in 1850 was taken for several years. This testimony tended to prove that the river was actually located in the position asserted by the State of Texas. Thereafter, L. M. Crawford, the owner of certain lands under the Santa Teresa Grant in the Country Club area, was permitted to intervene in the case as *amicus curiae*. Crawford asserted that the boundary was not a fixed line, but was subject to the doctrine of accretion and avulsion. The Supreme Court then referred the question of the location of the boundary line to a court-appointed special master.

Special Master Charles Warren, on April 21, 1926, reported that in 1850 the river ran down the approximate center of the Mesilla Valley, as contended by the State of Texas. The master further found that the boundary was not a fixed line, but was subject to the doctrine of accretion and avulsion. He concluded by ruling that the boundary had shifted eastward by accretion.[30]

On December 12, 1927 the United States Supreme Court held that the only proper questions in issue in the case were whether the master's findings as to the location of the river in 1850 were correct, and if so, whether the boundary had subsequently changed by accretion. The Court held that the Act of September 9, 1850 established the Texas-New Mexico

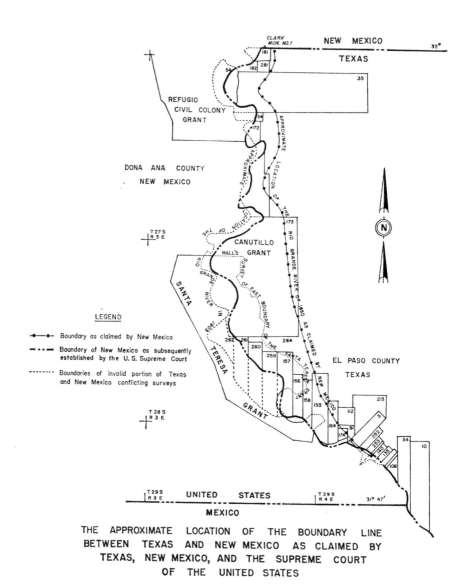

THE APPROXIMATE LOCATION OF THE BOUNDARY LINE
BETWEEN TEXAS AND NEW MEXICO AS CLAIMED BY
TEXAS, NEW MEXICO, AND THE SUPREME COURT
OF THE UNITED STATES

boundary as a fixed line in the middle of the Rio Grande channel between 32° and 31° 47′ north latitude, and that the master's report as to the location of the river in 1850 was substantially correct. The Court rejected the master's findings that the boundary had changed by accretion.[31]

Samuel S. Gannett was appointed Commissioner by the United States Supreme Court to survey and mark the fixed boundary line. Gannett's survey showed that the boundary line between 32° and 31° 47′ was 25.17 miles in length. The line was marked by one hundred five permanent monuments, which are approximately .24 of a mile apart. The Commissioner also established and marked forty-five reference points and six triangulation stations. The number, elevation, and geographic position of each individual monument, reference point, and triangulation station were inscribed on a bronze tablet imbedded in the top of a marker which designated such site. The survey was completed on July 17, 1930, and it was subsequently approved by the Court.[32]

As a result of the Supreme Court's decision, patents issued by the United States government covering 4,627 acres of land in Texas were invalidated and Texas patents to 2,499 acres of land in New Mexico were set aside.[33]

L. M. Crawford filed a suit in the Texas District Court against Z. T. White and nine other defendants on January 25, 1928. Crawford alleged that the Supreme Court decision had fixed the boundary lines as of September 9, 1850, but that the line had subsequently moved eastward by accretion. He asserted that, as the owner of the adjoining lands, he had acquired all lands lying west of the river in the Country Club bend area under the doctrine of accretion. The trial court instructed a verdict in favor of the defendants, on the grounds that this precise issue had previously been adjudicated by the United States Supreme Court.[34]

The Eighth Court of Civil Appeals affirmed the trial court's decision and held that the Texas-New Mexico boundary was a fixed line, and that title to the lands adjoining the Rio Grande was not affected by the doctrine of accretion and avulsion.[35]

Here is an unusual case from the records of state and federal courts. The net effect of this strange decision was that the forces of nature are, in effect, declared subject to man's jurisdiction. One is dealing with a legal fiction when he considers the court's statement that the proper legal boundary between Texas and New Mexico is a fixed line, and, in addition, that the fixed line is the channel of the Rio Grande. Under the decision of the court, the river may, and had, moved physically, but not legally. Seen through the eyes of the court, the Rio Grande must flow eternally through its channel of 1850.

One material advantage resulted from defining the bonudary between Texas and New Mexico as a fixed line was that property rights were securely tied down and no longer subject to change or alteration through accretion by the annual Rio Grande floods of the ever-shifting river. During the more than a quarter of a century it took to settle the Texas-New Mexico interstate boundary controversy which had evolved out of the Santa Teresa-Canutillo dispute, a majority of the landowners whose farms were intersected by the boundary line had purchased the conflicting title to their land, and therefore they held under both United States and Texas chains of title. Both the United States and Texas passed relief legislation which permitted persons who had held actual bona fide possession of land under patent or color of title from the previous sovereign, but whose title had been invalidated by the Supreme Court's decision, to purchase the same under certain conditions from the new sovereign, if such lands were a part of the vacant public domain.[36]

The confirmation of the grant and final adjudication of its disputed eastern boundary, together with the completion of the Elephant Butte Dam and irrigation system, greatly increased the value of the 5,774.51 acres of choice valley remaining in the Santa Teresa Grant.

REFERENCES

[1] Milton Quaife, *The Southwestern Expedition of Zebulon Pike* (Chicago, 1925), 166.

[2] Santa Teresa Grant, Report No. 111 (Mss., Records of the Surveyor General's Office, Bureau of Land Management, Santa Fe, New Mexico).

[3] *Ibid.*   [4] *Ibid.*

[5] *Deed Records* (Mss., Records of the Doña Ana County Clerk's Office, Las Cruces, New Mexico), VI, 515-517.

[6] *Ibid.,* VI, 517-519.

[7] *Ibid.,* VI, 519-521.

[8] *Land Claims Records* (Mss., Records of the Surveyor General's Office, Bureau of Land Management, Santa Fe, New Mexico), VI, 48-51. This latter assumption by the Surveyor General was subsequently proven erroneous in the Refugio Civil Colony Grant case. In that case, it was held that the call for the Refugio Civil Colony Grant to extend south to the lands of José María García meant for the grant to extend only to the southern boundary of the Refugio Civil Colony lands, which had been allotted to José María García by Commissioner Ortiz, and not to the north boundary of the Santa Teresa Grant, which was then owned by José María García and his co-heirs. The Grant of the Colony of Refugio v. United States (Mss., Court of Private Land Claims, Records of the Bureau of Land Management, Santa Fe, New Mexico), No. 150.

[9] Santa Teresa Grant File 111 (Mss., Records of the Cadastrial Engineer's Office, Santa Fe, New Mexico).

[10] *Senate Executive Documents,* 50th Cong., 1st Sess., Document No. 19, 2-3 (1887).

[11] *Senate Executive Documents,* 51st Cong., 1st Sess., Document No. 170, 2-5 (1890).

[12] *Ibid.,* 6-15.

[13] *United States Statutes at Large,* XXVI, 854 (1892).

[14] Pendell v. United States (Mss., Court of Private Land Claims, Records of Bureau of Land Management, Santa Fe, New Mexico), No. 168.

15 *Ibid.*

16 *Deed Records* (Mss., Records of the Doña Ana County Clerk's Office, Las Cruces, New Mexico), XVII, 138.

17 There is an interesting but somewhat vague series of documents in the Archives of New Mexico touching upon this point. It appears that some one apparently attacked the validity of the Santa Teresa Grant on the grounds that it conflicted with the grant which had been previously issued to the Town of El Paso del Norte. When a thorough search of the Archives of El Paso del Norte failed to produce El Paso del Norte's Grant, Fernando García, Lieutenant Governor and Alcalde of El Paso del Norte, referred the matter to Facundo Melgares, Governor of the Province of New Mexico, on June 19, 1820. By a memorandum dated July 19, 1820, the Governor acknowledged receipt of the Lieutenant Governor's letter. This document specifically mentions that a copy of the grant to Francisco García had accompanied the Lieutenant Governor's letter. On December 18, 1820 the Governor advised the Lieutenant Governor that he had not been able to find any document in the archives of New Mexico which described the limits of the Town of El Paso del Norte, and that he understood that the lands in question were unappropriated. Therefore, Francisco García was entitled to take whatever might correspond to him. Archives of New Mexico (Mss., Records of the Museum of New Mexico, Santa Fe, New Mexico), Document No. 128.

18 United States v. Chaves, 175 U.S. 509 (1899). In the *Chaves Case* the Supreme Court held that long and uninterrupted possession of real property, in the absence of rebutting circumstances, creates a presumption that formal records of title have once existed, even though they cannot be found.

19 Pendell v. United States (Mss., Court of Private Land Claims, Records of the Bureau of Land Management, Santa Fe, New Mexico), No. 168.

20 *Ibid.*

21 *Journal* (Mss., Court of Private Land Claims, Records of the Bureau of Land Management, Santa Fe, New Mexico), IV, 208-210.

22 *Report of the United States Attorney dated August 29, 1900, in Pendell v. United States* (Mss., Records of the General Services Administration, National Archives, Washington, D.C.), Record Group 60, Year File 9865-92.

23 United States v. Pendell, 185 U.S. 189 (1902).

24 Santa Teresa Grant, Map File 111 (Mss., Records of the Cadastrial Engineer's Office, Santa Fe, New Mexico).

25 Santa Teresa Grant, Report No. 111 (Mss., Records of the Surveyor General's Office, Bureau of Land Management, Santa Fe, New Mexico).

26 Pendell v. The Unknown Heirs, Executors and Administrators of George Baggs, Dec. (Mss., Records of the Doña Ana County District Clerk's Office, Las Cruces, New Mexico), No. 2741.

27 *Deed Records* (Mss., Records of the Doña Ana County Clerk's Office, Las Cruces, New Mexico), XXXV, 252.

28 Turney, Burges, Culwell & Pollard, *The Texas and New Mexico Boundary Along the Rio Grande Valley Between the 32nd Parallel of North Latitude and the Parallel 31° 47' North Latitude (Latter Parallel Being the International Boundary Line Between the United States and Mexico)* El Paso, 1930, 18.

29 State of New Mexico v. State of Texas, 275 U.S. 279 (1927).

30 *Report of the Special Master in the Case of the State of New Mexico v. The State of Texas* (Washington, D.C., 1926), 6, 75, 78, 90.

31 State of New Mexico v. State of Texas, 275 U.S. 279 (1927).

32 *Report of the Boundary Commissioner, The State of New Mexico v. The State of Texas* (Washington, D.C., 1930), 1-9, 20, 54.

33 Turney, Burges, Culwell & Pollard, *The Texas and New Mexico Boundary*, 25.

34 Crawford v. White, (Mss., Records of the District Clerk's Office, El Paso, Texas), No. 29011.

35 Crawford v. White, 25 S.W. 629 (1930).

36 *United States Statutes at Large*, XLV, 1069 (1929); and *Vernon's Annotated Revised Civil Statutes of the State of Texas, Revision of 1925* (Kansas City, 1947), XV, 641. Article 5421-d of the Texas Civil Statutes authorized persons holding bona fide possession of vacant land located within the boundaries of the State of Texas under United States patents to petition the Commissioner of the General Land Office for a Texas patent to such land. Pursuant to this Act, the State of Texas issued patents on thirteen separate tracts covering a total of 37.797 acres of land.

CHAPTER 4

The Sanchez Grant ₹❧

● JUAN JOSE SANCHEZ, the Jefe Político of El Paso del Norte, petitioned Guadalupe Miranda, Commissioner of Emigration, for a league of land located on the west bend of the Rio Grande between Refugio Civil Colony and the Santa Teresa Grant. Sánchez stated he needed the land to pasture his livestock because his lands at El Paso del Norte had been largely destroyed and washed out by the annual river floods.

Upon investigating the petition, Commissioner Miranda found that the lands requested by Sánchez were rough, deeply cut by arroyos, and therefore unsuited for colonization and farming. The Commissioner further found that conveyance of the land to such an industrious individual would be to the public welfare, as its occupation would help protect the colonists of Refugio and the town of El Paso del Norte from the frequent attacks of the hostile Apache Indians. Commissioner Miranda, on June 29, 1853, granted the following described lands, located some fifteen miles northwest of El Paso del Norte, to Juan José Sánchez, to wit:

Beginning at the southeast corner of the Refugio Civil Colony Grant; thence running south 5,000 varas along the west bank of the Rio Grande River to a mound near the river; thence west 5,000 varas to a mound on the top of the foothills; thence north 5,000 varas to the south line of the Refugio Civil Colony Grant; thence east 5,000 varas along the south line of the said grant to the place of beginning.

In the *testimonio* of the grant, Commissioner Miranda stated that the concession was made in accordance with Article 3 of the State Colonization Law of January 15, 1849 and Article 18 of the State Colonization Regulations of May 22,1851. Paragraph three of the State Colonization Law of January 15, 1849 authorized the Commissioner of Emigration gratuitously to grant a league of pasture land to any livestock owner who emigrated to Chihuahua from the area ceded to the United States under the Treaty of Guadalupe Hidalgo. The Commissioner of Emigration was authorized by Paragraph eighteen of the State Colonization Regulations of May 22, 1851 to make fee simple conveyance of the lands granted to such emigrants.

Juan José Sánchez immediately took legal possession of the lands, but the frequent Indian raids prevented him from establishing his proposed ranch on the grant. When the danger of such Indian attacks subsided, Sánchez would temporarily move his herds from his lands at El Paso del Norte to the grant. He also made a few trips to the grant to gather fire wood. Sánchez gave Mariano García, one of the Refugio colonists, permission to graze his stock on the grant, which he did between the years 1860 and 1876; however, neither Sánchez nor García ever constructed any permanent improvements on the grant. Such irregular use of the lands covered by the grant continued up until the time of Juan José Sánchez' death in 1893. Upon his death, the grant passed to Blaza Alvarez de Sánchez, widow of Esperedón Sánchez, and her five children: Jesús Sánchez, Guadalupe Sánchez de Martínez, Josefa Sánchez de Alvarez, Silvarino Sánchez and José J. Sánchez. Blaza Alvarez de Sánchez was the only child of Juan José Sánchez and Josefa García Sánchez.

No action was taken by the owners of the grant to secure recognition of their claim by the United States government until April 7, 1902. On this date the heirs of Juan José Sánchez filed suit in the Court of Private Land Claims, seeking confirmation of the Sánchez Grant.[1]

In their petition, the claimants alleged that a valid grant had been made by Commissioner Miranda on June 29, 1853 in favor of Juan José Sánchez; that Miranda was authorized to make the grant; that the grant was recorded in the Archives of Mexico; that the grantee had improved and used the lands covered by the grant for more than thirty-five years prior to his death; and that the grant should be confirmed into the petitioners.

The case came up for trial on June 24, 1903, at which time the plaintiffs offered in evidence their muniments of title and a substantial amount of oral testimony and depositions supporting their position. The government did not offer any evidence in the case, but by cross-examining the plaintiff's witnesses, the government's attorney, Matt G. Reynolds, showed that Juan José Sánchez was an inhabitant of El Paso del Norte at the time the grant was issued, and that he had never actually resided upon the grant.

In his argument, Reynolds contended that the claim should be rejected on the grounds that the Act of January 15, 1849, and the Regulations of

May 22, 1851, authorized Commissioner Miranda to grant land only to emigrants from New Mexico, and the title papers and testimony clearly showed that the grantee was a citizen of El Paso del Norte on the date the grant was made. In the alternative, the government asserted that the ground should be rejected, because the Act and Regulations, under which the grant was allegedly made, confined the authority of the Commissioner solely to the founding of civil colonies and distributing land to the members of such colonies. The government pointed out that the title papers in the case clearly disclosed that Sánchez was not a member of any civil colony, that the conveyance was not the distribution of colony land, but that the grant was an individual grant, made wholly independent of the founding and administration of any colony.[2]

The court, in an unanimous opinion dated June 26, 1903, rejected the claim on the grounds that Commissioner Miranda had no authority, under the Act of January 15, 1849 or the Regulations of May 22, 1851, to make a grant of land to an individual. The court held that it was necessary that the recipient of an allotment, under the Act of January 15, 1849 and the Regulations of May 22, 1851, be an actual settler in a colony formed by the Commissioner of Emigration.[3] However, the court did not pass on the question as to whether a member of a colony established under said Act and Regulations had to be an emigrant from New Mexico in order to receive an allotment of the colony's land. The claimants gave notice of their intention of appealing the decision to the United States Supreme Court, but failed to perfect it.[4] They apparently realized that they would have a very difficult burden of convincing the Supreme Court that Commissioner Miranda had authority to issue a valid land grant to an individual citizen, and the Court of Private Land Claims' decision should be reversed. After the decision became final, the land was returned to the vacant public domain. It subsequently was appropriated by the residents of La Union under the Act of February 3, 1911, which authorized the persons who claimed and occupied land covered by the rejected portion of the Refugio Civil Colony Grant to make an entry on such lands.[5]

R E F E R E N C E S

1 Alvarez v. United States (Mss., Court of Private Land Claims, Records of the Bureau of Land Management, Santa Fe, New Mexico), No. 280.

2 *Report of the United States Attorney dated August 4, 1903, in the Case Blaza Alvarez de Sánchez et al v. United States* (Mss., Records of the General Services Administration, National Archives, Washington, D.C.), Record Group 60, Year File 9865-92.

3 Alvarez v. United States (Mss., Court of Private Land Claims, Records of the Bureau of Land Management, Santa Fe, New Mexico), No. 280.

4 *Journal* (Mss., Court of Private Land Claims, Records of the Bureau of Land Management, Santa Fe, New Mexico), IV, 341 and 342.

5 United States Statutes at Large, XXXVI, 896 (1912).

CHAPTER 5

The Refugio Civil Colony Grant ᖚ

● THE VILLAGE OF REFUGIO DE LOS AMOLES,[1] like Mesilla and Santo Tomás, was established in 1850 by fifty families of Mexican citizens who elected to be repatriated after their native lands were ceded to the United States under the Treaty of Guadalupe Hidalgo. Shortly after formation of the settlement of Refugio de los Amoles, its inhabitants petitioned the Governor of Chihuahua for a land grant. On June 4, 1851 Commissioner of Emigration, Ramón Ortiz, was directed to grant the colonists the lands upon which they had settled. Arriving at the new settlement on February 2, 1852, Ortiz found that the colonists were primarily immigrants from New Mexico and that they had already appropriated and improved a tract of rich agricultural land embracing an area of 6,900 varas from north to south and 2,475 varas from east to west. Commissioner Ortiz granted said land to the colony and allotted each of its eighty-three inhabitants a *suerte*[2] of land. This agricultural block was bounded on the east by the Rio Grande and on the west by the slopes of the foot hills. The north line of the grant extended east and west along the north line of the *suerte* which had been allotted to José de la Luz Jaquez. The south line of the grant was an extended line running along the south boundary of the *suerte* which had been awarded to José María García. The eighty-three *suertes* embraced the entire agricultural block. Once the individual agricultural tracts were allocated and the owners placed in legal possession, the Commissioner proceeded with the partitioning of the townsite at Refugio de los Amoles, and awarded each family a residential lot. Lots were set aside for a plaza and public buildings. The Commissioner also set aside a one and one-fourth league tract of land immediately north of the agricultural block as a common pasture. This tract measured 6,250 varas north and south by 3,125 varas east and west. The bosques and woods along the river were also set aside for the common benefit of all the inhabitants of the colony. The lands were granted to the inhabitants of the Refugio Civil Colony by Commissioner Ortiz in accordance with the Federal Decree of August 19, 1848, and the State Regulations of May 22, 1851, as amended by the Act of December 23, 1851. Only a few of the individual settlers could afford to pay the six *pesos* fee required by the Commissioner in order to receive title documents for their individual allotments of land within the grant. The original Refugio Civil Colony Grant papers were duly filed in the Archives of the Ayuntamiento of El Paso del Norte by Commissioner Ramón Ortiz.[3] No further allotments of land were made within the Refugio Civil Colony Grant under authority of the Mexican Government.

In 1865 or 1866, a group of two hundred men, together with their families, moved from the village of La Mesa, New Mexico and settled on the Colony's common pasture tract. These new settlers formed the town now known as "Old" Chamberino. About this same time another group of new settlers, together with some of the flood refugees from Refugio de los Amoles, occupied the lands lying between the grant's southern boundary and the north line of the Santa Teresa Grant. These settlers formed the village of La Union. The inhabitants of La Union undoubtedly believed that their settlement, together with their adjoining farms, comprised a part of the Refugio Civil Colony Grant. They apparently interpreted the language in the original grant, which fixed the grant's southern boundary at the lands belonging to José María García, to mean the Santa Teresa Grant, which were then also owned by García, instead of the lands allotted to him by Ortiz.[4]

Frequent boundary disputes arose in the colony because only a few of the original grantees and none of the subsequent settlers had title papers to the lands which they claimed and occupied. In an effort to resolve these disputes, the interested parties called a special meeting at La Union on November 16, 1870. At this meeting, José María García was appointed special commissioner, with outhority to issue deeds to the persons who claimed and occupied land within the grant.[5]

Commissioner García recalled all of the Ortiz allotment documents, and in lieu thereof issued new deeds to the original grantees. He also issued deeds to the new settlers for the lands which they were occupying within the grant.[6]

When the claimants of the Refugio Civil Colony Grant learned of the efforts of the inhabitants of the Doña Ana Bend Colony and the Mesilla Civil Colony to secure confirmation of their grants, they also retained John P. Bail to represent them. On February 2, 1874 Bail, as attorney for the claimants of the Refugio Civil Colony Grant, petitioned James K. Proudfit, Surveyor-General of New Mexico, requesting him to investigate the validity of the grant.

In his petition to the Surveyor-General, Bail stated that the boundaries of the grant were correctly set out in an affidavit by Clemente Nañez, who was one of the founders of the town of Chamberino. Nañez asserted that the grant was bounded on the north by a monument, on the east by the river, on the south by El Alto de los Cuarones, and on the west by a line running one mile west of the top of the foothills.

By decision dated May 18, 1874, Surveyor-General Proudfit held that the Refugio Civil Colony Grant had been lawfully made in 1852 by the proper authorities of the Mexican Republic, that the colonises had held peaceful possession of such lands since the date of issuance of the grant, and that he believed the petitioners had a legal and equitable claim to the land. He concluded his decision by recommending that the grant, as described in the record, be confirmed by Congress to the inhabitants of the Civil Colony of Refugio.[7]

In order to assist it in reaching its final determination on the validity of private land claims, Congress required a preliminary survey be made on each grant approved by the Surveyor-General after 1862. This preliminary survey was to be executed by a United States Deputy Surveyor, but at the sole cost and expense of the grant's claimant. United States Deputy Surveyors were nominally officers of the government, but they were in fact merely independent contractors. Being paid per-mile of line surveyed, they naturally were interested in extending, rather than limiting, the extent of a grant. They invariably interpreted the vague terms and boundary calls contained in the grant papers in favor of the claimant.

On August 15, 1877 the government entered into Contract Number 80 with John T. Elkins and Robert Marmon, United States Deputy Surveyors, for the surveying of the Refugio Civil Colony Grant. Upon arriving at the grant, Elkins requested Clemente Nañez to show him the four corners of the grant. Nañez pointed out an old worn post on top of Tejano Hill, and stated that the northwest corner of the grant was located one mile west of the post. He also pointed out a mound of loose rocks at the place known as El Alto de los Cuarones, which he represented as the southeast corner of the grant. Based on this information and the specific language contained in the Surveyor-General's decision, Elkins and Marmon proceeded to survey the grant in March, 1879. No attempt was made to re-survey the two tracts of land in accordance with the boundaries as prescribed by Commissioner Ramón Ortiz when he originally issued the grant. The Refugio Civil Colony Grant, according to Elkins and Marmon's survey, covered 26,130.19 acres of land, instead of merely two leagues. The survey was approved by Surveyor-General Henry M. Atkinson on April 5, 1879.[8]

The United States Congress had not acted on the Surveyor-General's decision recommending confirmation of the Refugio Civil Colony Grant prior to creation of the Court of Private Land Claims. The grant's claimants were therefore obligated to institute suit against the United States in an effort to obtain recognition of their claim. The claimants of the grant incorporated their interests on March 7, 1884, and appointed three commissioners to hold title to and manage the grant. The commissioners of the Grant of the Colony of Refugio and William Desauer, the owner of several tracts located in the grant, instituted proceedings against the United States in the Court of Private Land Claims on February 8, 1893, seeking confirmation of the grant.[9]

A similar suit was brought against the United States in the Court of

Private Land Claims on March 2, 1893, by Jesús Ochoa, Jesús Henriques and Vincente García, the owners of certain tracts of land located within the grant.[10]

Due to the similarity of issues involved in the two cases, they were consolidated by the Court on September 5, 1896. Ione L. Morley, the owner of a one hundred-sixty acre tract of land located in the northwest corner of the grant, intervened in the case.

The Cause came up for hearing on July 5, 1898. The plaintiffs offered a large amount of oral testimony and documentary evidence in support of their petition. The United States, in turn, presented no evidence in opposition to the confirmation of the grant, but asserted that the agricultural tract should be limited to the area described in the original grant, and that the pasture tract should be restricted to one league of land.

In a preliminary opinion, the Court, on September 4, 1898, announced that the grant was entitled to confirmation, but that such confirmation should be confined to the area set forth in the government's argument. By limiting the pastoral tract to one league, the tract claimed by Mrs. Morley was excluded from the grant. Mrs. Morley promptly requested permission to introduce further evidence in order to prove that her tract was actually located within the grant. This permission was granted, and additional testimony was taken by the Court on the subject of boundaries. The Court, in its decision of July 13, 1901, adhered to its original opinion, and fixed the boundaries of the two tracts covered by the grant.

The first, or agricultural tract, all of which had been allotted to and distributed among the colonists by Commissioner Ortiz, was confirmed to the Corporation of Refugio in trust for the persons to whom it had been allotted, their heirs and assigns. The first tract commenced on the west bank of the Rio Grande as the same was situated in 1852, at a point where an extension of the south boundary line of the José María García agricultural allotment intersected the western bank of said river; thence west along an extension of the south boundary line of said allotment to a point at the foot of the slopes or drainage of the foothills; thence in a northerly direction along the foot of the foothills, to a point where a prolongation of the northern boundary line of the lands allotted to José de la Luz Jaques struck the foot of the slopes; thence east along said line to the west bank of the river; thence south along the west bank of the river to the point of beginning.

The second, or pastoral tract, was confirmed to the Corporation of Refugio. The north boundary of the first tract formed the southern boundary of the second tract. The eastern and western boundaries of the second tract were extensions of the first tract. The northern boundary line of the second tract was to be parallel to the southern boundary line, and was to be located far enough north so as to embrace one league of land within the boundaries of the second tract. The Court restricted the size of the pasturage tract to one square league of land because the plaintiffs did not adequately prove that Commissioner Ortiz had authority to grant one and a fourth leagues to the colony for grazing purposes.

The Court also refused to recognize the allotments made by Commissioner García to the new settlers in the area south of the grant in the vicinity of La Union. Title to the strip of land claimed by the colony lying between the base of the foothills and one mile west of the top of the foothills was also rejected by the Court. The Court qualified its decision, however, by stating that if the Rio Grande of 1852 was found to be located within the boundaries of the State of Texas, then the eastern boundary lines of said tracts were to extend only to the western boundary of Texas, instead of to the old riverbed. The decision also excepted all gold, silver and quicksilver mines, and minerals located upon and within the grant premises.[11]

The United States Attorney reported that he did not believe the government should appeal the decision. He reasoned that the boundaries as fixed by the Court were as favorable to the government as could be hoped for in any event.[12]

After the Court handed down its decision, the Surveyor-General advised the Court that it was encountering difficulty in securing a contract with a Deputy Surveyor for the surveying of the grant because of the confusion and doubt concerning the proper location of the river as it existed in 1852. If the Court rejected the survey on the grounds that it did not accurately located the riverbed, the Deputy Surveyor would then have to bear the financial loss. The Surveyor-General felt that the location of the river was a question of fact, to be determined by the Court, instead of a Deputy Surveyor. The Court's attention was also called to the fact that in 1852 the boundary between the United States and Mexico was located in the center of the Rio Grande bed.

The Court, on December 14, 1901, amended its original decision by providing that the east boundary of the grant should be located in the center of the riverbed of 1852, instead of along its western bank. In order to obtain a more definite description of the location of the center of the Rio Grande as it ran in 1852, the Court appointed Clayton G. Coleman as a Special Commissioner, with authority to determine by a metes and bounds survey the location of the middle thread of the Rio Grande as it ran in 1852.[13]

The Court, by decree dated August 20, 1902, approved the survey and report of Commissioner Coleman as correctly locating the center of the river as it ran in 1852. After the location of the center of the river as it ran in 1852 had been judicially determined, an official survey of the grant was ordered. Tracts one and two of the Refugio Civil Colony Grant were surveyed in December, 1903 by Wendell V. Hall, U.S. Deputy Surveyor, under Contract No. 362. Tract one of this survey contained 7,184.02 acres, and Tract two embraced 3,450.38 acres.[14]

The Commissioners of the Refugio Colony Grant, on May 12, 1904, filed a protest against the approval of the Hall Survey. Among other objections, they stated that the survey did not follow the middle of the Rio Grande River bed as it ran in 1852, and that Tract two did not contain one league of land. These objections were based on a resurvey of the grant made by Charles L. Post. The Post Survey of the grant attempted to show that the Coleman Survey located the east boundary line of the grant some distance to the west of the center of the Rio Grande as it ran in 1852. The Post Survey placed the Rio Grande bed in approximately the same position as the Elkins and Marmon Survey of 1877. The Court of Private Land Claims rejected the protest and approved the Hall Survey on June 14, 1904.[15]

A patent covering the 11,524.3 acres of land covered by the two tracts which comprised the Refugio Civil Colony Grant was issued to the Corporation of Refugio on June 6, 1910. Gold, silver and quicksilver mines and minerals were reserved by the United States in this patent.[16]

Under the provisions of the Act of February 3, 1911,[17] persons claiming title to land within the rejected portion of the Refugio Civil Colony Grant under conveyances issued by the grant officers prior to August 20, 1902, were authorized to "make an entry" for the land they occupied and claimed.

Pursuant to the provisions of this special relief act, most of the innocent parties who had developed and improved specific tracts of land in good faith and belief that their lands were embraced within the grant finally received legal title to their homes and farms.

A further reduction of the acreage contained within the Refugio Civil Colony Grant occurred in 1928, as a result of the United States Supreme Court's decision in the case styled "State of New Mexico v. State of Texas."[18] In this case, the Court held that the boundary between New Mexico and Texas from 32° down to 31° 47' north latitude was located in "the middle of the channel of the Rio Grande River as it existed on September 19, 1850," and in that year the river was actually located west of a portion of the patented east boundary line of the Refugio Civil Colony Grant. The patent to the Refugio Civil Colony Grant was therefore declared invalid, insofar as it covered any land located within the boundaries of the State of Texas.

The final settlement of its boundary dispute along the Rio Grande, for all practical purposes, marks the end of the history of the Refugio Civil Colony Grant. All of the colony's lands have long since been distributed among its inhabitants and the original settlement of Refugio de los Amoles, from which the colony took its name, is no longer in existence.

REFERENCES

1 Refugio de los Amoles was located on the west bank of the Rio Grande, Doña Ana County, New Mexico, approximately one and a half miles west of the present town of Anthony, Texas. The settlement was damaged during a river flood in 1865, and was finally destroyed by the floods of 1884 and 1885.

2 The Spanish term "suerte" was used to designate an individual allotment of irrigable land. The word means "chance" and arose from the practice of distributing land by lot. By virtue of this practice, the word is now defined in some Spanish dictionaries as any tract of land with specific boundaries. A suerte in the Refugio Civil Colony Grant denoted a 700 by 250 vara tract, or approximately 29.75 acres of land. Colony of Refugio v. United States (Mss., Court of Private Land Claims, Records of the Bureau of Land Management, Santa Fe, New Mexico), No. 150.

3 Senate Executive Documents, 43rd Cong., 1st Sess., Document No. 56, 41-61 (1874).

4 The fallacy of this interpretation is clearly evident when the Sánchez Grant is considered. The Sánchez Grant was made shortly after the Refugio Civil Colony Grant and covered the land located between the García allotment and the Santa Teresa Grant. Alvarez v. United States (Mss., Court of Private Land Claims, Records of the Bureau of Land Management, Santa Fe, New Mexico), No. 280.

5 Deed Records (Mss., Records of the Doña Ana County Clerk's Office, Las Cruces, New Mexico), IV, 345.

6 Colony of Refugio v. United States (Mss., Court of Private Land Claims, Records of the Bureau of Land Management, Santa Fe, New Mexico), No. 150.

7 Land Claims Records, (Mss., Records of the Surveyor-General's Office, Bureau of Land Management, Santa Fe, New Mexico), V, 105.

8 Refugio Civil Colony Grant, Map File 90 (Mss., Records of the Cadastrial Engineer's Office, Santa Fe, New Mexico).

9 Colony of Refugio v. United States (Mss., Court of Private Land Claims, Records of the Bureau of Land Management, Santa Fe, New Mexico), No. 150.

10 Ochoa v. United States (Mss., Court of Private Land Claims, Records of the Bureau of Land Management, Santa Fe, New Mexico), No. 193.

11 Journal (Mss., Court of Private Land Claims, Records of the Bureau of Land Management, Santa Fe, New Mexico), IV, 247-250.

12 Report of the United States Attorney Dated July 29, 1901, in the Case of The Colony of Refugio and William Desauer v. United States (Mss., Records of the General Services Administration, National Archives, Washington, D.C.), Record Group 60, Year File 9865-92.

13 Journal (Mss., Court of Private Land Claims, Records of the Bureau of Land Management, Santa Fe, New Mexico), IV, 283 and 284.

14 The Refugio Civil Colony Grant, Report No. 90 (Mss., Records of the Surveyor-General's Office, Bureau of Land Management, Santa Fe, New Mexico).

15 Journal (Mss., Court of Private Land Claims, Records of the Bureau of Land Management, Santa Fe, New Mexico), IV, 351 and 352.

16 Deed Records (Mss., Records of the Doña Ana County Clerk's Office, Las Cruces, New Mexico), XLIII, 45.

17 United States Statutes at Large, XXXVI, 896 (1912).

18 State of New Mexico v. State of Texas, 275 U.S. 279 (1927).

CHAPTER 6

The José Manuel Sánchez Baca Grant ॐ

● JOSE MANUEL SANCHEZ BACA was a wealthy patriotic New Mexican
who elected to retain his Mexican citizenship after the Treaty of Guadalupe Hidalgo. At his own expense, he transported his family, peons, and
some 6,000 sheep to Mexico. Baca temporarily moved to San Ignacio and
then, in December, 1852, to the new colony of Santo Tomás de Yturbide.
He petitioned the Commissioner of Emigration, Ramón Ortiz, for a land
grant in accordance with Article 3 of the Act of the State of Chihuahua of
January 15, 1849. This article authorized the Commissioner to grant im-
migrating livestock owners a league of vacant public grazing land as
pasture land for their animals. Complying with Baca's request, Commissioner Ortiz designated the limits of the proposed grant. Baca immediately
constructed corrals for his livestock and jacals for his peons on such lands
and commenced using them as pastures for his animals. Ramón Ortiz was
removed as Commissioner of Emigration before he was able to issue the
grant to Baca and place him in possession of such lands. Guadalupe Miranda was appointed as his successor, with instructions to complete all un-
finished business in connection with the colonies of La Mesilla, Santo Tomás de Yturbide, Refugio, Guadalupe, San Ignacio, and San Joaquin.
Guadalupe Miranda, as Commissioner General for Emigration of the
Supreme Government and the State of Chihuahua on June 5, 1853, granted
unto José Manuel Sánchez Baca a *sitio de ganado mayor*.

The grant commenced at the southeast corner of the Santo Tomás de
Yturbide Colony Grant, and ran south 5,000 varas along the west bank of
the river to a large rock; thence west 5,000 varas to a mesa in front of two
mountain peaks in the prairie; thence north 5,000 varas to the point of a
black mesa; and thence east along the south line of the Santo Tomás de
Yturbide Colony Grant 5,000 varas to the place of beginning on the edge
of the Rio Grande. The concession was given in consideration of the loyal
services rendered by Baca in migrating to Chihuahua at great personal
expense.

The grant was made subject to the conditions that he could not sell or
encumber the lands for a period of four years, that he occupy and build
upon it, and that he cultivate the tillable portions thereof. Commissioner
Miranda personally surveyed the grant and placed Baca in legal possession
of the lands contained therein. He then issued a *testimonio* evidencing
Baca's title to the grant, and filed the original *expediente* in the Archives
of the Ayuntamiento of El Paso del Norte.

Baca and his family resided at Santo Tomás, as the constant threat of Indian attacks made it impossible for them to live on the grant. However, Baca constructed a small log cabin near the northwest corner of the grant, in which he lived whenever possible. However, he continuously grazed his large herds of sheep and livestock on the grant. In 1852 Baca began cultivating a 200 acre tract of land which was located in the northeastern portion of the grant. In order to irrigate this tract, he built an *acequia* which commenced on the river north of the grant at a point near the Arroyo de Agua and extended to this farm tract.

The José Manuel Sánchez Baca Grant is situated in Doña Ana County, New Mexico, and is a portion of the lands within the area ceded to the United States by Mexico under the Gadsden Purchase. Perfected property rights were recognized and guaranteed by the Treaty of Mesilla which culminated this purchase. On March 24, 1856 José Manuel Sánchez Baca petitioned the Surveyor General of New Mexico, requesting permission to prove the validity of his grant.[1]

Between 1850 and 1856 the population of the Mesilla Civil Colony and Santo Tomás de Yturbide Colony Grants greatly increased. Many of the more recent residents of these colonies found they could not obtain any lands within the limits of the colonies upon which to earn a livelihood. During January of 1857 a meeting was held at Mesilla to discuss the plight of these landless colonists. After this meeting approximately three hundred men proceeded to establish the new settlement known as La Mesa, upon which the then vacant public domain located between the José Manuel Sánchez Baca and the Refugio Civil Colony Grants. In order to irrigate their newly appropriated lands, the La Mesa settlers commenced consturcting an *acequia* from Mesilla down to the lands which they were preparing for cultivation.[2]

When the *acequia* reached Baca's Grant, he denied the La Mesa settlers permission to construct their ditch across his land. The colonists offered to purchase the grant, but Baca refused to sell. Knowing that the grant was valid, they maliciously requested United States Attorney for New Mexico, William Claude Jones, to file a protest against confirmation of the grant. Complying with their request, on January 25, 1857 Jones addressed such a protest to the Surveyor General, alleging that the grant should be rejected on the grounds that (1) the grant was anti-dated; (2) under the Laws and Colonial Regulations, Commissioner Miranda had no authority to issue such a grant; and (3) the conditions specified in the grant had never been fulfilled. In conclusion, Jones stated that the grounds upon which the protest was based were incontrovertible, and that he was thoroughly convinced that Baca's claim to one of the best tracts of land in Doña Ana County was invalid.[3]

When Baca learned of the protest, he decided to comply with the unjust demands of the La Mesa settlers. On April 20, 1857 he conveyed all of his interest in the grant, except for his two hundred acre farm tract which was known as Los Chulos, to William Claude Jones, Eugenio Leonard, Marcial Padillo, and Pablo Albillar, Trustee for the Town of La Mesa, in exchange for and in consideration of 3,000 sacks of corn.[4] After the La Mesa residents purchased the grant, Jones withdrew his protest, stating that he was unable to sustain the allegations mentioned therein.

Shortly thereafter, the La Mesa *acequia* was completed, and the La Mesa colonists proceeded to distribute the land which they had appropriated among themselves. The Commissioners of La Mesa issued deeds to the colonists for their individual allotments. The colonists who had been allotted land on the José Manuel Sánchez Baca Grant moved to the grant and proceeded to establish the new town known as San Miguel, New Mexico, for their mutual convenience and protection.

In order to cure the title defect which resulted from Baca's violating the condition which prohibited him from selling the grant for a period of four years, Eugenio Moreno and the other settlers who had acquired portions of the José Manuel Sánchez Baca Grant obtained a new deed from Baca on November 28, 1857, covering all of his interest in the grant except for Los Chulos Tract. Baca was also given the right to use water from the La Mesa *acequia* for irrigation of his land.[5]

After establishment of the settlement of San Miguel, Baca moved to the Los Chulos Tract and cultivated it until his death about 1860 or 1861. He died at Valverde, New Mexico, while enroute to Santa Fe for medical treatment. By verbal will, Baca bequeathed the Los Chulos Tract to his brother, Cristóbal Sánchez Baca. Cristóbal Sánchez Baca and Lajara Baca, widow of José Manuel Sánchez Baca, sold the Los Chulos Tract to Nester Telles on January 6, 1868 for $2,000.00[6]

Due to the death of the grantee, no further steps were taken to secure confirmation of the grant until January 25, 1882. On that date W. L. Rynerson, attorney for the claimants of the grant, petitioned the Surveyor General, requesting the lands be segregated from the public domain, and the claimants be permitted to prove the validity of their claim to the lands upon which they had resided for more than a quarter of a century.

By opinion dated May 20, 1882, Henry M. Atkinson, Surveyor General, held that the grant to José Manuel Sánchez Baca had been properly made by Commissioner Guadalupe Miranda under the National Law of August 19, 1848, and the Laws of the State of Chihuahua dated January 15, 1849 and May 22, 1851, that the conditions contained in the grant had been fulfilled, and that the grant had been duly filed in the Mexican Archives. He advised Congress that in his opinion the grant was valid and title thereto should be confirmed unto the heirs, assigns and legal representatives of José Manuel Sánchez Baca. The Surveyor General expressly excepted from his approval any minerals, which were reserved by the Mexican Government on the date of the issuance of the concession.[7]

The grant was officially surveyed in April, 1888 by John Shaw, United States Deputy Surveyor. The survey showed that the grant contained a total of 3,601.18 acres of land. The Surveyor General approved the survey on November 28, 1883.[8]

Anticipating early approval of their claim, the owners of the grant formed a corporation known as the Corporation of the José Manuel Sánchez Baca Grant. Such a corporation would be necessary in order to settle the numerous legal problems which undoubtedly would arise once the grant was confirmed. Francisco Rivera, Melquiades Telles, and José María Romeres were appointed Commissioners of the Corporation.

No further action was taken on recognition of the grant until after the Court of Private Land Claims was established. On February 28, 1898 the Corporation of the Grant of José Manuel Sánchez Baca and several other claimants of the grant filed suit against the United States in the Court of Private Land Claims for confirmation and recognition of the grant.[9]

The plaintiffs alleged in their petition that the grant had been duly and properly made by Commissioner Guadalupe Miranda under the laws of the Mexican Government and the State of Chihuahua, in consideration for the patriotic services rendered by Baca to the Republic of Mexico. They further alleged that the conditions contained in the grant had been satisfied, that the claimants had derived their title therein through the original grantee, and that the *testimonio* of the grant had been properly filed in the Archives of Mexico. The petition closed with a prayer that the title to the grant be investigated and confirmed in its one hundred an two claimants.

The cause originally came up for hearing on March 21, 1896, but was postponed until July 5, 1898. When the hearing was resumed, a large amount of oral and documentary evidence was introduced by the plaintiffs tending to substantiate the allegations set forth in their petition.

The government offered no evidence in contradiction to that presented by the plaintiffs. In its argument, the government contended that the granting authority was not authorized to issue the concession, and that the *expediente* of the grant had not been duly recorded in the Archives of Mexico as required by the Gadsden Treaty.

In a preliminary opinion dated September 4, 1899, the court, through Justice William W. Murray, overruled the government's contentions and confirmed the grant. The court held that Commissioner Miranda was authorized, under Article 3 of the Act of January 15, 1849, to grant a *sitio de ganado mayor* to an individual stockraiser who had emigrated to Mexico from the territory ceded to the United States under the Treaty of Guadalupe Hidalgo.[10]

The difficulties previously encountered by surveyors in locating the Rio Grande riverbed of 1853 prompted the Justice Department to send Special Agent Clayton G. Coleman to the premises for purposes of investigating the boundaries and extent of the lands which had been confirmed by the Court. Clayton reported that the grant:

. . . commenced at a point on the west boundary of the Hugh Stephenson Grant directly east of the most prominent point of a black mesa (which point of mesa is a mile or more northwest of the Plaza of San Miguel and is mentioned as a southern limit of the Santo Tomás de Yturbide Grant) and running thence for the east boundary in a southeasterly direction along the west boundary of the Hugh Stephenson Grant to a point which is two miles 48.33-1/3 chains by a direct line from the beginning; thence for the south boundary west two miles 48.33-1/3 chains; thence for the west boundary by a line parallel to a direct line between the northeast and south-east corners two miles 48.33-1/3 chains; and thence for the north boundary by a direct line to the beginning.[11]

The Court of Private Land Claims entered its Final Decision in the case on May 2, 1900. This decision formally confirmed title to the grant in the Corporation of the José Manuel Sánchez Baca Grant in trust for its one hundred and two claimants. The court, in describing the lands which it had confirmed, adopted the boundaries designated by Coleman in his report. The decree expressly provided that title to any gold, silver and quicksilver mines and minerals situated on the lands were to remain the property of the United States.[12]

In his report on the case to the United States Attorney General, Matthew G. Reynolds pointed out that in this case the claimants of the grant had very strong equities in their favor. He noted that many of the claimants, or their ancestors, had held peaceful possession of their individual tracts of land for approximately fifty years. Continuing, the government's attorney stated that while he had some doubts as to the correctness of the court's decision, he was not so confident of his position as to feel justified in recommending an appeal of the case.[13]

Once the court's decision became final, the Commissioner of the General Land Office issued Contract Number 350 to Jay Turley, United States Deputy Surveyor, for the surveying of the grant. Turley was instructed to survey the grant in strict conformity with the description contained in the Private Land Claims' decision of May 2, 1900. Turley surveyed the grant on the 30th and 31st of January, 1901, and filed his field notes and plat of the grant with the Surveyor General on April 27, 1901. Turley's survey showed that the grant contained 3,530.6 acres of land.[14]

The United States Attorney protested the approval of the Turley survey on the grounds that the survey included lands in excess of and beyond those contemplated by the court in its decree of confirmation, and such excess resulted due to the failure of the Deputy Surveyor strictly to follow the boundary calls set forth in the court's decision. The Surveyor General appointed Thomas M. Hurlburt as a Special Examiner to investigate the merits of the government's protest. Hurlburt reported that Turley had executed his survey in an accurate manner, and he knew of no reason why the survey should not be accepted. The Court of Private Land Claims overruled the government's protest and approved Turley's survey of the grant on April 8, 1902.[15]

The years of persistent and tireless effort to secure recognition of the José Manuel Sánchez Baca Grant were culminated in victory on March 19, 1906. On that date Theodore Roosevelt, as President of the United States, executed the long coveted patent for the 3,530.6 acres of land covered by the grant. The patent was issued to the Corporation of the José Manuel Sánchez Baca Grant in trust for the persons to whom the same was assigned and sold and who are now the owners thereof, their heirs and successors in interest. The patent excluded all right and title to gold, silver and quicksilver mines and minerals located on the grant.[16]

REFERENCES

1 José Manuel Sánchez Baca Grant, Report No. 129, (Mss., Records of the Surveyor General's Office, Bureau of Land Management, Santa Fe, New Mexico).

2 In the Southwest, no land can be cultivated without irrigation. The meager rainfall during the months of July and August is not sufficient to support dry land farming. Irrigation in the El Paso area was originally introduced by the Spaniards. The first *acequia* — or gravity canal — was constructed at El Paso del Norte in about 1660. The *acequia* irrigation system was widely utilized by the inhabitants of the Mesilla Valley. This system employs the basic principle that as a river flows down a valley there is a continuous fall in the elevation of the land traversed away from the head of the valley. There is also a gradual sloping of the side of the valley toward the river. Therefore, the lands on both sides of the river are considerably higher than the riverbed at a particular point, but lower than the river at a point further upstream. By diverting water from the river upstream through an *acequia* which follows a contour with a somewhat higher elevation than the river, the strip of land lying downriver between the *acequia* and the river could be successfully irrigated. F. C. Baker, *Irrigation in Mesilla Valley, New Mexico, Water Supply and Irrigation Paper No. 10* (Washington, 1898), 21.

3 José Manuel Sánchez Baca Grant, Report No. 129, (Mss., Records of the Surveyor General's Office, Bureau of Land Management, Santa Fe, New Mexico).

4 The deed dated April 20, 1857 from José Manuel Sánchez Baca to William Claude Jones *et al* was not recorded in Doña Ana County, New Mexico, but the original deed was filed in the Surveyor General's Office. *Ibid.*

5 *Deed Records* (Mss., Records of the Doña Ana County Clerk's Office, Las Cruces, New Mexico), XIV, 27.

6 *Deed Records* (Mss., Records of the Doña Ana County Clerk's Office, Las Cruces, New Mexico), IV, 380-384.

7 *Land Claims Records* (Mss., Records of the Surveyor General's Office, Bureau of Land Management, Santa Fe, New Mexico), VI, 767 and 768.

8 José Manuel Sánchez Baca Grant, Map File 129 (Mss., Records of the Cadastrial Engineer's Office, Santa Fe, New Mexico).

9 The Corporation of the Grant of José Manuel Sánchez Baca v. United States (Mss., Court of Private Land Claims, Records of the Bureau of Land Management, Santa Fe, New Mexico), No. 138.

10 Ibid.

11 José Manuel Sánchez Baca Grant, Report No. 129 (Mss., Records of the Surveyor General's Office, Bureau of Land Management, Santa Fe, New Mexico).

12 Journal (Mss., Court of Private Land Claims, Records of the Bureau of Land Management, Santa Fe, New Mexico), IV, 151-153.

13 Report of the United States Attorney dated June 20, 1900, in the Case of The Corporation of the Grant of José Manuel Sánchez Baca v. United States, (Mss., Records of the General Services Administration, National Archives, Washington, D.C.), Record Group 60, Year File 9865-92.

14 José Manuel Sánchez Baca Grant, Map File 129 (Mss., Records of the Cadastrial Engineer's Office, Santa Fe, New Mexico).

15 José Manuel Sánchez Baca Grant, Report No. 129 (Mss., Records of the Surveyor General's Office, Bureau of Land Management, Santa Fe, New Mexico).

16 Deed Records (Mss., Records of the Doña Ana County Clerk, Las Cruces, New Mexico), XXIX, 398.

CHAPTER 7

The Santo Tomás de
Yturbide Colony Grant 🙠

● AFTER THE SIGNING of the Treaty of Guadalupe Hidalgo in 1848, numerous residents of New Mexico who did not desire to become citizens of the United States moved to Mexico. Many of these emigrants settled in the area west of the Rio Grande in the upper Mesilla Valley, which was located within the State of Chihuahua. Upon assuming his duties as General Commissioner of Emigration in 1849, Ramón Ortiz found that these emigrants had established settlements at Mesilla and Santo Tomás and were cultivating most of the bottom lands adjacent to these towns. The residents of Santo Tomás petitioned Commissioner Ortiz for a colony grant, but he denied the request on the grounds he did not consider the settlement at Santo Tomás as a separate and distinct colony, since there was only a short interruption between the houses of the two villages. Commissioner Ortiz then proceeded to establish a single colony embracing both settlements. On January 20, 1852 he set aside to the Mesilla Colony three and one-half leagues of land for agricultural purposes, and one and one-fourth leagues for general grazing purposes. He also designated lands for a public park, the gathering of fire wood, and pasture for domestic animals. Commissioner Ortiz allotted and distributed a large number of individual agricultural tracts and town lots within the Mesilla Colony to the inhabitants of Mesilla and Santo Tomás during the years 1852 and 1853.[1]

Before Commissioner Ramón Ortiz had performed all acts necessary to vest title to the grant in the inhabitants of the Mesilla Colony, President Mariano Arista's government was overthrown and Commissioner Ortiz was removed from office early in the year 1853. Guadalupe Miranda was appointed as Ortiz' successor. In order to avoid confusion and future difficulties, Commissioner Miranda held that the settlement of Santo Tomás constituted a separate colony and proceeded to divide the original Mesilla Colony into the Mesilla Civil Colony and the Santo Tomás de Yturbide Colony. On August 3, 1853 Commissioner Miranda granted two leagues of land to the Colony of Santo Tomás de Yturbide. The grant was made under authority of and in conformity with the Regulation of May 22, 1851,[2] and covered the following tracts of land:

A league of agricultural land beginning at a monument on a little arm of the river which marks the southeast corner of the Mesilla Civil Colony Grant; thence west 5,000 varas along the south line of the Mesilla Civil Colony Grant to a monument on top of a sand hill opposite the ruins of the Querras Corral; thence south along the foothills 7,500 varas to a monument located on the north line of the José Manuel Sánchez Baca Grant; thence east 2,500 varas to a monument located on the river bank; thence north along the west river bank to the place of beginning.

A league of common pasture land commencing at the northwest corner of the agricultural tract; thence west 2,500 varas; thence south 7,500 varas; thence east 2,500 varas to the southwest corner of the agricultural tract; thence north 7,500 varas along the west boundary of the agricultural tract to the place of beginning.

After Commissioner Miranda had completed surveying the Grant, he placed the inhabitants of the Santo Tomás de Yturbide Colony in legal possession of the above described lands. In addition to recognizing the individual allotments of land which had previously been issued by Commissioner Ortiz, Miranda proceeded to distribute the remaining unappropriated agricultural lands located within the grant to the new colonists, who had not received a *suerte* of land. On September 4, 1853 Commissioner Miranda reported to the Governor of Chihuahua that he had allotted land and given deeds to the inhabitants of the colonies of Mesilla, Santo Tomás, Guadalupe and San Ygnacio in accordance with his duties as General Commissioner of Emigration. The governor approved Miranda's report on September 10, 1853, and ordered that the colonists be secured in their rights.[3]

No attempt was made to secure recognition of the Santo Tomás Yturbide Colony Grant until January 24, 1885. On that date Mariano Barela and twelve other interested parties petitioned the Surveyor General's Office of the Territory of New Mexico for confirmation of the grant. In support of their claim, they filed what purported to be a certified copy of the original grant papers, and also introduced oral testimony tending to show that the Colony's copy of the grant papers had been lost during a flood of the Rio Grande in 1862. On May 16, 1885 Surveyor General Clarence Pullen reported to the Commissioner of the General Land Office that the Santo Tomás de Yturbide Colony Grant was a valid land grant, and recommended its confirmation by Congress.[4]

President Grover Cleveland, shortly after his inauguration in 1885, appointed William A. J. Sparks as Commissioner of the General Land Office and George W. Julian as Surveyor General of the Territory of New Mexico. Both Sparks and Julian believed that Pullen and his predecessors had failed to investigate adequately the validity of Spanish and Mexican land grants in New Mexico, and had thereby caused the government to be despoiled of a million acres of land. Based upon this assumption, Commissioner Sparks promptly instituted a partisan investigation of all New Mexican private land claims. Pursuant to this policy, Commissioner Sparks returned the report to Surveyor Pullen and instructed him to refer the claim to George W. Julian when he arrived in New Mexico for his further investigation.

Shortly after he entered office, Julian proceeded to re-examine the Santo Tomás de Yturbide Colony Grant. In a supplemental opinion dated August 25, 1885, he conceded that Commissioner Miranda had authority to issue the valid colony grant, but recommended the claim be rejected because there was no evidence that the grant papers introduced by Mariano Barela were genuine, that the grant had been recorded in the Archives of Mexico as required by the Gadsden Treaty, or that the claimants were the original grantees or their successors.[5]

Mariano Barela, purchaser of a large number of the individual tracts which comprised the Santo Tomás de Yturbide Colony Grant, realized that unless the objections raised in Surveyor General Julian's supplemental opinion of August 25, 1885 were cured, Congress would undoubtedly refuse to confirm the grant. In order to satisfy these objections, Barela obtained an exemplified copy of the grant papers from the Archives of El Paso del Norte and field it in the Surveyor General's Office. He also filed an abstract which evidenced his title to a major portion of the grant. Surveyor General Julian, in a letter to the Commissioner of the General Land Offiffice dated July 1, 1886, stated that if these documents had been before him when he made his Supplemental Report of August 25, 1885, he would have reached a different conclusion.[6]

The reluctance of the Congress of the United States to confirm Spanish and Mexican land grants in New Mexico after 1869 delayed further action on the Santo Tomás de Yturbide Colony Grant until after establishment of the Court of Private Land Claims in 1891. Mariano Barela died on September 26, 1892, and his interest in the grant was devised to his mother, Rafaela G. Barela, a widow.

Rafaela G. Barela and Ramón Gonzales, the owner of a number of individual tracts in the Santo Tomás de Yturbide Colony Grant, instituted proceedings in the Court of Private Land Claims against the United States on February 28, 1893, requesting confirmation of the grant. The suit was brought by the plaintiffs in their individual capacity and as a class action for the benefit of all others who owned or claimed an interest in the grant.[7]

The cause was heard by the court on July 5, 1898. At the trial, the plaintiffs introduced voluminous oral and documentary evidence supporting their position. The government introduced no contradictory evidence. The United States Attorney attacked the claim on the grounds that the plaintiffs did not have authority to institute the suit on behalf of the other claimants, that the granting officer had no power to issue the concession, and that it had not been duly recorded as required by the Gadsden Treaty. In a Preliminary Decree dated September 4, 1899, the court held that a class action could be brought by the plaintiffs for the benefit of all the claimants of the grant, that Commissioner Miranda had authority to make the concession, that the Archives of the Ayuntamiento of El Paso constituted a record within the meaning of the Gadsden Treaty, and that the Santo Tomás de Yturbide Colony was a valid grant which the government was bound to recognize under the Gadsden Treaty. The court, therefore, held that a decree of confirmation should be entered in the case. Subsequent to the announcement of its preliminary decree, the court appointed a Special Agent to investigate the boundaries and extent of the grant. The Agent's report was accepted by the court and embodied in its final decree of May 2, 1900.[8]

The Court of Private Land Claims, in its final decision dated May 2, 1900, found that the Santo Tomás de Yturbide Colony Grant was a valid grant which the United States was obligated to recognize. The court held that the grant consisted of a tract of agricultural land and a tract of pasture land described as follows:

TRACT 1

Beginning at the foothills on the west side of the present bed of the Rio Grande del Norte where there is a hill on top of which was placed the original landmark (a pile of stone which can still be seen), running thence for the west boundary in a southeasterly direction along the slopes or drainage of the hills to the most prominent point of a black mesa, which is a mile or more northwest of the Plaza of San Miguel; thence for the south boundary east to an intersection with the west boundary of the Hugh Stephenson Grant; thence for the east boundary in a northeasterly direction along the west boundary of said Hugh Stephenson Grant to the northwest corner thereof; and thence for the north boundary by a direct line to the beginning, excluding any portion of the Hugh Stephenson Grant which may be included within these boundaries by reason of the last named or north boundary crossing the boundary of said Hugh Stephenson Grant.

TRACT 2

Beginning at the northwest corner of Tract 1, and running thence for the north boundary west two miles 48.33-1/3 chains; thence for the west boundary in a southeasterly direction on a line parallel to the west boundary of Tract 1 two miles 48.33-1/3 chains; thence for the south boundary east to an intersection with the west boundary of Tract 1; and thence along the west boundary of Tract 1 to beginning.

The court concluded its decision by confirming title to the grant insofar as it covered the agricultural tract in the numerous individuals to whom it had been completely distributed by Commissioners Ortiz and Miranda. Title to the pasture tract was vested in the persons who were bona fide residents of the Colony on December 30, 1853. The government, however, reserved all gold, silver and quicksilver mines and minerals located on or within the grant lands.[9]

Matthew G. Reynolds, the United States Attorney in the case, reported to the Attorney General that although he had some doubts as to the correctness of the decree insofar as it held that the grant had been legally made and duly recorded, he was not sufficiently confident of his position to feel justified in recommending an appeal be taken to the Supreme Court. As a result of Reynolds' report, the United States did not appeal the action, and the court's decree of confirmation became final.[10]

An official survey of the Santo Tomás de Yturbide Colony Grant was made in January, 1901 by Jay Turley, United States Deputy Surveyor, under Contract Number 350. Turley was instructed by the Surveyor General's Office to locate the east line of the Santo Tomás de Yturbide Colony Grant coincident with the west line of the Bracito Grant[11] as surveyed in 1893 by Leonard M. Brown. Based upon Turley's survey, the grant contained three separate tracts. The first tract contained 2,137.89 acres; the second tract covered 3,033.91 acres, and the third tract embraced 88.13 acres — or a total of 5,259.93 acres — instead of 8,000 acres as originally claimed by the petitioners. Rafaela G. Barela objected to approval of the Turley survey, insofar as it pertained to a position of the east boundary lines of the first tract between stations numbered 45 and 96, inclusive, on the grounds that it did not depict the true location of the west boundary of the Bracito Grant. She pointed out that the east bank of the river, as it ran in 1854, formed the west boundary of the Bracito Grant. She contended that Turley had erroneously located the east boundary of the Santo Tomás de Yturbide Grant approximately two miles west of its true location, and that as a result of this error approximately 4,690 acres of land had been excluded from Tract 1. In support of her claim, Mrs. Barela attached a survey plat prepared by Fred H. Prietz showing the location of the east boundary of said Tract 1 under her theory.

Clayton G. Coleman, Special Agent for the Department of Justice, was appointed to investigate Mrs. Barela's protest. He made on-the-ground investigation of the area in conflict and report that Turley's survey of the grant did not depict correctly the location of the east bank of the old river-bed of 1854 below Station 45, but departed therefrom at a right angle crossing an eight-foot river bank, and running west approximately two miles to the foot of the slopes; thence south approximately five miles; and thence east until it intersected the true river channel as it ran in 1854 at Station 96. Coleman concluded his report by stating that the Prietz survey represented the river channel of 1854 as he found it on the ground. After considering Mrs. Barela's protest, Mr. Coleman's report and Mr. Turley's testimony that he had been instructed to follow the Brown survey of 1893, the Court of Private Land Claims, in a decision dated April 5, 1902, re-jected Jay Turley's survey of the Santo Tomás de Yturbide Colony Grant insofar as it covered the east boundary of the first tract between Stations 45 and 96. The court then ordered a re-survey of the east boundary of said tract between those two stations, and directed that the re-survey be made so as to conform with the east bank of the river channel as it ran in 1854, as delineated by Clayton G. Coleman.[12] Jay Turley re-surveyed the Santo Tomás de Yturbide Colony Grant in December, 1902, in accordance with the court's instructions. His re-survey disclosed that Tract 1 contained 6,500.3 acres, instead of 2,137.89 acres. The Turley re-survey showed that the Santo Tomás de Yturbide Grant combined a total of 9,622.34 acres of land.

Upon learning of Turley's re-survey, Nathan D. Lane, owner of a sub-stantial portion in the Bracito Grant, protested the approval of the Turley re-survey of the Santo Tomás de Yturbide Colony Grant. His objections were based on the grounds the re-survey failed to locate the bed of the Rio Grande as it existed in 1854, but had placed the common boundary between the two grants ½ mile to 3 miles east of its true location. Lane requested the court to order a new survey of the common boundary be-tween the two grants in accordance with the Stephen Archer Survey of 1854. The Court of Private Land Claims dismissed Lane's protest as being unsupported by the evidence, and approved Jay Turley's re-survey of the grant in its decision dated June 26, 1903.[13]

After the decision of June 26, 1903, the government proceeded to issue a patent to the forty-two original grantees and any other persons who were bona fide residents of the Santo Tomás de Yturbide Colony on December 30, 1853. The patent was dated October 17, 1905, and covered the 9,622.34 acres of land embraced within three separate tracts. All gold, silver and quicksilver mines and minerals were reserved and retained by the United States.[14]

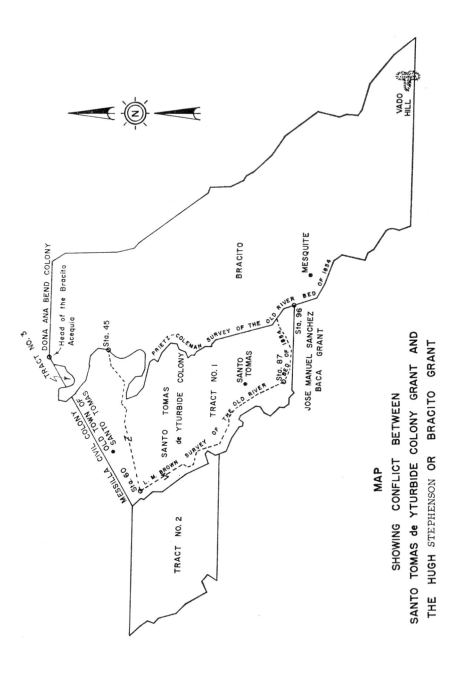

MAP

SHOWING CONFLICT BETWEEN

SANTO TOMAS de YTURBIDE COLONY GRANT AND

THE HUGH STEPHENSON OR BRACITO GRANT

After Elephant Butte Dam was constructed, land in the Mesilla Valley became very precious. The timely patenting of the Santo Tomás de Yturbide Colony Grant, together with settlement of its conflicting boundary dispute with the Bracito Grant, naturally increased the value of the lands embraced within the grant. The grant is truly a monument to the brave and loyal colonists who forsook the safety of their former homes in order to return to their native country. Deep in the heart of the hostile Indian country, they encountered many dangers and hardships in return for a small tract of land. It is only just that the United States, after a delay of more than half a century, finally recognized the rights of these courageous individuals who formed the Santo Tomás de Yturbide Colony.

R E F E R E N C E S

1 Santo Tomás de Yturbide Colony Grant, Report No. 139, (Mss., Records of the Surveyor General's Office, Bureau of Land Management, Santa Fe, New Mexico).

2 *Senate Executive Documents,* 43rd. Cong., 1st Sess., Document No. 56, 21 (1874).

3 Santo Tomás de Yturbide Colony Grant, Report No. 139 (Mss., Records of the Surveyor General's Office, Bureau of Land Management, Santa Fe, New Mexico).

4 *Land Claims Records* (Mss., Records of the Surveyor General's Office, Bureau of Land Management, Santa Fe, New Mexico), VII, 232-252.

5 *House Executive Documents,* 49th Cong., 1st Sess., Document No. 196, 1-3 (1886).

6 *Senate Executive Documents,* 49th Cong., 2nd Sess., Document No. 113, 8 (1887).

7 Barela v. United States (Mss., Court of Private Land Claims, Records of the Bureau of Land Management, Santa Fe, New Mexico), No. 137.

8 *Ibid.*

9 *Journal* (Mss., Court of Private Land Claims, Records of the Bureau of Land Management, Santa Fe, New Mexico), IV, 153-156.

10 *Report of the United States Attorney dated June 26, 1900, in the case Rafaela G. Barela and Ramón Gonzales v. United States,* (Mss., Records of the General Services Administration, National Archives, Washington, D.C.), Records Group 60, Year File 9865-92.

11 After Hugh Stephenson acquired the north two-thirds of the Bracito Grant in 1851, it was frequently referred to as the Hugh Stephenson Grant.

12 *Journal* (Mss., Court of Private Land Claims, Records of the Bureau of Land Management, Santa Fe, New Mexico), IV, 298-300.

13 *Ibid.,* IV, 344-345.

14 *Deed Records* (Mss., Records of the Doña Ana County Clerk's Office, Las Cruces, New Mexico), XLVI, 615.

CHAPTER 8

The Mesilla Civil Colony Grant ह**

● THE CALIFORNIA GOLD RUSH in 1849 caused large numbers of Anglo-Americans to take the southern overland route to the west coast. The advantages, both agricultural and commercial, existing at the Mexican settlement of Doña Ana, New Mexico caused many weary and disillusioned "forty-niners" to settle in the valley. This settlement was ideally located at the north end of the fertile Mesilla Valley at the junction of the Camino Real and the west-bound migration over the Emigrant Trail. The upper Mesilla Valley was especially inviting after the United States established a military post at Doña Ana in the latter part of 1849, to protect the area from the hostile Apache Indians.

The Doña Ana colonists soon found that title to their land was being challenged by the Anglo-Americans on the ground that the Mexican officials had no authority to issue a valid concession in 1839 covering lands east of the Rio Grande, since, under the Boundary Oct of December 19, 1836, such land belonged to Texas. Based on the assumption the Doña Ana Bend Colony Grant was invalid, a number of Texas land speculators began locating Texas land certificates within the boundaries of the Doña Ana Bend Colony Grant.[1]

Under the provisions of the Eighth Article of the Treaty of Guadalupe Hidalgo, residents of New Mexico were given the choice of retaining their Mexican nationality or becoming citizens of the United States. In an effort to assist any loyal Mexican citizens who desired to return to their native country, the Mexican government created a special fund of two hundred thousand pesos, on June 4, 1848, to help pay their moving expenses. José Joaquin de Herrera, President of the Republic of Mexico, promulgated the National Regulations of August 19, 1848, governing the repatriation of any such citizens.[2] These regulations provided that the government would pay twenty-five *pesos* toward repatriation expenses of each adult, and twelve *pesos* for each child who moved to Mexico from the territory which had been ceded to the United States under the Treaty of Guadalupe Hidalgo. The National Regulations directed the Governors of the Northern States of Mexico to issue regulations governing establishment of colonies within their respective boundaries and the distribution of lands to the emigrants.

Ramón Ortiz, Cura of El Paso del Norte, was appointed[3] Commissioner by the Republic of Mexico to supervise removal of any New Mexican who wished to emigrate to Chihuahua. However, Ortiz' activities were severely limited when the National Government appropriated only twenty-five thousand *pesos* from the special fund for fulfillment of his phase of the repatriation project.[4] Complying with the National Regulations of 1848, the State of Chihuahua promulgated the Regulations of May 22, 1851, which governed the organization of the civil colonies established within the State.[5] Ramón Ortiz was appointed Commissioner of Emigration by the State of Chihuahua.

When the United States and Mexican boundary Commissioners met at El Paso del Norte on December 3, 1850 a serious question existed as to where the International Boundary between the United States and Mexico would be located. Conflicting interpretation of Article V of the Treaty of Guadalupe Hidalgo were compromised on Christmas Day. On April 24, 1851 representatives of both nations formally established the initial point of the International Boundary at a point 219.4 meters west of the center of the Rio Grande upon the 32° 22' parallel of north latitude. The establishment of the boundary at this point appeared to insure Mexico's continued control over the lands in the Mesilla Valley west of the Rio Grande.

After the Boundary Commissioners had reached their compromise concerning the location of the initial point, Ortiz exhorting the inhabitants of New Mexico to retain their native citizenship and to move to Mexican territory as soon as feasible. However, Ortiz' repatriation efforts were only moderately successful. Even before the bondary question had been settled, a number of loyal Mexican citizens from New Mexico immigrated to the western portion of the upper Mesilla Valley. The fear of an armed conflict over the lands in the Doña Ana Bend Colony Grant with the Texas land speculators and the patriotic desire to live in their native land prompted Rafael Ruelas[6] and sixty citizens from Doña Ana voluntarily to abandon their land on March 1, 1850, in order to settle upon a low plateau known as La Mesilla, which was situated on the west side of the Rio Grande about eight miles south of Doña Ana.[7]

By January, 1852 approximately 2,000 New Mexican emigrants had settled on the lands now covered by the Refugio, Santo Tomás de Yturbide, and Mesilla Civil Colony Grants. These settlers appropriated most of the tillable lands along the west bank of the Rio Grande lying between the International Boundary Line and the pass just above El Paso. On January 20, 1852 Commissioner Ortiz formally established the Mesilla Colony and set aside, for the benefit of the colonists, a rectangular tract of land containing three and one-half leagues of land for agricultural purposes and an additional one and one-fourth leagues of land as a common pasture.[8] The bosque lands lying between the river and the agricultural and pasture lands were designated as common wood lands. A narrow strip of land situated between the agricultural and pasture lands and the mesas was also given to the colonists as a public park and domestic cattle pasture. The colony included the settlements of Mesilla and Santo Tomás, which were both located upon the agricultural tract and separated only by a short interruption in the houses. During the years 1852 and 1853 Ortiz distributed and allotted numerous farm tracts and city lots to the more than 2,000 inhabitants who resided within Mesilla Colony, in accordance with the Regulations of May 22, 1851. Before Ortiz had performed all the acts necessary to convey legal title to the lands set aside for the benefit of the Mesilla colonists, there was a revolution in Mexico. The Arista government was overthrown and Ramón Ortiz was removed from office. Guadalupe Miranda was appointed as his successor on April 28, 1853.[9]

The residents of Santo Tomás, prior to Ortiz' removal, had requested him to divide the Mesilla Colony into two separate colonies and give them a separate land grant. After Miranda took office, they renewed their requests for a distinct land grant, which they felt they were entitled to under the Regulations of 1851. In order to avoid further strife and confusion between the inhabitants of the two settlements, Miranda divided the Mesilla Colony into the Mesilla Civil Colony and Santo Tomás de Yturbide Colony on August 3, 1853. He also divided the land formerly set aside for the benefit of the Mesilla Colony into two distinct grants, one for each of the two new colonies. The following day he proceeded to survey the boundaries of the Mesilla Civil Colony Grant and granted legal title to such lands to its colonists in accordance with the Regulations of May 22, 1851. The Mesilla Civil Colony Grant contained two leagues of agricultural lands and two leagues of pasture lands. The survey of the agricultural tract was commenced at a point upon the west bank of the Rio Grande, being the southeast corner of the grant and also the northeast corner of the Santo Tomás de Yturbide Grant, and ran thence west along the north line of the Santo Tomás de Yturbide Grant 5,000 varas to a hill, in front of which were the ruins of the Querras Corral; thence north 19,500 varas along the slope of hills to the point where Peñasco Prieto Hill strikes the west bank of the Rio Grande north of Picacho Mountain and Apache Ford; thence down the west bank of the river 20,000 varas to the place of beginning. The survey of the pasture tract was commenced at Peñasco Prieto Hill, and ran thence west 5,000 varas across the hills; thence south 10,000 varas; thence east 5,000 varas to a point in the west boundary line of the agricultural tract upon the slope of the mesa; and thence north to the point of beginning.[10]

Due to the Mesilla Civil Colony's large population, the Commissioner recommended that a new settlement be founded at the foot of Picacho Mountain, and that a portion of the inhabitants of Mesilla be moved to the new town. In order to induce establishment of the new village, Miranda granted the colony two leagues of common pasture land, instead of one. He advised the colonists that such common pasture lands should be proportionately divided between the two settlements. Shortly thereafter, a new town know as Picacho was established at a point about three miles south of Peñasco Hill.

Miranda recognized and confirmed all the allotments of farm and city tracts which had previously been issued by Ortiz to individual settlers. He also made allotments to new settlers as they moved to the colony until the agricultural tract was fully appropriated and distributed. Miranda's acts as Commissioner were approved by the General Government and the State of Chihuahua. The village at Mesilla soon developed into the largest and strongest settlement in the Rio Grande Valley south of the Jornada del Muerto and north of El Paso.[11]

Shortly after the Initial Point of the International Boundary had been established in accordance with the Bartlett-García Conde Compromise, the American Surveyor, Andrew B. Gray, refused to sanction the compromise on the ground that the International Boundary west of the Rio Grande should have been located eight miles north of El Paso del Norte, as shown on the Disturnell map. Partisan activities in Washington led to the dismissal of Bartlett and suspension of the International Boundary survey. In the meantime, William Carr Lane, Governor of New Mexico, issued a proclamation claiming jurisdiction over the disputed area, and Angel Trias, Governor of Chihuahua, prepared to resist Lane's claim by force of arms. For a while it looked as though the United States and Mexico might be drawn into an armed conflict due to the territorial dispute. A new treaty appeared to be the only possible way to peacefully settle the controversy.

The Gadsden Treaty of December 30, 1853 finally provided the solution to the controversy. The United States purchased Mexico's interest in, among other lands, the western portion of the Mesilla Valley lying between 31° 47′ and 32° 22′ north latitude. This treaty guaranteed that the United States would recognize all valid land grants that had been located, perfected and recorded in the Archives of Mexico prior to September 25, 1853.[12]

One of the most memorable days in the history of the Mesilla Valley was the raising of the American flag on July 4, 1854 over the Plaza at Mesilla. This flag raising marked confirmation of the Treaty and transfer of jurisdiction over the area to the United States. The eastern portion of the territory acquired under the Gadsden Purchase was annexed to Doña Ana County. The loyal Mexicans, who just a few years previously had migrated to Mesilla in order to retain their native citizenship, once again found themselves on foreign soil. Most of the Mesillans, however, were content and elected to accept American citizenship.

In the Spring of 1865 there was a severe and disastrous flood in the Mesilla Valley, which caused the Rio Grande to change its course, and heavily damaged vast areas of cultivated land. After this flood, the river was located west of the town of Mesilla. Many of the inhabitants whose lands were destroyed moved to the Tularosa area. The inconveniences of being separated by the river from the other settlements caused the gradual abandonment of the town of Picacho.

The danger and expense connected with a journey from Mesilla to Santa Fe caused the claimants of the Mesilla Civil Colony Grant to postpone until 1874 the filing with the Surveyor General of the necessary documentary proof and testimony supporting their grant. The more than one thousand claimants of the grant, through their attorney, John D. Bail, petitioned the Surveyor General on January 23, 1874, and requested confirmation of their title to the grant. This was the first claim to be presented to the Surveyor General for approval of land lying within the area covered by the Gadsden Purchase.

By letter dated February 17, 1874, the Secretary of Interior decided that the Surveyor General had the same authority and jurisdiction to pass on the validity of title to land embraced within the Gadsden Purchase as he had possessed for lands acquired under the Treaty of Guadalupe Hidalgo. Surveyor General James K. Proudfit, in his opinion dated February 12, 1874, held that the grant had been duly and properly made by Commissioner Guadalupe Miranda on August 4, 1854, that claimants had undisputed possession of the lands, and that valuable improvements had been made and placed upon the lands by the claimants. The Surveyor General concluded his report by recommending to Congress that title to the Mesilla Civil Colony Grant be confirmed to its inhabitants.[13]

In order to withdraw the acreage covered by the grant from the public domain, the claimants retained John T. Elkins and Robert Marmon, United States Deputy Surveyors, to survey the claim. Their survey, which was made in March, 1878, showed that the grant contained a total of 33,960.33 acres. The Elkins and Marmon survey of the Mesilla Civil Colony Grant was formally approved by Surveyor General Henry M. Atkinson on May 15, 1879.[14]

Contemplating early confirmation of the grant by Congress, the claimants secured passage of a special act by the New Mexico Territorial Legislature on February 15, 1878, which incorporated their various interests under the grant as the Incorporation of Mesilla. The corporation was to be managed by three elected Commissioners who had the right to sue, be sued, hold, lease or rent the lands embraced within the grant, and power to sell and convey such lands with consent of two-thirds of the claimants.

No further action was taken toward approval of the Mesilla Civil Colony Grant until after establishment of the Court of Private Land Claims. On February 28, 1893 the Incorporation of Mesilla and Thomas J. Bull, owner of an interest in the Mesilla Civil Colony Grant, for themselves and on behalf of all others who owned or claimed an interest in the grant, brought suit in the Court of Private Land Claims against the United States for approval of the grant.[15]

The case was originally set for hearing on July 5, 1898, but was postponed until August 28, 1899. At the hearing, the plaintiffs introduced a large amount of oral and documentary evidence in support of their claim. The government objected to confirmation of the grant on the grounds that Commissioner Miranda lacked authority to issue the concession, and that it had not been recorded in the Archives of Mexico, as required by Article VI of the Gadsden Treaty.

The court, in its decision dated September 5, 1899, held that Commissioner Miranda had been duly appointed as Commissioner to supervise repatriation of emigrants from New Mexico. The court further found Miranda, as Emigration Commissioner, had authority to establish new colonies and allot land to settlers in accordance with the Federal Decree of August 19, 1848, and the State Regulations of May 22, 1851. Continuing, the court held that Miranda had made a valid colony grant to the persons who constituted the Mesilla Civil Colony on the date of the signing of the Gadsden Treaty. Commenting on the issue of whether the title papers of the grant had been duly recorded as required by the Gadsden Treaty, the court noted that the Mexican laws required the *expediente* of this grant to be filed in the Archives of the Ayuntamiento of El Paso del Norte, instead of in the National Archives at Mexico City. Next, the court noted that the grant had been made for two separate tracts, one for agricultural purposes and the other for pasture. The evidence showed that all the agricultural lands had been allotted or distributed among the colonists, and that the pasture lands were being held by the Corporation for the benefit of the claimants. In connection with the grant of pasture lands, the court held such concession — insofar as it exceeded one square league of land — was void for want of authority. In conclusion, the court confirmed title to the following described tract of agricultural land as Tract Numbered One to the Corporation of Mesilla in trust for all persons to whom the same was allotted and such others who were bona fide residents on the grant on December 30, 1853, their heirs and successors, to wit:

Commencing at a point on the west margin of the Rio Grande del Norte as the same was situated in the year 1853, on a small hill on the line which divides the colonies of Santo Tomás and of Mesilla, being the point fixed by the United States Government survey as the southeast corner of said grant; thence for the southern boundary running west five thousand varas to a hill in front of the ruins of a corral called the Querras corral, or the place where said corral and the ruins thereof were formerly situated; thence for the westerly boundary running in a northerly direction, west of north, along the slope or drainage of the hills in a direct line toward the Picacho Mountain on the river side where it touches the hills; and thence continuing along the margin of said river to the Peñasco Prieto Hill, which is to the north of a small bend called the Apache Ford a little above Picacho, making nineteen thousand, five hundred (19,500) varas; thence for the easterly boundary continuing toward the south, and east of south, to the place of beginning, following along the west margin of said river as the same was situated in the year 1853, except where the said grant lies opposite to the Doña Ana Bend Colony Grant, heretofore confirmed as Cause No. 24, and as to such portions of the easterly boundary the line shall follow the western boundary of said Doña Ana Bend Colony Grant as finally located under the confirmation aforesaid. The north boundary of this tract shall be an east and west line running from the northwest corner at the Peñasco Prieto Hill to the northeast corner on the west boundary of the Doña Ana Bend Colony Grant.

The court also confirmed title to the following described tract of pasture land as Tract No. 2 to the Corporation of Mesilla, to wit:

Commencing at a point on the westerly boundary of Tract No. 1 as above described, and five thousand varas from the northwest corner thereof, said five thousand varas being measured by following the meandered west boundary of Tract No. 1, from the northwest corner of said Tract No. 1; from said point on said west boundary five thousand varas from said northwest corner, measured as aforesaid, running due west five thousand varas; thence southerly and parrallel to said western boundary of Tract No. 1, five thousand varas; thence due east five thousand varas to the intersection of said first mentioned boundary; thence northerly along said first mentioned boundary, five thousand varas to the place of beginning, making a tract one square league, more or less.[16]

The United States Attorney, Matthew G. Reynolds, reported that while he had some doubt as to the correctness of the court's decision holding that the grant had been made by proper authorities and had been duly recorded as required by the Gadsden Treaty, he did not believe that the Supreme Court would reverse the decision. Therefore, he recommended that no appeal be taken by the government.[17]

Once the decree became final, a contract with Jay Turley, Deputy United States Surveyor, was entered into for the surveying of the grant. Turley's survey disclosed that Tract No. 1 contained 17,784.43 acres, and Tract No. 2 embraced 3,844.09 acres. The survey was approved by the Court of Private Land Claims on April 8, 1902.[18] The final step in confirmation of the grant was taken on November 15, 1909, when the United States issued a patent to the Corporation of Mesilla.[19]

Since issuance of the patent, the history of the grant has been one of economic and cultural development. Construction of Elephant Butte Dam in 1916 checked the disastrous spring freshets, and conserved the floodwaters for future use during drought periods. Fertile soil, coupled with successful reclamation and irrigation projects, has transformed the Mesilla

Valley into one of the true garden spots of the southwest. Despite these changes, Old Mesilla stubbornly holds fast to her memorable traditions and historic past.

R E F E R E N C E S

1 The Texas Legislature passed an Act on December 2, 1850, which directed the Commissioner of the General Land Office to issue a patent to the owners of these surveys; however, the Commissioner of the General Land Office refused to patent the lands, since prior to the passage of this Act the lands covered by the surveys had been ceded to the United States. William Campbell Binkley, *The Expansionist Movement in Texas* (Berkeley, 1925), 171, 181-182; *Appendix to the Journals of the Senate of the Third Legislature, State of Texas, Second Session* (Austin, 1850), 4; H.P.N. Gammel, *The Laws of Texas* (10 Vols., Austin, 1898), III, 853; and Bexar 2-398 (Mss., Records of the General Land Office, Austin, Texas).

2 A copy of these regulations is contained in *Senate Executive Documents*, 43rd Con., 1st Sess., Doc. No. 56, 27-30 (1873).

3 Fidelia Miller Puckett, "Ramón Ortiz: Priest and Patriot," *New Mexico Historical Review* (1950), XXV, 265-295.

4 Hubert Howe Bancroft, *History of Arizona and New Mexico* (San Francisco, 1889), 472 and 473.

5 A copy of these regulations is contained in *Senate Executive Documents*, 43rd Cong., 1st Sess., Document No. 56, 21-26 (1873).

6 Rafael Ruelas was formerly a resident of El Paso del Norte and had received a land grant in the El Paso Valley in 1847.

7 John Russell Bartlett, *Personal Narrative of Explorations and Incidents in Texas, New Mexico, California, Sonora, and Chihuahua, connected with the United States and Mexican Boundary Commission during the Years 1850, '51, '52 and 53,* (2 Vols., London, 1854), I, 212-214.

8 Article 23 of the Act of December 23, 1851 allegedly superseded the Regulations of May 22, 1851, by authorizing the Commissioner of Emigration to grant colonies of 1,000 inhabitants or more one and one-fourth leagues of land for common pasturage purposes, instead of only one league.

9 Mesilla Civil Colony Grant, Report No. 86 (Mss., Records of the Surveyor General's Office, Bureau of Land Management, Santa Fe, New Mexico).

10 *Senate Executive Documents*, 43rd Cong., 1st Sess., Document No. 56, 16-20 (1873).

11 Mesilla Civil Colony Grant, Report No. 86 (Mss., Records of the Surveyor General's Office, Bureau of Land Management, Santa Fe, New Mexico).

12 *House Executive Documents*, 33rd Cong., 1st Sess., Document No. 109, 1-5 (1853).

13 *Land Claims Records* (Mss., Records of the Surveyor General's Office, Bureau of Land Management, Santa Fe, New Mexico), V, 21 & 22.

14 Mesilla Civil Colony Grant, Map File 86 (Mss., Records of the Cadastrial Engineer's Office, Santa Fe, New Mexico).

15 The Incorporation of Mesilla v. United States (Mss., Court of Private Land Claims, Records of the Bureau of Land Management, Santa Fe, New Mexico), No. 151.

16 *Journal* (Mss., Court of Private Land Claims, Records of the Bureau of Land Management, Santa Fe, New Mexico), IV, 122-125.

¹⁷ *Report of the United States Attorney dated June 21, 1900, in the Case Incorporation of Mesilla v. United States* (Mss., Records of the General Services Administration, National Archives, Washington, D.C.), Record Group 60, Year File 9865-92.

¹⁸ Mesilla Civil Colony Grant, Map File 86 (Mss., Records of the Cadastrial Engineer's Office, Santa Fe, New Mexico).

¹⁹ *Deed Records* (Mss., Records of the Doña Ana County Clerk's Office, Las Cruces, New Mexico), XXXVIII, 180.

CHAPTER 9

The Santa Rita del Cobre Grant ⧈

● THE PRINCIPAL MOTIVE for exploration and conquest of the northern frontiers of New Spain by the Spaniards was the search for precious metal. Although the Indians of the Southwest had obtained copper from the extensive natural deposits in the Santa Rita Basin¹ prior to the sixteenth century to make ceremonial bells and crude utensils, the Spaniards had somehow overlooked these diggings for centuries.² It was not until 1800 that an Indian guide pointed out the rich field of red metal to Lieutenant Colonel José Manuel Carrasco. The deposit was situated in a small narrow valley which was practically encircled by lofty mountain peaks. The floor of this valley was composed of feldspar and red oxide of copper, intermixed with native metal. While he was a military man and not a trained prospector, Carrasco immediately realized the value of his discovery. On June 30, 1801 he filed a formal Denouncement covering the Santa Rita del Cobre Mine.³

Carrasco commenced working an outcrop, and made at least one very profitable trip to Chihuahua with copper ore. However, he did not have sufficient capital to develop the mine, and his military duties prevented him from devoting his full attention to its operation. Therefore, he sold⁴ the claim in 1804 to Francisco Manuel de Elguea, who made plans to develop and improve the property. Through his extensive political connections, Elguea was able to secure establishment of a penal colony at Santa Rita del Cobre. Approximately 600 convicts were sent to the colony. The Chihuahuan government also permitted him to work the prisoners in the mine in consideration of his paying their maintenance. A triangular *presidio* or fort was erected near the mine on a small rise which commanded the approach to the valley.⁵ It was built for the dual purpose of providing protection against the hostile Apaches and also as a prison to house the convict laborers. A primitive smelter was established at the mine to reduce the native copper and copper ore into ingots weighting one hundred and fifty pounds each.

Life at Santa Rita del Cobre was monotonously routine, involving only hard work and continual harassment from the Indians. Since the miners were mostly convicts, there were few armed persons at the settlement. The isolated location of the settlement, coupled with the meager defenses afforded by the fort, caused inhabitants of Santa Rita del Cobre to be deathly afraid of the Apaches. Food was also a major problem at the mine. Since the valley was so highly mineralized, it was impossible to grow sufficient agricultural products to support the community. Therefore, the miners were totally dependent upon Janos and Casa Grandes for food.[6]

While the supply caravans were used to carry ingots on their return trips, most of the copper was transported under military protection by pack train to Chihuahua and thence to Mexico City.[7] The deep, narrow ruts hewn by the sharp hooves of innumerable Spanish mules, which are still visible in the foothills near Santa Rita, evidence the vast amount of copper which was taken from the mine during the Spanish and Mexican periods.[8] Due to the superior quality of the copper and the extreme scarcity of copper coins[9] in Mexico during the early part of the nineteenth century, the Royal Mint entered into a contract with Elguea to purchase the entire output of the mine for coinage. In 1807 Lieutenant Zebulon M. Pike mentions that the mine was producing twenty thousand mule loads, or approximately six million pounds, of copper annually.[10] Elguea died in 1809, and shortly thereafter his widow and son leased the mine to Juan Oniz.

When Sylvester Pattie and his party of American trappers arrived at Santa Rita del Cobre on July 8, 1825, the Apaches were especially troublesome. Therefore, Juan Oniz requested them to remain with him for two or three months and assist in protecting the miners from the Indians. Oniz offered to pay each of the trappers a dollar a day, and agreed that they could freely trap the mountains surrounding the mine. The party consented to stay, but refused to accept any pay for their services, since the area had an abundance of fur-bearing wildlife. Pattie contacted the Apaches and threatened them with the entire American army if they molested either the miners or Pattie's party. This was talk the Indians understood. The bluff worked, and the Apaches advised Pattie that they had no objections to making peace with the Americans, but would never make a treaty with the Spaniards. His success in dealing with the Indians prompted Pattie to try to acquire the property. Having tired of operating the mine under such harsh and dangerous conditions, and fearing the Indian atrocities would resume if the Americans left, Oniz subleased it to Pattie for five years in consideration of an annual rental of one thousand dollars.[11]

The arrangement proved to be exceedingly profitable for Pattie, and by 1827 he made a profit in excess of thirty thousand dollars from the mine.

On April 18, 1827 Pattie sent a trusted employee to Santa Fe with thirty thousand dollars in gold to purchase goods and equipment for the future operation of the mine. The clerk embezzled the gold and absconded. When he failed to return to the mine, Pattie's son, James O. Pattie, went in search of him. Failing to find the clerk in Santa Fe or El Paso del Norte, James O. Pattie had no alternative but to report the dilemma to the owner of the mine,[12] for he knew his father did not have sufficient assets to re-order supplies and provisions, and without them he could not continue to operate the mine. James O. Pattie found the owner of the mine in a state of anxiety and grief, for the President of Mexico had just issued a Decree which ordered all persons born in Spain to leave Mexico within one month. Being a Spaniard, the mine owner was faced with the problem of either selling the mine or entering into some type of permanent arrangement covering its operation. He especially regreted Sylvester Pattie's misfortune, for he had hoped to sell the mine to him. Since Pattie was financially ruined, the mine owner had no alternative but to make other arrangements. Pattie delivered possession of the mine to its owner on July 1, 1827. He and his son set out for Santa Fe, with plans to join the first trapping expedition leaving that city for the Red River country.[13]

In 1828 the mine was being operated by a Frenchman named Stephen Coursier under an agreement with its proprietors.[14] During the next seven years Coursier was able to monopolize the copper trade in the State of Chihuahua. It has been reported, and is generally believed, that he made at least half a million dollars out of the mine. Much of his success is attributed to the fact that he was able to secure permission to work the mine from Juan José Compa, the leading Apache Chief. Age and booty had taken much of the rancor out of Chief Compa's once proud and fierce nature. However, the sight of the miners peacefully working in the very heart of Apachería ate like a cancer in the hearts of the young braves. Finally, in 1834, the Warm Springs Apaches, under the leadership of Mangas Coloradas, refused to continue to follow the fat and lazy Chief. After this date, Coloradas and his followers continuously harazzed the mine and its supply and pack trains. This renewal of Indian hostilities finally forced Coursier to abandon operation of the mine.[15]

Robert McKnight, an American adventurer, commenced operating the mine for its proprietors in either 1835 or 1836. While the Indians undoubtedly gave McKnight some trouble, he was able to work the mine for several years at a profit.[16]

Meanwhile, the State of Chihuahua took a desperate step in an effort to solve its Indian problem. A barbarous law was promulgated in 1837, entitled *Proyecto de Guerra*, which offered a bounty for Apache scalps. A party of scalp hunters, led by James Johnson, planned to exterminate the entire tribe of Mimbreño Apaches, who were then living in the vicinity of the mine. The plan was to invite the Mimbreños to a *fiesta,* and once they were gorged and drunk, the scalp hunters would massacre them. This macabre party was held on April 22, 1837 at Sierra de las Animas, which is located in Hidalgo County, New Mexico. It has been estimated that four hundred Indians — men, women and children — were killed.[17]

The atrocity, instead of causing the Apaches to fear the white man, prompted swift retaliation. The method chosen was to starve the miners out of Santa Rita del Cobre by severing all lines of communication. It was well known that the mine had only a limited food reserve and was dependent upon the periodic supply caravans. Therefore, they attacked the next wagon train from Chihuahua in a canyon near the Pueblo de Corralitos. The teamsters and guards were forced to abandon the wagons in order to escape the ambush. The Indians took all of the mules and most of the supplies before setting fire to the wagons. They sent word to the inhabitants of Santa Rita del Cobre that they would not let any further supplies reach the mine. Thus, the Apaches let it be known that they would no longer tolerate the working of the Santa Rita del Cobre mine. It soon became apparent to McKnight and his miners that they would have to abandon the mine if they were to escape with their lives. The whole population of some three or four hundred persons immediately prepared to make the one hundred fifty mile flight to safety to the Presidio de Janos. They made one fatal mistake, in that they attempted to salvage their personal possessions, and thereby sacrificed speed for what proved to be millstones around their necks. The slow-moving party was ambushed, and only a handful of survivors were able to reach Janos.[18]

Leonardo Pesqueira made several attempts to re-open the mine in the 1840's and 1850's under an arrangement with Francisco Elguea and his mother. However, the Apaches successfully thwarted each of such efforts.[19] In 1846 Lieutenant W. H. Emory reported that the mine was deserted.[20] It was still shut down five years later when the United States Boundary Commission temporarily occupied the deserted settlement while running the International Boundary between the United States and Mexico. Commissioner John Russell Bartlett found the presidio in an excellent state of preservation, and with just a little effort it was converted into a comfortable dwelling for the Commission and its military escort. Many of the more than fifty outlying buildings were also in good condition, except for their roofs. In describing the mine, Bartlett stated: "One of the largest shafts had been filled up in consequence of the earth's caving in. . . . Others are obstructed by water, which accumulated near their entrances. Some of the excavations are still accessible."[21]

In June, 1851 Mangas Coloradas and a large band of Apaches camped near the mine. At first they were friendly, and their conduct was beyond reproach; however, the amicable relationship between the Americans and

Indians changed, and it was clearly evident that the Apaches were anxious for the white man to depart. The Indians apparently were afraid that the protection offered by the military forces would encourage re-opening of the mine.[22]

The Santa Rita del Cobre Mine played an important role in the Bartlett-García Conde Compromise which fixed the location of the initial point of the International Boundary west of the Rio Grande. Bartlett was extremely anxious to secure this valuable natural resource for the United States. Since the Treaty Map, coupled with Article V of the Treaty of Guadalupe Hidalgo, could be interpreted as placing the mine in Mexico, Bartlett was willing to interpret the ambiguous Treaty Map in a way which would give Mexico, among other lands, the western portion of the Mesilla Valley in exchange for the mine.[23] The controversy which developed in the United States as a result of this compromise was not settled until the United States acquired the disputed area from Mexico in 1853 under the Gadsden Purchase.[24]

A small contingent of dragoons from Fort Fillmore occupied the presidio when the Boundary Commission moved out in October, 1851. A post was formally established there on January 23, 1852 and was known as Fort Webster. It was created for the dual purpose of protecting the immediate area from Indian depredations and to deter the Apaches from raiding Mexico, as required by the Treaty of Guadalupe Hidalgo. On September 9, 1852 Fort Webster was moved to a site on the Mimbres River about twelve miles east of Santa Rita del Cobre, in order to afford better pasturage for its animals. The fort proved difficult to supply and defend, and was therefore permanently abandoned on December 20, 1853.[25]

While the Apaches had successfully prevented Leonardo Pesqueira from working the mine for nearly two decades, he never gave up hope of making a fortune from the rich copper deposits. When his original arrangement with the mine owners expired in 1858, he obtained a new sublease from Elguea's widow and his son's heir, Dolores Elguea. The sublease ran for a term of seven years, and contained an option to renew same for an additional seven years. The copper ore was there, but he was able to work the mine only spasmodically. The continuous hostilities of the Apaches, coupled with the lessening of demand for copper in Mexico, finally prompted Pesqueira to sell his interest in 1861 to J. B. Sweet and L. W. Lacorte, merchants of San Antonio, Texas.[26]

Sweet and Lacorte, through their agent, Dr. Alexander Brand, promptly commenced working the mine with a crew of one hundred and twenty miners. Fort McLane was established about this time at a site approximately fifteen miles south of the mine. The Santa Rita del Cobre and another copper mine[27] were producing approximately twelve tons of copper per week, when the Civil War commenced.

Shortly after the Confederate Army, under General Henry H. Sibley, invaded New Mexico, in June, 1861, the Union forces abandoned Fort McLane. When the Confederates were forced to retreat from northern New Mexico, they confiscated a large amount of copper and most of the mine's provisions. The lack of protection from the Indians and the shortage of supplies forced abandonment of the mine on May 10, 1862.[28] After the Civil War, the mine was re-opened and worked from time to time by Sweet and Lacorte until their lease expired in 1865.

Noting that the property was unoccupied, James H. Carleton and six associates formed a company known as the Santa Rita Mining Association, and filed an application in August, 1866 for a patent covering a 31.26 acre tract under the New Mexico Territorial Mining Act of January 18, 1865 and the Federal Mining Act of July 26, 1866.[29] The Santa Rita del Cobre Mine was located on this tract. The only work conducted on the tract by the Association was the sinking of a new shaft, at a cost in excess of one thousand dollars, between November, 1866 and February, 1867. This work was done apparently for the sole purpose of complying with the provisions of the mining laws.

By decision dated December 22, 1869, James S. Wilson, Commissioner of the General Land Office, pointed out that the petitioners' application was for a patent under the Federal and Territorial Mining Laws, based upon an allegation that they had discovered and opened a new mine. Since the Santa Rita del Cobre was the most famous mine in New Mexico and had been worked continuously for more than sixty years, except for short periods when operations were suspended due to hostilities, he denied the application.[30]

The next move by the Santa Rita Mining Association was to apply for a patent under the mining law upon a theory that the mine had been abandoned and was therefore subject to relocation. By decision dated May 22, 1870, Commissioner Wilson held that the mine could be relocated only if it had been abandoned for more than ten years and had not been granted in fee simple by competent authority under the government of Spain or Mexico. He found that Santa Rita del Cobre was not subject to relocation, since it had been occupied by Sweet and Lacorte under an agreement with María Guero and Dolores Elguea during a portion of the critical period. An appeal was taken from this decision to the Secretary of Interior. On April 15, 1873 the Secretary held that the claimants had no right to the mine which had been known to the Department of Interior for more than half a century as belonging to the Elguea estate.[31] This decision made it obvious that the interest of the Elguea estate was protected by the Treaty of Guadalupe Hidalgo.

Meanwhile, María Guero and Dolores Elguea filed a petition with the Surveyor General on November 15, 1872, requesting an investigation of their claim to a grant covering four square leagues of land, being a league

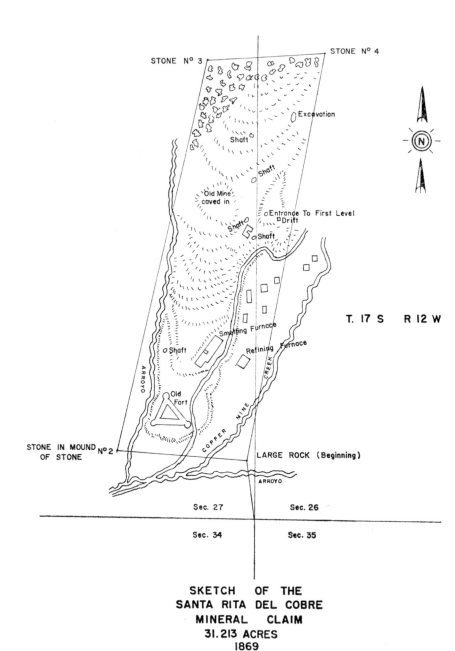

STONE N° 3

STONE N° 4

Excavation

Shaft

Shaft

Old Mine
caved in

Entrance To First Level

Drift

Shaft

Shaft

T. 17 S   R 12 W

Smelting Furnace

Shaft

Refining Furnace

ARROYO

CREEK

Old
Fort

COPPER MINE

STONE IN MOUND N° 2
OF STONE

LARGE ROCK (Beginning)

ARROYO

Sec. 27   Sec. 26

Sec. 34   Sec. 35

SKETCH   OF   THE
SANTA RITA DEL COBRE
MINERAL   CLAIM
31.213 ACRES
1869

in each direction from the center of the main shaft of the Santa Rita del Cobre Mine. The petitioners alleged that Elguea had acquired title to such land by virtue of a grant from the king of Spain, but that the *testimonio* evidencing same had been lost or destroyed. They contended that the grant should be recognized and confirmed, notwithstanding their inability to produce any written evidence of the grant. They based this contention upon their continuous undisputed possession of the mine for more than sixty years prior to the unlawful entry on the grant by the Santa Rita Mining Association.[32]

Meanwhile, M. B. Hayes purchased all of María Guero and Dolores Elguea's interest in the grant and mine. The deed to Hayes was dated October 27, 1873, and recited a consideration of $15,000.[33] Hayes, in turn, conveyed an undivided 1/6th interest in the grant and mine to David H. Moffet, Jr., and a similar interest to Joel P. Whitney.[34] Hayes and his associates presented their claim to the Santa Rita del Cobre Mine and grant to Surveyor General H. M. Atkinson. On July 6, 1882 the Surveyor General held that the petitioners had failed to produce sufficient evidence to establish the existence of a valid grant in favor of Francisco Manuel Elguea. Therefore, he dismissed their petition.[35] Hayes and his associates appealed this decision to the Secretary of Interior. In a letter[36] dated February 13, 1883, the Commissioner of the General Land Office advised the attorneys for the applicants that their appeal had been denied, because the evidence presented to the Surveyor General could not be construed as a basis of a claim under the treaty provisions. The Commissioner stated that since there was "no evidence of the existence of any claim or right or title in the alleged grantor of your client, there was nothing to be sent to Congress, and your request was accordingly declined." This letter was supplemented by a decision[37] dated March 3, 1883 by Surveyor General H. M. Atkinson, in which he pointed out that:

Under the Spanish and Mexican governments, grants to mines could only be made by the supreme authorities of those governments, and mines were usually held by possession and working merely, the claim and right thereto being liable to forfeiture and denouncement unless certain conditions of working and retaining possession of same were complied with (excepting where the supreme authority referred to had granted the mine and adjacent land in fee). These mining claims, which were held for purposes of working only and to which no title in fee had been acquired, were often sold and conveyed by deed to the purchaser, as under our laws before application for patent; hence the abstract of title which you furnished is not deemed sufficient evidence of title, in fee, to the tract claimed to warrant the presumption that a grant was made to Elguea or his grantors, which invested the fee to the Santa Rita del Cobre tract in him. In order to maintain a claim for a tract of land a league square, partly non-mineral, such as pasture and woodland, there must have been a grant from the proper authority empowered to alienate and convey to the grantee, the fee to the mine and adjacent land, but if the mines were held under the usual forfeitable tenure, then the claim would be confined to the right to hold the maximum amount of ground, which could have been embraced in any mining claim or claims, under the Spanish or Mexican law, at the date of the denouncement thereof, and it would in that case devolve upon the claimants to show the nature of the claim, that it was valid and unforfeited at the date of the acquisition of this territory by the United States to the mine or several mines, as the case may be, and that no forfeiture has since occurred. . . . If a grant in fee is claimed to the square leagues, some proper evidence of the original concession must be filed as the basis of the petition and claim. If the mines are claimed by mere denouncement and possessory title, it will be necessary to amend your petition to cover the facts in the case as herein indicated.

The rejection of each of these applications presented a stranger paradox. The applications made under the mining laws were denied on the grounds that the Santa Rita del Cobre Mine was neither a newly discovered mine nor an abandoned mine. On the other hand, the petition for confirmation of the Santa Rita del Cobre Grant, under the Act of July 22, 1854, was rejected because the applicants had failed to show that their predecessors had received a valid grant covering the copper deposits.

Realizing that there was little possibility of securing recognition of the Santa Rita del Cobre Grant, Hayes and his associates decided to perfect their title to the mine by securing patents on the copper deposits under the mining laws. In 1873 a large number of mining entries were filed in the name of F. D. Moffet, Jr. By acquiring the rights of María Guero and Dolores Elguea, Hayes removed the two obstacles which had prevented the previous location of such lands. Since it had been determined that there had been no grant in fee covering the mine, and in view of the fact that Moffet was claiming the mine as a successor of Francisco Manuel Elguea, the applications proceeded to patent without further question. In May, 1883 approximately fifty mining claims were patented to D. H. Moffet, Jr. These patents covered the area then occupied by the Santa Rita del Cobre Mine.[38]

Once title to the mine was finally cleared, full scale operations were resumed at one of the most historic mines in the United States. Santa Rita del Cobre has since developed into the largest open pit copper mine in the world.

REFERENCES

[1] The Santa Rita Basin lies in the Central Mining District of New Mexico. It is located in Grant County, and is situated about 12 miles east of Silver City. The basin is relatively small, covering an area of only approximately 35 square miles. It was situated in the heart of the Warm Springs and Mimbreño Apache country. The cool timbered mountains surrounding the Santa Rita Basin abounded with game and contained a profusion of springs. Therefore, it is not difficult to see why the nomadic desert dwellers considered

the area as their sacred homeland. A. C. Spencer and Sidney Paige, *Geology of the Santa Rita Mining Area, New Mexico* (Washington, D.C., 1935), 3; and Dale Collins, *Frontier Mining Days in Southwestern New Mexico* (Mss., Master's Thesis, Texas Western College, El Paso, Texas), 17.

2 Warren B. Beck, *New Mexico, A History of Four Centuries* (Norman, 1962), 242-244.

3 Francisco R. Almada, *Resumen de Historia del Estado de Chihuahua* (Mexico, D.F., 1955), 137. Law 8, Title 1, Book 6, of the Nueva Recopilacion provided that all metals were the property of the sovereign, and that the permission of the Crown was necessary in order to mine them. On May 22, 1783 Charles III promulgated a royal mining ordinance applicable to all the Spanish Americas except Peru. This ordinance established a procedure known as Denouncement, whereby the discoverer of a new mineral deposit could acquire the privilege of mining a 200 vara square tract of land surrounding the new mine. As work progressed, additional lands could be denounced. The Crown reserved a royalty on all minerals mined. Frederic Hall, *The Laws of Mexico* (San Francisco, 1885), 362, 368; and Wallace Hawkins, *El Sal del Rey* (Austin, 1947), 7-9.

4 Santa Rita del Cobre Grant, Files Nos. 107 & 194 (Mss., Records of the Surveyor General's Office, Bureau of Land Management, Santa Fe, New Mexico).

5 John Russell Bartlett, *Personal Narrative of Explorations and Incidents in Texas, New Mexico, California, Sonora, and Chihuahua* (2 Vols., London, 1854), I, 235.

6 *Ibid.*, I, 228; and Dale Collins, *Frontier Mining Days in Southwestern New Mexico*, 14.

7 John Russell Bartlett, *Personal Narrative of Explorations and Incidents in Texas, New Mexico, California, Sonora, and Chihuahua*, I, 228.

8 A. C. Spencer and Sidney Paige, *Geology of the Santa Rita Mining Area, New Mexico*, 9.

9 C. H. Haring, *The Spanish Empire in America* (New York, 1947), I, 311.

10 Elliott Coues, *The Expedition of Zebulon Montgomery Pike* (3 Vols., New York, 1895), II, 728.

11 Milo Milton Quaife, *The Personal Narrative of James O. Pattie* (Chicago, 1930), 115-123.

12 James O. Pattie states the mine was owned by Francisco Pablo de Lagera. *Ibid.*, 209. However, it should be remembered that Pattie wrote his narrative from memory some three years after the occurrence of this incident. There is a possibility that his memory was hazy when he mentioned the name of the owner of the Santa Rita del Cobre Mine. He was probably making reference to either Pablo Guero, who had married Elguea's widow or to Elguea's only child, Francisco Elguea. All were expelled from Mexico in 1827.

13 Milo Milton Quaife, *The Personal Narrative of James O. Pattie*, 208-209.

14 A. Wislizenus, *Memoir of a Tour to Northern Mexico* (Washington, 1848), 57-58.

15 John M. Sully, "The Story of the Santa Rita Copper Mine," *Old Santa Fe* (1916), III, 138; Paul I. Wellman, *The Indian Wars of the West* (Garden City, 1954), 247-250; and A. Wislizenus, *Memoir of a Tour to Northern Mexico*, 58.

16 The Apaches directed their hostilities against only the Spanish and Mexicans. In the late 1830's there were only a few white trappers and traders in the Apache county, and toward these, the Apaches had a more or less friendly attitude. Except for petty thefts and occasional horse stealing, the Apaches showed remarkably little animosity against the white man. Paul I. Wellman, *The Indian Wars of the West*, 251.

17 John C. Ceromony, *Life Among the Apaches* (San Francisco, 1868), 31-32; and Francisco R. Almada, *Diccionario de Historia, Geografía y Biografía Sonorenses* (Chihuahua, 1952), 74.

18 John C. Ceromony, *Life Among the Apaches*, 32; and Paul I. Wellman, *The Indian Wars of the West*, 258-260.

19 John M. Sully, "The Story of the Santa Rita Copper Mine," *Old Santa Fe* (1916), III, 138.

20 Ross Calvin, *Lieutenant Emory Reports* (Albuquerque 1951), 97.

21 John Russell Bartlett, *Personal Narrative of Explorations and Incidents in Texas, New Mexico, California, Sonora, and Chihuahua*, I, 229, 235-236.

22 *Ibid.*, I, 322-323.

23 *Ibid.*, I, 201-208; and William H. Goetzman, *Army Exploration in the American West* (New Haven, 1959), 173-175.

24 Paul Neff Garber, *The Gadsden Treaty* (Gloucester, 1959), 146.

25 M. H. Thomlinson, "Forgotten Fort," *The New Mexico Magazine* (1943), XXIII, 39-41; and Wm. G. B. Carson, "William Carr Lane, Diary," *New Mexico Historical Review* (1964), XXXIX, 217-218.

26 Dale Collins, *Frontier Mining Days in Southwestern New Mexico*, 31.

27 This mine was the Hanover Copper Mine, which was located near Santa Rita, New Mexico, in the Arroyo de Alamo.

28 Dale Collins, *Frontier Mining Days in Southwestern New Mexico*, 34; and A. C. Spencer and Sidney Paige, *Geology of the Santa Rita Mining Area, New Mexico*, 6.

29 Santa Rita del Cobre Grant, File No. 107 (Mss., Records of the Surveyor General's Office, Bureau of Land Management, Santa Fe, New Mexico).

30 *Ibid.*   31 *Ibid.*   32 *Ibid.*

33 *Deed Records* (Mss., Records of the Grant County Clerk's Office, Silver City, New Mexico), I, 543.

34 *Ibid.*, I, 627; and VII, 250.

35 Santa Rita del Cobre Grant, File No. 194 (Mss., Records of the Surveyor General's Office, Bureau of Land Management, Santa Fe, New Mexico).

36 *Decisions of the Department of Interior and General Land Owce in Cases Relating to the Public Lands* (37 Vols., Washington, D.C., 1887), I, 579.

37 Santa Rita del Cobre Grant, File No. 194 (Mss., Records of the Surveyor General's Office, Bureau of Land Management, Santa Fe, New Mexico).

38 W. J. Anderson to J. J. B., May 25, 1964.

CHAPTER 10

The Doña Ana Bend Colony Grant ⁊

● In the history of colonization of the Mesilla Valley of New Mexico, the Doña Ana Bend Colony and its land grant has played a leading role. Old Doña Ana, the initial settlement on the grant and the first permanent settlement located in the Valley, was founded upon the old Doña Ana campsite.[1] This village afforded the only protection for travelers using the Camino Real between El Paso del Norte and Socorro. It undoubtedly took great courage for the members of the Doña Ana Bend Colony to move from the security of El Paso del Norte to that isolated outpost in the middle of the hostile Indian country. However, through their efforts, the nucleus was formed for ultimate settlement and developments of the entire Mesilla Valley.

As early as 1822, unappropriated land suitable for agriculture in the vicinity of El Paso del Norte became very scarce. Since farming was the principal occupation, it became apparent, due to the city's continuous increase in population, that many of its citizens would not be able to earn a livelihood unless the rich lands in the Mesilla Valley were opened for cultivation. John Heath's thwarted plan of 1823 to establish a colony at Bracito only highlighted the practicability of developing the fertile valley lands.

Realizing that the lands near the old Doña Ana campsite were ideal for cultivation, José María Costales, a citizen of El Paso del Norte, consulted the Prefect of the El Paso District, Cayetano Justiniani, concerning the possibilities of his obtaining a grant of land at the place known as the Doña Ana Bend. The lands in which Costales was interested are located forty to fifty miles north of El Paso del Norte on the east bank of the Rio Grande. The prefect advised Costales that he was not authorized under the law to make a grant to him individually, but that if he could interest one hundred other men in joining him in the formation of a new settlement, he would grant them land at Doña Ana Bend.

On September 18, 1839 Costales and one hundred fifteen other citizens of the Town of El Paso del Norte presented a formal petition to José Ygnacio Ronquillo, then prefect of El Paso del Norte, requesting that the lands known as Doña Ana Bend be granted to them for colonization purposes. The prefect referred the petition to the Governor of the State of Chihuahua, J. María Yrigoyen, on October 18, 1839. In his accompanying report to the governor, the prefect stated that the lands requested were fertile and capable of being cultivated by irrigation; that the proposed settlement would be beneficial to the general welfare; and that he knew of no reason why the application should be denied. Governor Yrigoyen sent the application to the Departmental Assembly for its approval. On December 5, 1839 the Assembly recommended granting of the concession to the applicants, subject to the laws pertaining to colonization. No further action was taken on this application during the term of Governor Yrigoyen.

On July 3, 1840 the applicants submitted a new application for the same lands to José Morales, Prefect of El Paso del Norte. In this petition they stated that they direly needed the lands which they had requested, because they had been idle and without means for subsistance since 1828, when the river had flooded and ruined their lands at El Paso del Norte. They concluded by pointing out that the new settlement would promote industry and communication, and would also serve as a bulwark against the hostile Indians. This new application was likewise transmitted by the prefect to the then Governor of Chihuahua, Francisco García Conde. In his report to the governor, the prefect recommended issuance of the grant, as it would alleviate the miseries of the landless applicants. The prefect further reported that if the river flooded the area again in the coming year as it had in the past, one-half of El Paso del Norte, San Lorenzo del Real, and other adjoining towns would be lost.

After carefully considering the proposal, the governor, with the consent and approval of the Departmental Assembly, granted the request on July 8, 1840, subject to promulgation of proper regulations governing colonization and distribution of the granted lands. On the same day the governor requested the Director of the Geographical Bureau of the State of Chihuahua to prepare such regulations. On July 31, 1840 the Director of the Geographical Bureau, José Rodrigo García, promulgated regulations[2] governing establishment of the Doña Ana Bend Colony. On August 5, 1840 the governor ordered the prefect of El Paso del Norte to proceed with establishment of the colony and granting of the lands at Doña Ana Bend to the settlers, in accordance with terms and conditions prescribed by the Geographical Bureau. The governor informed the Supreme Government, on August 5, 1840, that he had made a colonization grant to the petitioners.

When the prefect of El Paso del Norte received the governor's order, he published notice of his intention to establish the Doña Ana Bend Colony. On the day appointed for the settlers to migrate to Doña Ana Bend, the colonists advised the prefect that they were unable to proceed with the project due to their poverty, the unusual hostility of the Indians, and other just circumstances. Therefore, they requested the prefect to extend the date for migration to February 1, 1843. The prefect granted their request.

On January 26, 1843 thirty-three of the original applicants advised the prefect that they were ready to proceed with formation of the colony. The prefect appointed one of the colonists, Bernabé Montoya, as his agent to supervise establishment of the colony, and authorized these colonists to proceed to their grant. He also issued special instructions[3] pertaining to construction of the community irrigation system. This group emigrated to Doña Ana and commenced construction of the *acequia madre*.

For various reasons, some of the colonists lost interest in the colonization scheme. One by one they began abandoning the project until, on April 16, 1843, only fourteen settlers remained on the grant. In order to save the enterprise from failure, the remaining settlers requested the governor to send a detachment of troops with sufficient arms and ammunition to the grant for their protection. They also requested that ten men be sent from each district to help them complete the irrigation ditch, that they be permitted to cultivate the lands that they had already cleared, without prejudice to their rights to select other land as their own individual farm tracts in the future, and that they be exempt from military service and taxes. In response to this urgent request, a detachment of seven men with eleven muskets were rushed to Doña Ana to protect the settlers from the hostile Indians, who were then terrorizing the community. At the same time, the governor advised the settlers that they would be exempt from military service and could cultivate any land within the grant until it was officially distributed in accordance with the regulations, but that he could not, under the law, exempt them from taxation or furnish them with workmen from other districts to work on their local irrigation project. There is no question but that the prompt relief measures extended to the colonists by the governor saved the project from being abandoned during its first year.[4]

Living conditions at the Doña Ana Bend Colony during its first year were primitive. On one of his occasional visits to the colony, the military commander of the frontier, General Mauricio Ugarte, was met by only four of the settlers. When he inquired of the others, he was advised they were in hiding because they were without any wearing apparel. Ugarte promptly outfitted the entire colony with military uniforms, and gave each a horse and a mule. These were the only domestic animals in the settlement.

Construction of the irrigation system was the first community project undertaken by the colonists. Working solely with crude wooden spades, they were able to complete the *acequia madre* during the month of April, 1843. Thereafter, they proceeded to plant the small tract of land which they had previously cleared, in order to raise sufficient crops to see them through the ensuing winter.

Life at the isolated colony was hazardous, for the fierce Apaches freely roamed the area. Each morning one-half of the settlers would venture forth, armed to the teeth, to work the fields. A sentinel was always posted to prevent a surprise attack. The remaining colonists would work in town on the construction of adobe homes and jacals. The signal for an Indian attack was a single pistol shot, and under no circumstances was a shot fired, except as an Indian warning. If a field worker fired the shot, the town workmen would rush to their assistance. If the signal came from town, the field hands would drop their tools and rush to the rescue of the besieged.

Provisions for the new colony had to be packed in from El Paso del Norte. Whenever the colony's supplies were nearly exhausted, a minimum of six men would make the tedious excursion. The trip was so dangerous that all of their traveling was done at night. The settlement could spare scarcely one man, much less half of its members.[5]

A bumper harvest of corn, beans and vegetables, coupled with the successful negotiation of a temporary peace treaty with the Mescalero Indians by General Mauricio Ugarte, encouraged many of the original applicants and a large number of new settlers to migrate to the colony.

On January 9, 1844 the colonists petitioned the prefect of El Paso del Norte, Antonio Rey, requesting a distribution of the lands which they were entitled to receive under the regulations governing the colony. In response to this petition, Rey personally went to the colony on January 19, 1844, and promptly surveyed the boundaries of the grant. The survey commenced at the head of the Doña Ana Acequia, and ran thence down the east bank of the Rio Grande to the head of the Bracito Acequia; thence east to a point one league east of the foothills; thence north to a point located one league east of the foothills and due east of the head of the Doña Ana Acequia; and thence west to the point of beginning.

After the prefect had completed his survey of the grant he proceeded to take a census of the colony in preparation for distribution of the individual tracts of land to the settlers. The census disclosed that the population of the colony had already increased from fourteen to two hundred sixty-one inhabitants. It also showed there were forty-seven families and twenty-two single men on the grant who were eligible to receive individual allotments of land in accordance with the Regulations of July 30, 1840.

The prefect laid out forty-seven *caballerías* of agricultural land for the married men and twenty-two farm tracts for the single men. The original fourteen settlers were given the preferential right to choose their tracts. After the original settlers had selected their tracts, the new settlers were awarded their tracts at a public drawing. Next, a townsite was set aside upon the grant and subdivided into residential lots. Each of the sixty-nine allottees received a residential lot. The prefect, on January 24, 1844, placed each allottee in lawful possession of the tracts which had been awarded to him, but no title papers were issued to the colonists at that time.

When the prefect created the townsite, he set aside a tract of land located in the center of the settlement as the public plaza, and ordered the colonists to construct a church and other public buildings on the lots located on the south side of the plaza. He also set aside the grant land lying east of the foothills as a common pasture. The wooded areas adjoining the river were set apart for the use and benefit of all inhabitants of the colony. All unallotted land located within the grant was reserved for the benefit of any new settlers who might subsequently join the colony.

The prefect concluded his visit by appointing Pablo Melendrez to the office of Alcalde and José María Costales as alternate Alcalde. Upon returning to El Paso del Norte, Rey transmitted a written report of his actions to the Governor of Chihuahua.[6]

Upon being advised that the Doña Ana Bend colonists had not received title papers to their individual allotments, Guadalupe Miranda, then prefect of El Paso del Norte, on January 22, 1846, authorized Pablo Melendrez, as the principal Alcalde for the colony, to issue the necessary muniments of title. Acting upon this authorization, Melendrez proceeded to issue title papers to the original allottees. He continued to allot and grant land to the settlers who subsequently moved to the grant prior to the signing of the Treaty of Guadalupe Hidalgo in 1848.[7]

After the lands near the village of Doña Ana were appropriated, the subsequent colonists were obliged to receive allotments in the southern portion of the grant. As the population of the grant increased, new settlements were formed to protect the new colonists. The villages of Las Cruces and Tortugas were thus established for the convenience of the farmers cultivating the lands adjacent to the new towns.

The inhabitants of the Doña Ana Bend Colony petitioned the Surveyor General to investigate their claim on January 23, 1874. Surveyor General James K. Proudfit, in an opinion dated March 31, 1874, stated that the records showed the colony had been established by the lawful authorities of the Republic of Mexico; that the colonists or their successors were in peaceful possession of the land; that they had never been disturbed in their possession except by hostile Indians; and that he believed their claim had been legally perfected. In conclusion, he recommended Congressional confirmation of the grant.[8]

A preliminary survey of the grant was made under the direction of the Surveyor General in March, 1878 by John T. Elkins and Robert Morman. Their survey disclosed that the grant contained 29,323.57 acres. The Surveyor General approved the survey on April 5, 1879.[9]

The claimants' petition for recognition of the Doña Ana Bend Colony Grant was pending in Congress when the Court of Private Land Claims was created. Numa Reymond, John D. Barncastle, Josefa Barncastle and Manuel Baregas, as owners of certain interests in the grant, filed suit in the Court of Private Land Claims against the United States on July 26, 1892, for confirmation of the Doña Ana Bend Colony Grant.[10]

Numa Reymond claimed two tracts of land under the grant which he had purchased from two of the original grantees. Josefa Barncastle, wife of John D. Barncastle, was the daughter and heir of Pablo Melendrez and had inherited all of her father's lands located within the grant. Manuel Baregas was one of the original grantees.

At the trial, the plaintiffs introduced a copy of the grant papers, together with a transcript of the proceedings before the Surveyor General. They also introduced oral testimony which established the boundaries of the grant and substantiated the allegation that the claimants had held peaceful and continuous possession of the grant ever since its issuance.

The government acknowledged the genuineness of the grant papers, but opposed confirmation of the grant on the grounds that the Governor and Departmental Assembly had no authority to make a valid concession. Prior to 1835, Mexico had contracted a large national debt, which it was having difficulty in repaying. On April 4, 1837 the Mexican Congress passed an act providing for the refunding of the debt through the sale of the public domain. To secure this indebtedness, an act was passed on April 12, 1837, which mortgaged one hundred million acres of public lands in California, Chihuahua, New Mexico, Texas and Sonora. The government contended that the Act of April 4, 1837 expressly repealed the National Colonization Act of 1824 and the Regulations of 1828; and therefore, a gratuitous colonization grant made after that date would be void.

The plaintiffs answered this contention by arguing that the Act of April 4, 1837 applied only to the lands owned by the National Government which were actually mortgaged by the Act of April 12, 1837. In view of the fact that there was no evidence that the lands in question were owned by the National Government or had been mortgaged under the Act of April 12, 1837, the plaintiffs contended that it could reasonably be presumed that the lands in question belonged to the State of Chihuahua, and were, therefore, subject to colonization under the State's Colonization Act of May 25, 1825.

In the alternative, the government argued that, assuming the granting authorities had the power to make a gratuitous colonization grant, they had only granted a small tract of farm land and a residential lot to each individual settler, and that the fee title to all the remaining unallotted land located within the boundaries of the grant was retained by the government of Mexico. The government also asserted that only the tracts which had been awarded by the prefect, Antonio Rey, on January 22, 1844, by virtue of the governor's expressed orders, should be confirmed because the regulations did not authorize an Alcalde to grant land to settlers.

The plaintiffs answered the contention by arguing that the grant was a Colony Grant made for the benefit of all its inhabitants, and that on July 30, 1840 the sovereign had conveyed all its title to the lands embraced within its boundaries to the original and any future settlers. They contended that all of the subsequent distribution of land by the Alcalde among its inhabitants was merely a partitioning of the lands which previously had been owned by the colony.

The Court of Private Land Claims, in its majority opinion dated March 25, 1896, held that the National Colonization Laws of August 18, 1824, and State of Chihuahua's Colonization Law of May 25, 1825, were repealed only insofar as they pertained to the public lands which were mortgaged by the Act of April 12, 1837, and that there was no evidence indicating that the lands covered by the Doña Ana Bend Colony Grant had been mortgaged. The court further held that the Governor of Chihuahua, with the consent and approval of the Departmental Assembly, had authority to make a valid colonization grant. The court noted that the Governor, the Departmental Assembly, the Geographical Board, and the prefect were all involved in the making of the grant. The court stated it could reasonably be presumed that these public officials knew the law, and had properly discharged their duties. The court further asserted that the validity of the grant was supported by the fact that the colony, which was well known and whose boundaries were well defined, had held peaceful uninterrupted possession of the land from the time of its inception up to and ever since the change of sovereignty. Continuing, the court held that the grant had been made for the benefit of the original settlers and all future settlers who might join the colony at a later date. The court concluded its majority opinion by confirming title to the Doña Ana Bend Colony Grant to all bona fide residents living upon the grant on the date of the signing of the Treaty of Guadalupe Hidalgo. The court established the boundaries of the grant at the points specified by Guadalupe Miranda in his testimony before the Surveyor General. Miranda's testimony was particularly pertinent in view of his having accompanied the prefect of El Paso del Norte when the tract was originally surveyed.

In a dissenting opinion, Justice William N. Murray stated that he believed that each of the arguments which had been presented by the government against confirmation of the grant was well founded.[11]

Through accident or mistake, the court, in its decree confirming the Doña Ana Bend Colony Grant, failed to reserve for the United States the title to all gold, silver and quicksilver mines, and minerals located upon and within the grant, as required by the third paragraph of Article 13 of the Act of March 3, 1891. The court corrected this oversight by *nunc pro tunc* order dated May 4, 1897.[12]

In his report on the case to the Attorney General of the United States, Matthew G. Reynolds, the government's attorney, recommended that the case be appealed to the Supreme Court of the United States, despite the strong equities in favor of the plaintiffs. Reynolds pointed out that the Court of Private Land Claims had rejected a number of private land claims where there were strong equities, because the power to initiate title was lacking. He called the Attorney General's attention to the fact that under the views entertained by the government and sustained by one member of the court, the Doña Ana Bend Colony Grant was not made by lawful authority. Due to the fact that the case involved many new issues and interpreted several recently discovered Mexican Statutes concerning the authority of Mexican officials to issue land grants after April 4, 1837, Reynolds felt it would be advisable to have the case reviewed by the Supreme Court.[13]

Acting upon Reynolds' recommendation, the government appealed the Court of Private Land Claims' decision to the United States Supreme Court.[14] Shortly after the government had perfected its appeal in the case, Reynolds reversed his original recommendation and advised the Attorney General that, as a result of the Supreme Court's decision in the Chaves Case,[15] he was satisfied that the long, continuous, peaceful possession and development of the grant lands by its numerous claimants would prompt the court to overrule his purely technical objection on the grounds that it

would be presumed that the granting authorities had the power to issue
the concession, or at least hold that the government was estopped to deny
such a lack of authority by reason of its laches. Continuing, Reynolds advised his superiors that in the event the grant was finally rejected, the claimants could possibly obtain title to their holdings under the Public Land
Laws, but that they might suffer undue hardships if unscrupulous speculators jumped their claims. In conclusion, Reynolds recommended that the
appeal be dismissed, because he was satisfied that no peculiar interests of
the United States would be subserved by further prosecution of the claim.[16]
The government dismissed its appeal on March 15, 1897.[17]

Subsequently, the Commissioner of the General Land Office ordered the
grant be officially surveyed in accordance with Article 10 of the Act of
March 3, 1891. Such a survey was made on March 8, 1901 by Jay Turley,
under Contract No. 352. Turley's survey disclosed that the grant contained
35,399.017 acres of land, and was approved by the Court of Private Land
Claims on April 4, 1902.[18]

By Patent dated February 8, 1907, the United States conveyed, subject
to the reservation of gold, silver, and quicksilver mines, and minerals, all
its title in the following described lands in Doña Ana County, New Mexico,
to the Doña Ana Bend Colony, its successors and assigns, to wit:

> Commencing at a point on the east bank of the Rio Grande River, where
> the original settlers of said Grant took from the river the water for the
> Doña Ana Acequia, being the same point at which the mouths of the Las
> Cruces and Mesilla Acequias were afterwards located; it being the same
> point fixed by the U. S. Government survey as the northwest corner of said
> grant; then following the east bank of the Rio Grande, as that river ran
> in the year 1844, in a southerly direction about thirteen miles to a point on
> the east bank of said Rio Grande at a place called high banks, said point
> being the head or mouth of an Acequia known as the Acequia of the Bra-
> cito Grant (said Grant sometimes called the Hugh Stephenson Grant),
> and also being the southwest corner of the said Doña Ana Bend Colony
> Grant as fixed by the United States Government Survey, including all the
> lands lying between the said Rio Grande and the foothills on the east bank
> of said river, which are between the old head of said Acequia of Doña Ana,
> Las Cruces, and Mesilla, and the said high banks and head of said Bracito
> Acequia, also a strip of land one league in width lying east of a line drawn
> along the foothills which lie to the east of said strip of land bordering on
> the river, which said last mentioned strip of land one league in width was
> granted to said colonists for pastoral purposes.[19]

This Patent by the United States cleared titles of more than 3,000 inhabitants who resided on the grant. The Patent protected the claimants'
investments and homes in Las Cruces, Doña Ana and Tortugas, all of
which were located upon the grant. The Doña Ana Bend Colony Grant is
unquestionably one of the most fertile and valuable tracts of land located
in the State of New Mexico.

On March 18, 1897 the New Mexico Legislature passed an act which authorized the claimants of an interest in a Spanish or Mexican Colony Grant to form a corporation to represent their interests. Each colony corporation has the power to sue or to be sued in the corporate name, and to distribute, sell, convey or otherwise dispose of the commonly owned lands. The corporation is managed by a Board of Trustees.[20]

Such a corporation was necessary to clear the land titles of the individual owners of the lands embraced within the Doña Ana Bend Colony Grant after it was patented to the Doña Ana Bend Colony. The grant was incorporated in accordance with the Act of 1897, and on February 18, 1907 Isidoro Armijo, Secretary of the Board of Trustees of the Doña Ana Bend Colony Grant, received and signed for the Patent to the grant.[21]

Though the lands of the grant have all long since passed into the hands of individual owners, the Doña Ana Bend Colony Corporation is still in existence. It is joined as a necessary party to quiet title suits involving lands within the grant. It also occasionally issues a quitclaim deed to the owner of lands within the grant in the event original title papers have not been recorded or have been lost or destroyed.

Belated recognition is indeed due the fourteen courageous colonists[22] who, despite the extreme dangers and hardships encountered during the first year of the Doña Ana Bend Colony's existence, remained at their frontier outpost to save the enterprise from failure. Men of lesser stamina undoubtedly would have abandoned the project in view of the difficulties encountered for such small return — a meager plot of land. The rapid settlement and development of the entire Mesilla Valley can be attributed to efforts of these men. The City of Las Cruces, New Mexico, together with its surrounding agricultural fields, are dynamic monuments to the memory of these brave pioneers.

R E F E R E N C E S

[1] The campsite or *paraje* known as Doña Ana is one of the earliest landmarks in southern New Mexico. It was located in El Ancón de Doña Ana, approximately fifty miles north of El Paso del Norte in the northern portion of Doña Ana County, New Mexico. Perhaps the earliest reference to the Doña Ana Paraje is Governor Otermin's notation that he camped there on February 4, 1682, following his unsuccessful expedition of 1681 and 1682 to crush the Pueblo Revolt. Charles F. Coan, *A History of New Mexico*, (3 Vols., New York, 1925), I, 211.

[2] A copy of these regulations is contained in *Senate Executive Documents*, 43rd Cong., 1st Sess., Document No. 43, 45-48 (1873).

[3] *Ibid.*, pp. 65-67.

[4] *Ibid.*, pp. 70-73.

[5] Maude Elizabeth McFie, *A History of the Mesilla Valley* (Thesis, New Mexico A. & M. College, 1903), 24, 25.

6 *Senate Executive Documents,* 43rd Cong., 1st Sess., Document No. 43, 74-87 (1873).

7 Doña Ana Bend Colony Grant, Report No. 85 (Mss., Records of the Surveyor General's Office, Bureau of Land Management, Santa Fe, New Mexico).

8 *Land Claims Records* (Mss., Records of the Surveyor General's Office, Bureau of Land Management, Santa Fe, New Mexico), IV, 536.

9 Doña Ana Bend Colony Grant, Map File 85 (Mss., Records of the Cadastrial Engineer's Office, Santa Fe, New Mexico).

10 Reymond v. United States (Mss., Court of Private Land Claims, Records of the Bureau of Land Management, Santa Fe, New Mexico), No. 24.

11 *Journal* (Mss., Court of Private Land Claims, Records of the Bureau of Land Management, Santa Fe, New Mexico), III, 31-33.

12 *Ibid.,* III, 178.

13 *Report of the United States Attorney dated December 9, 1896, in the Case of Numa Reymond et al v. United States,* (Mss., Records of the General Services Administration, National Archives, Washington, D.C.), Record Group 60, Year File 9865-92.

14 United States v. Reymond, (Mss., Records of the United States Supreme Court, Washington, D.C.), No. 706 of the October, 1896 Term.

15 United States v. Chaves, 159 U.S. 452 (1895).

16 *Supplemental Report of the United States Attorney in the Case of Numa Reymond et al v. United States,* (Mss., Records of the General Services Administration, National Archives, Washington, D.C.), Record Group 60, Year File 9865-92.

17 United States v. Reymond, 166 U.S. 72 (1897). For some unknown reason, the United States Attorney did not raise the issue in this case that the Doña Ana Bend Colony Grant was invalid due to the fact that the grant had been issued after the Texas Boundary Act of December 19, 1836, and covered lands embraced within the then Republic of Texas. For a detailed discussion of the interesting question, see Judge Federici's dissenting opinion in Cartwright v. Public Service Company of New Mexico, 342 P. 2d 654 (1959).

18 Doña Ana Bend Colony Grant, Map File 24 (Mss., Records of the Cadastrial Engineer's Office, Santa Fe, New Mexico). The Doña Ana Bend Colony Grant is one of the few claims confirmed by the Court of Land Claims for more land than contained in the plaintiff's petition. The claimants of the grant asserted that the grant covered only 29,323.57 acres, but the court confirmed title to a total of 35,399.017 acres.

19 *Deed Records,* (Mss., Records of the Doña Ana County Clerk's Office, Las Cruces, New Mexico), XX, 55.

20 *Acts of the Legislature of the Territory of New Mexico* (Santa Fe, 1897), 111-121.

21 Doña Ana Bend Colony Grant, Report No. 85 (Mss., Records of the Surveyor General's Office, Bureau of Land Management, Santa Fe, New Mexico).

22 The names of the fourteen colonists are: Pablo Melendrez; José María Costales; Juan José Benavidas; Francisco Rodriquez; Jesus Olivarez; José María Bernal; José María Perea; Francisco Lucero; Geronimo Lujan; Saturnino Abillar; José Ines García; Gabriel Dabalos; Ramón de la Serna; and one other whose name is unknown. Maude Elizabeth McFie, *A History of Mesilla Valley* (Thesis, New Mexico A. & M. College, 1903), 28.

CHAPTER 11

The Heath Grant ॐ

● THE LONG DEPRESSION in the United States following the panic of 1819 caused many adventurous Americans to consider Mexico's generous offers of land for colonists who would settle upon its northern frontiers. East Texas was rapidly settled and developed under the Empresario System. However, the only serious attempt to colonize the southwest under this system was made by John G. Heath.[1]

Heath was intimately acquainted with Stephen F. Austin and his Texas colonization grant. He was also acquainted with Captain William Becknell and other Missouri traders who were engaged in the Santa Fe trade. From Austin, Heath learned the procedure to be followed in securing an Empresario Grant. The Santa Fe traders probably advised Heath that the lands at El Bracito[2] were ideal for colonization.

Fired with the spirit of conquest, Heath petitioned Emperor Agustín de Iturbide, through the Ayuntamiento of El Paso del Norte, for the lands known as El Bracito on December 27, 1822. The tract was located approximately thirty-three miles northwest of El Paso del Norte on the Rio Grande, and previously had been occupied by Juan Antonio García. García had petitioned the Comandante General of Durango for a grant covering the lands at El Bracito in 1821, but the request was still pending in the summer of 1821, when Indian hostilities compelled García to withdraw from the land. On April 3, 1823 Heath was advised by the Ayuntamiento that no action had been taken on his petition because, on January 4, 1823, a colonization law[3] had been enacted by the National Assembly.

Heath, under his Spanish name of Juan Gid, again petitioned the Ayuntamiento of El Paso del Norte on April 3, 1823, for a grant of twenty-five leagues of land in the form of a square, with the head of the Bracito Acequia as its central point. As consideration for the grant, Heath agreed to establish a colony of thirty Catholic families on the land, among whom were to be representatives of various trades and professions. He further agreed to furnish all agricultural implements necessary to cultivate the lands, and promised to build and equip a hospital, a drug store, a warehouse, a powder factory, and a textile mill on the grant. The Ayuntamiento found the proposition was beneficial to the general welfare of the area. In accordance with the previsions of Article 4 of the National Colonization Law of 1823, the Ayuntamiento proceeded, on April 3, 1823, to grant Heath a square tract of land extending two and one-half leagues in each direction from the mouth of the Bracito Acequia. The grant was made subject to the understanding that any Mexican citizen desiring the lands would have preferential right to acquire them upon the same terms offered by Heath. The Ayuntamiento stated the grant was made subject to the securing of final approval by the Governor of New Mexico. Finally, the Ayuntamiento gave public notice of a meeting to be held at the Town Hall on April 13, 1823, at which time any interested party would be given an opportunity to voice his objections to the making of the concession. A large group of citizens from the area attended the meeting, but no one objected to the granting of the lands to Heath. At the end of the meeting the Ayuntamiento appointed a Commission, composed of Alcalde José Morales, Alderman José María Valverde, Public Attorney Lorenzo Provincio, and Secretary Juan María Ponce de León, to survey the grant. The Commission was also ordered to place Heath in possession of the lands covered by its survey.

At a meeting of the Ayuntamiento, two days later, Agapito Albo protested the granting of the lands to Heath on the grounds that the new settlement would endanger the future prosperity of El Paso del Norte by appropriating all of the river water during the frequent periods of drought. The objection was dismissed when Heath pointed out that the Ayuntamiento had authority to regulate the equitable distribution of water.

On April 17, 1823 the Commission commenced its survey, beginning at the mouth of the Bracito Acequia, and proceeded thence north two and one-half leagues to a point on the summit of a hill which marked the center of the north line. They proceeded from this point east two and one-half leagues to a point upon a hill called "La Cueva" in the Organ Mountains for the northeast corner of the grant. Returning to the center point on the north line, they ran thence west two and one-half leagues to a monument on "Mount Roblecito" for the northwest corner of the grant. They then returned to the central point at the mouth of the Bracito Acequia and ran thence south two and one-half leagues to a point for the center of the south line. They went thence west two and one-half leagues to "Cuba de los Organos" for the southwest corner. After returning to the central point on the south line, they ran thence east two and one-half leagues to a point on the east peak of the El Paso Mountains which is called "Paso de los Alamitos" for the southeast corner. The east and west lines of the grant were not actually surveyed on the ground, but were merely projected for the established corners.

After the survey was concluded, the Commission placed Heath in possession of the lands, and instructed him to use the bottom lands only for agricultural purposes. Heath was also notified that he could use water from the river to run his machines as long as they did not interfere with the welfare of the new colony or the town of El Paso del Norte. The Commission filed a written report of its actions with the Ayuntamiento on April

21, 1823, which it accepted and approved on the next day. A plat of the Heath grant, prepared by William Box, Master Mathematician, was also approved by the Ayuntamiento and attached to the title papers of the grant. A copy of the *expediente* of the grant was transmitted on April 26, 1823 to the governor.

In its letter transmitting the copy of the proceedings to the governor, the Ayuntamiento justified the issuance of concession on the grounds that it had jurisdiction over the territory extending up the river from El Paso del Norte to San Diego. It pointed out that once the new colony had completed its irrigation system, all the valley land lying between the grant and El Paso del Norte could be opened up for agricultural purposes, and many of the landless residents of El Paso del Norte would be willing to settle in the Mesilla Valley. The Ayuntamiento also noted that the Heath colony would tend to restrain the Indians from attacking any new settlements established in the valley, as well as El Paso del Norte and travelers on the Camino Real. In regard to the objection that the colony would prejudice the water rights of the farmers at El Paso del Norte, the Ayuntamiento asserted that it had sufficient authority to regulate the equitable distribution of water between the interested parties. Based upon these benefits, the Ayuntamiento contended that it was justified in issuing the concession under Articles 4 and 5 of the Colonization Law, but, in order to avoid any question concerning the validity of the grant, it had made the grant subject to his approval.

Upon receipt of the copy of the proceedings, the governor presented the matter to the Provincial Deputation for its consent and advice. The assembly, on June 19, 1823, repudiated the actions of the Ayuntamiento, primarily on the grounds that the Colonization Law of 1823 had been repealed before all action necessary to convey a valid grant had been completed. In admonishing the Ayuntamiento, the assembly expressed its contempt for the "violent and mistaken actions" taken by the Ayuntamiento in granting land to a foreigner, not only in prejudice to the inhabitants of its jurisdiction, but also in violation of the very law under which it purported to act. In conclusion, the assembly advised the Ayuntamiento that in order to avoid liability for damages, it should immediately notify Heath, through the Mexican Plenipotentiary to the United States, that the grant had been issued under a mistaken opinion and wrong understanding of the Colonization Law, which had already been repealed.[4]

Shortly after receiving the grant from the Ayuntamiento, Heath returned to Missouri and organized a company of one hundred fifty colonists. He disposed of his extensive holdings in Missouri on April 17, 1824, and, with the proceeds therefrom, purchased a large quantity of agricultural implements, machinery, and all necessary supplies and paraphernalia for the enterprise. Early in the spring of 1824 Heath and his colonists bade farewell to their friends and commenced their migration to Mexico from the "old city of Franklin, Missouri." The colonists traveled down the Missouri and Mississippi Rivers to New Orleans on a fleet of flatboats. At New Orleans, the colonists chartered a boat to transport them and their supplies to the Mexican harbor of Soto la Marina. They traveled thence overland to the grant by way of Chihuahua and El Paso del Norte.

Immediately after establishing his colony on the grant, Heath was advised by the Mexican authorities at El Paso del Norte that Iturbide's government had been overthrown by a revolution, and that the Governor and Provincial Deputation of New Mexico had repudiated the grant on June 19, 1823. Thereupon the colonists were ejected from the grant. Heath protested, on the grounds that he had faithfully fulfilled all of the provisions of his agreement, and was therefore entitled to the land. Heath made numerous applications to the Ayuntamiento of El Paso del Norte and to other authorities of Mexico for ratification or confirmation of the grant, all of which were refused. The colonists temporarily moved to El Paso del Norte, but returned to Missouri in 1825, when it became obvious that Heath would not be able to secure recognition of the grant. Finally, in 1826, under penalty of death, Heath was forced by the Mexican government to abandon all of his personal property and leave the country. Upon his return to Missouri, he was financially ruined. It has been estimated that the venture cost him over $75,000.[5] Until his death Heath never gave up hope of obtaining recognition of his claim. He died intestate in Boone County, Missouri in August, 1851.

Heath's heirs, prior to 1893, took no formal action to secure recognition of their claim by the United States due to a lack of funds and the loss of Heath's copy of the grant papers. They had been destroyed in 1863, when the Union forces burned the home of Heath's son at Gasconade, Missouri. The heirs retained Attorney J. B. Cessna to secure confirmation of the grant, and gave him a half interest in the claim in consideration of his services. On January 9, 1893 Cessna and the heirs of John Heath filed suit against the United States and the unknown claimants of the Doña Ana Bend Colony Grant, the Mesilla Civil Colony Grant, and the Bracito Grant, in the Court of Private Land Claims, for recognition and confirmation of the Heath Grant.[6]

The plaintiffs alleged that they were the owners of the twenty-five league tract of land which had been duly granted to Heath by the Ayuntamiento of El Paso del Norte on April 3, 1823. They proved that Heath, in reliance upon the grant, had induced more than thirty Catholic families to settle upon the grant, and had therefore fulfilled the conditions contained in the grant insofar as he was permitted to do so by the Mexican authorities. They contended that once Heath had commenced the performance of such conditions in good faith, that title to the grant became vested and could be repudiated only by judicial action. In support of their claim, they introduced into evidence a copy of the grant papers which they had found in the Archives of New Mexico.[7] The plaintiffs claimed that since the subsequent repudiation of the Heath Grant by the New Mexican authorities was illegal, their claim was protected under the terms of the Treaty of Guadalupe Hidalgo and the Gadsden Purchase.

The defendants answered that the Heath Grant was invalid because it did not conform with the provisions of the National Colonization Act of 1823. They further alleged that the Ayuntamiento of El Paso del Norte had no authority to grant the tract to Heath after April 11, 1823 because the National Congress of Mexico, on that date, had revoked the Colonization Law of January 4, 1823. This point is particularly important, since the defendants took the position that the grant was not made on April 3, 1823, as alleged by the plaintiffs, but was actually issued April 21, 1823. They also called attention to the fact that the grant clearly stated on its face that it had been made subject to its being approved by the Governor of New Mexico, and that the Governor and Assembly of New Mexico had, on June 19, 1823, rejected the grant. They stated that it was evident that the Mexican government had considered the grant void, for it had subsequently conveyed a major portion of the land claimed by the plaintiffs to the Doña Ana Bend Colony, the Mesilla Civil Colony, the Santo Tomás de Iturbide Colony, and José Manuel Sánchez Baca. The defendants' next assertion was that even if the grant had been valid originally, Heath had abandoned it when he left Mexico in 1826. Noting that the Heath Grant was located on both sides of the Rio Grande, the defendants called the court's attention to the fact that under Mexican law private land surveys were prohibited from crossing perennial streams which were more than thirty feet wide. They also noted that the Heath Grant purported to cover a *hacienda* of land. The Colonization Law of 1823 defined a *hacienda* as five leagues of land. In conclusion, the defendants argued that this provision would limit the claim to five leagues, instead of the twenty-five leagues claimed by the plaintiffs.

The court found that the Ayuntamiento of El Paso del Norte had attempted to make a concession to John Heath in April, 1823, under authority of Article 4 of the National Colonization Law of January 4, 1823, but that that law did not authorize the Ayuntamiento to make a grant of any land lying outside the limits of the town's four-league grant. The court further found that if Article 4 of said law permitted the Ayuntamiento to dispense unlimited amounts of the public domain to foreign colonizers upon such terms as its officials might choose, that the grant was still invalid, because, prior to settlement, the Ayuntamiento was only authorized under the law to designate the lands which were to be occupied by Heath's proposed colony. The court was of the opinion that the concession had only authorized Heath to lead a group of colonists to the area covered in the grant, and thereafter to grant each settler a separate lot of land. Since the Ayuntamiento had no authority to make an absolute grant of such lands prior to actual introduction of the colonists, Heath's privilege of establishing a colony on the lands at Bracito had been lawfully revoked by the Mexican government prior to settlement of any emigrant on the grant. The court, therefore, rejected the plaintiffs' claim on June 26, 1895.[8]

The plaintiffs appealed the decision.[9] The Supreme Court affirmed the decision of the Court of Private Land Claims, and held that the Ayuntamiento was not authorized, under Article 4 of the National Colonization Law of 1823, to make a grant of land outside the limits of the El Paso del Norte Town Grant. Noting that Mexican villages customarily received a town grant of only four square leagues, the court concluded that the Heath Grant, which was located approximately thirty-three miles north of the town and covered twenty-five leagues, could not reasonably be presumed to be embraced within the town grant. The court further found that the Heath Grant, which had been made subject to approval of the Provincial authorities, had subsequently been rejected by that body. The court was of the opinion that the failure of Heath and his successors to assert their claim for more than seventy years after expulsion of the colony from Mexico, raised a presumption against the validity of the plaintiffs' claim that an absolute grant had been made by the Ayuntamiento in April, 1823. It concluded its opinion by holding that the United States was not obligated, under its Treaties of 1848 and 1853 with Mexico, to recognize any claims to land which had been previously repudiated by the government of Mexico and subsequently re-granted to innocent third parties.[10]

The Supreme Court's decision in this case removed a serious cloud from the title of the numerous claimants of the Doña Ana Bend Colony Grant, the Mesilla Civil Colony Grant, the Santo Tomás de Yturbide Grant, the José Manuel Sánchez Baca Grant, and the Bracito Grant. Each of these grants, which conflicted with the Heath Grant, have been confirmed and recognized by the United States government. It is interesting to speculate as to what role this Anglo-American Colony would have played in the history of the southwest if it had been permitted to remain in Mexico. The living standards of this poverty stricken area undoubtedly would have been raised as a result of the introduction of scientific farming practices, industry and skilled artisans. The new colonists and their modern firearms also would have been of avail to help check the frequent Indian uprisings. Alas, it is indeed disconcerting to learn that after the colonists withdrew from the country, Juan María Ponce de León, the Secretary of the Ayuntamiento of El Paso del Norte at the time of the colony's expulsion, stated that he and other officials at El Paso del Norte subsequently regretted not allowing Heath and his associates to remain at Bracito.

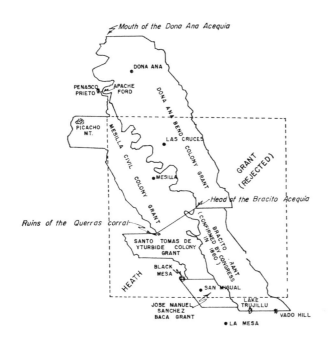

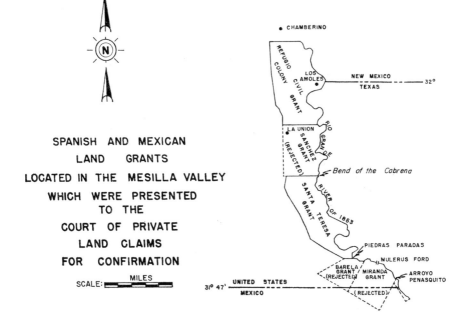

SPANISH AND MEXICAN
LAND GRANTS
LOCATED IN THE MESILLA VALLEY
WHICH WERE PRESENTED
TO THE
COURT OF PRIVATE
LAND CLAIMS
FOR CONFIRMATION

REFERENCES

1 John G. Heath was born in the State of New York. He was a nephew of General William Heath, of Revolutionary fame. On July 5, 1814 Heath married Hattie McDonald in St. Charles County, Missouri. He was elected to numerous political offices under the Territory and State of Missouri. Heath was well educated and spoke Spanish and French fluently. He was a qualified surveyor and engineer, as well as a licensed attorney and doctor of medicine. After having gained considerable wealth, Heath became interested in further conquests and state building. He was a man of fine business qualifications, and was always eager to engage in any enterprise where a legitimate profit was likely to be obtained. Tradition has it that he migrated to Texas with Stephen F. Austin, and that he settled at or near San Jacinto. After Heath returned from Mexico following the failure of his colonization venture, he settled in Cooper County, Missouri. Thereafter, he was engaged in the manufacturing of salt at "Heat's Salt Lick," which was located fifteen miles west of Boonesville, Missouri. Heath's death occurred in August, 1851. He was survived by his five children: Robert H. Heath, Joseph Heath, Eliza Heath Sherman, Harriet Heath and Margaret Heath. Wm. H. H. Allison, "John G. Heath," *New Mexico Historical Review* (1931), VI, 360-375.

2 El Bracito was the Spanish name for one of the regular campsites on the Camino Real. It was located about thirty-three miles north of El Paso del Norte and approximately fifteen miles south of Las Cruces. The El Bracito *paraje* was situated on a "Little Arm of the Rio Grande encircling a sandy island. The mesquite and chaparral near the site had been burned off by the travelers who rested there. The first reference to the Paraje de El Bracito is contained in the Diary of Nicolás de Lafora. He mentions that he camped at the Paraje de El Bracito on August 7, 1766. Lawrence Kinnaird, *The Frontiers of New Spain: Nicolás de Lafora's Description, 1766-1768* (Berkeley, 1958), 85.

3 A copy of this colonization law is contained in Francisco F. de la Maza, *Código de Colonización y Terrenos Baldíos* (México, 1893), 171-176.

4 Cessna v. United States *et al* (Mss., Court of Private Land Claims, Records of the Bureau of Land Management, Santa Fe, New Mexico), No. 59.

5 *Ibid.*

6 *Ibid.*

7 The original title papers to the Heath Grant are now contained in the Archives of New Mexico (Mss., Records of the New Mexico Museum, Santa Fe, New Mexico), Doc. No. 410.

8 *Journal* (Mss., Court of Private Land Claims, Records of the Bureau of Land Management, Santa Fe, New Mexico), II, 384 and 385.

9 Cessna v. United States (Mss., Records of the United States Supreme Court, Washington, D.C.), Cause No. 78 of the October, 1897 Term.

10 Cessna v. United States, 169 U.S. 165 (1898).

CHAPTER 12

The Bracito Grant ह✵

● ONE OF THE BEST KNOWN natural landmarks in the Mesilla Valley
was El Bracito ("Little Arm,"), the Spanish name applied to a sandy tract
of land situated within a prominent horseshoe bend of the Rio Grande,
which was located approximately thirty-three miles north of El Paso del
Norte. The bottom lands in the vicinity of this river bend were extremely
fertile and level. For centuries, El Bracito was used as a *paraje,* or campsite, by travelers up and down the Camino Real.

Shortly after the turn of the nineteenth century, the Spaniards discovered
valuable silver deposits in the Organ Mountains, but they could not be
developed until the miners were afforded adequate protection from the
hostile Indians. Realizing that the lands at El Bracito could be adapted for
agricultural purposes, Juan Antonio García de Noriega,[1] a retired Lieutenant of Dragoons of the Provincial Militia of El Paso del Norte, petitioned Joaquín Real de Alencaster, Governor of New Mexico, in 1805, for
a grant of land extending from El Bracito south to Lake Trujillo. In his
petition he agreed to build a house and corrals on the land, cultivate the
soil, maintain fifteen armed men on the lands for protection of the settlement, travelers, and the mines in the surrounding mountains, until a sufficient number of persons had been attracted to the area to form a permanent settlement. In answer to this petition, the Governor of New Mexico,
on August 4, 1805, decreed that the concession would be made whenever
a colony was established upon the lands requested. Juan Antonio García
immediately took possession of the lands, built a house thereon, constructed
the Bracito Acequia, and commenced farming the rich valley lands. García
successfully purchased peace with the hostile Apache Indians by giving
them the corn which he grew on the banks of his irrigation ditch.

Having thus formed the nucleus for the proposed new colony, García
petitioned Bernardo Bonavía, Comandante General of Durango, on November 29, 1816, for a grant covering the lands which he was occupying
at El Bracito. In his petition, he stated that there were eleven individuals
from El Paso del Norte who had volunteered to join him in formation of
the proposed settlement. He promised to continue planting a portion of
the lands for the Indians and furnishing them with provisions from his
fields, in order to keep them peaceful. The Comandante General referred
the petition to José Ordas, Lieutenant Governor of El Paso del Norte, for
his recommendation. The Lieutenant Governor recommended granting of

the lands to García on June 29, 1819. Eighteen days later the Comandante General requested the Lieutenant Governor to furnish him with a general description of the said lands and a list of the persons who had agreed to join García in the formation of the proposed settlement. In response to this request, the Lieutenant Governor replied that the proposed grant was located some fifteen leagues north of the last houses of the town of El Paso del Norte, and covered an area three leagues in length, and varied in width from one-fourth of a league to more than one league. He further stated that the lands offered every facility for cultivation, and that official residences, judicial and religious, could be established at the center of the grant. In conclusion, he attached the following list showing the persons who had agreed to settle upon the land:

> Don Juan A. García, with fourteen servants;
> Don José Barrios, with two servants;
> Don Juan Barrios, and his two brothers;
> Don Patricio Lucero;
> Don Miguel de Herrera, with two men;
> Don Simón Talamante;
> Don Ramón García, with two men;
> Don Antonio Provincio;
> Don Mateo Telles;
> Don Vicente Quarrón;
> Don Martías Valencia; and
> Don José García, with one man.

It became obvious to García that if the grant was issued it would be conditioned upon his agreeing to build homes for judicial and ecclesiastical officials, and with the understanding that the new settlement would be placed under the jurisdiction of El Paso del Norte for ecclesiastical and judicial purposes. Due to his reluctance to accept the grant under these conditions, on September 12, 1819 García requested the Lieutenant Governor to defer all further action upon his petition.

On February 18, 1820 Juan Antonio García again petitioned the Governor of New Mexico for the El Bracito lands. In this petition, he advised the Governor that the men who had previously volunteered to accompany him in the settlement of said lands had abandoned the project, but that he had continuously occupied and cultivated the land for at least eleven years. He concluded his petition by requesting the grant be made to him, individually. This petition was rejected by Facundo Melgares, Governor of New Mexico, on August 18, 1820, on the ground that he did not have jurisdiction over the lands.

García addressed a similar petition to the Comandante General of the State of Durango on July 28, 1821. This petition was referred to the Comptroller of the State for his approval and further action. The Comptroller recommended that the grant be issued to García if the land covered thereby was suitable for settlement and was a part of the unappropriated public domain. In order to satisfy these requisites, the Comptroller directed the First Justice of El Paso del Norte to appoint an Attorney General to represent the interest of the public revenue and to report upon the resources of the land and its suitability for farming and stock raising. In compliance with this request, the First Justice of El Paso del Norte, Jorge Guerina, on April 19, 1822, reported that the land was a part of the public domain, and that he had appointed Julián Bernal as the Attorney General to represent the interests of the public revenue, and José María Córdova, of El Paso del Norte, to report on the physical characteristics of the land. Córdova, in turn, reported that the land was suitable for both farming and stock raising.

Bentura Carbajal, José Velarde and José María García, three prominent citizens of El Paso del Norte, upon learning of García's application, went to Guerina and protested against the issuance of the grant on the ground that if the lands were granted to García, it would deprive the citizens of El Paso of certain privileges which were vital to the continued welfare of the town. They pointed out that even though the lands were a part of the public domain, they were being used by the inhabitants of El Paso del Norte as pasturage for their livestock. They further noted that the scattered groves of trees which were located on the grant furnished most of the city's lumber and fuel requirements. Before any further action could be taken upon García's request, the Apaches went on the warpath. It became too dangerous to live on the isolated rancho at El Bracito, and García was compelled to move back to El Paso del Norte.

Meanwhile, John G. Heath, an American from Missouri, petitioned the Ayuntamiento of El Paso del Norte for a grant covering the land at El Bracito. In consideration for the grant, Heath promised to establish a colony on the land. Due to the increased Indian hostilities, the Ayuntamiento realized that such a colony would be of benefit to the town of El Paso del Norte as a buffer zone between it and the Apaches. Therefore, the Ayuntamiento granted the land to Heath on April 3, 1823, subject to approval of the Governor of New Mexico. Upon learning of the grant, the officials of New Mexico formally censored the Ayuntamiento for its actions and repudiated the grant.[2]

Shortly after the repudiation of the Heath Grant, jurisdiction over the El Bracito area was transferred to the newly formed State of Chihuahua. Immediately after the change in sovereignity, Lieutenant Governor José Ordas proceeded to grant the lands at El Bracito to Juan Antonio García. García moved back to the grant in 1824 or 1825 and built a fine adobe house with his family. He cultivated most of the valley lands covered by the grant, and pastured large herds of sheep on his mesa lands.

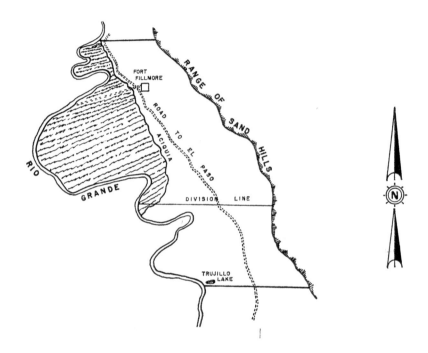

MAP OF THE BRAZITO TRACT OF LAND
SURVEYED AND MADE BY STEPHENSON ARCHER
DISTRICT SURVEYOR OF
EL PASO AND PRESIDIO DISTRICTS
1854
FOR HUGH STEPHENSON

In 1827, due to advanced age and illness, Juan Antonio García moved back to El Paso del Norte, but his servants continued to occupy and cultivate the grant properties. After García's death in 1828, all his personal influence over the Apaches was lost, and they soon made further living on the grant impossible. The properties were vacated shortly thereafter.

In 1851 the heirs of Juan Antonio García[3] entered into an agreement with Hugh Stephenson, wherein they agreed to sell him two-thirds of the grant for $1,000.[4] Stephenson agreed to pay all costs incurred in clearing title to the Bracito Grant, and immediately thereafter entered into actual possession of the grant.[5]

The García heirs gave Stephenson all of the papers they possessed pertaining to the grant, but they did not have a copy of the Lieutenant Governor Ordas' decree of 1823, which actually granted the land to Juan Antonio García. In an attempt to obtain this important link in his claim of title, Stephenson caused a diligent search to be made of the Archives of El Paso del Norte for the original grant papers, but they could not be located.

It was learned that after their victory at the Battle of Bracito, United States troops, under Col. A. W. Doniphan, had been quartered in the Municipal Building at El Paso del Norte. The public archives and records were deposited in this building. It is a known fact that these American troops destroyed a large portion of the public archives during their two-month stay in the town.[6]

Stephenson secured a number of affidavits, stating that the American forces used these priceless records to kindle fires and light candles, and that after the American troops left El Paso for Chihuahua the remaining records were found scattered about the chambers of the Ayuntamiento and in the streets. Stephenson asserted that it could reasonably be presumed that the original copy of the Bracito Grant papers, which had been deposited in the public archives of El Paso del Norte, had been lost or destroyed by the American troops under Colonel Doniphan. Affidavits by persons who had seen and handled the original grant papers further supported the theory that the grant had actually been made and the papers evidencing the grant had been deposited in the archives of the Ayuntamiento of El Paso del Norte.[7]

One of the cases heard during the May, 1853 term of the United States District Court for the Third Judicial District of the Territory of New Mexico was a friendly suit for the partitioning of the Bracito Grant by Francisco García and the other heirs of Juan Antonio García against Hugh Stephenson, in accordance with their agreement in 1851. The court recognized the validity of the Bracito Grant and ordered it surveyed and partitioned by Stephenson Archer, District Surveyor of the El Paso and Presidio Land District. The Archer survey showed the grant as containing

20,193 acres of land. The court then ordered Francisco García to deed the upper two-thirds of the grant to Hugh Stephenson, upon receipt of the $1,000 specified in the agreement. In compliance with the court's decree, Francisco García gave Stephenson a deed covering the northern two-thirds of the grant on November 16, 1854. At the same time, Stephenson paid García $1,000 in cash and gave him a deed covering the lower one-third of the grant.[8]

Fortified with the District Court's recognition of the Bracito Grant, Hugh Stephenson and the heirs of Juan Antonio García, through their attorney, John S. Watts, petitioned William Pelham, Surveyor General of New Mexico, on August 6, 1856, for confirmation of the Bracito Grant. After reviewing the evidence presented to him, the Surveyor General stated he was convinced that the grant was valid and had actually been issued to Juan Antonio García by Lieutenant Governor Ordas in 1823, and that he believed the original copy of the grant had been lost or destroyed in 1846 by the American troops. He was also of the opinion that the claimants' interests were fully protected by the Treaty of Guadalupe Hidalgo. The Surveyor General concluded by recommending that the grant, which was No. 6 in the report, be confirmed to Juan Antonio García, as the petitioners had not adequately shown that they were the legal heirs and assigns of Juan Antonio García. The Surveyor General transmitted all available papers and information concerning the grant, together with his favorable report to the Congress of the United States, for its further action.[9]

The Bracito Grant was confirmed by a special act of Congress on June 21, 1860. This Act merely referred to the grant by number, and stated it was confirmed in accordance with the Surveyor General's recommendation.[10]

In order to manage the public domain which adjoined the Bracito Grant, the United States needed to know the precise location and boundaries of the grant. John T. Elkins and Robert Morman, United States Deputy Surveyors, were directed to survey the grant by the Surveyor General of the Territory of New Mexico. Their work indicated that the grant contained only 10,612.57 acres. The Surveyor General approved the Elkins-Morman Survey on April 5, 1879, but the Commissioner of the General Land Office rejected it on February 20, 1893, on the ground that the west boundary of the Elkins-Morman Survey had not been correctly located on the east bank of the river as it ran in 1854.[11] The Surveyor General retained Leonard M. Brown to re-survey the grant. He was instructed to survey the east bank of the Rio Grande as it ran in 1854, but if he was unable to determine the location of the riverbed of 1854, he was directed to use the Archer Map as a guide. Brown's survey of the Bracito Grant showed it as containing 18,859.48 acres.[12]

For reason unknown, the owners of the Bracito Grant failed to procure a patent on the tract after the Brown survey was completed. Little did they realize that the El Bracito boundary problems were far from being settled.

No further action was taken in connection with the boundaries of the Bracito Grant until September 1, 1900. On that date the Court of Private Land Claims confirmed the Santo Tomás de Yturbide Colony Grant, which joined the Bracito Grant on the west. The court's decree defined the eastern boundary of the Santo Tomás de Yturbide Colony Grant as being the western boundary of the Bracito Grant. Jay Turley was hired by the Surveyor General to survey the Santo Tomás de Yturbide Colony Grant in January, 1901. Turley's survey of the common boundary line between the two grants was based on Leonard M. Brown's survey of 1893. The claimants of the Santo Tomás de Yturbide Colony Grant protested the approval of the Turley survey on the grounds that it failed to locate correctly the east bank of the river as it ran in 1854. They alleged that the major portion of the common boundary line between the two grants should be located approximately two miles further east. The court sustained the protest and held that the Turley survey did not correctly locate the east bank of the Rio Grande as it flowed in 1854. The court then ordered a re-survey of the line forming the common boundary between the two grants. Turley re-surveyed the Santo Tomás de Yturbide Colony Grant in December, 1902, in accordance with the special instructions given him by the court. The court approved Turley's re-survey of the Santo Tomás de Yturbide Colony Grant on June 26, 1903, and a patent, based on the Turley re-survey, was issued to the claimants of the grant on October 17, 1905.

After the Santo Tomás de Yturbide Colony Grant was patented, the owners of the Bracito Grant requested the Commissioner of the General Land Office to issue them a patent on the Bracito Grant, in accordance with the Leonard M. Brown Survey of 1893. Upon receipt of this request, the Commissioner of the General Land Office approved the Brown survey, and gave notice of his intention of patenting the Bracito Grant, even though it overlapped and conflicted with the Santo Tomás de Yturbide Colony Grant by approximately 5,000 acres. The claimants of the Santo Tomás de Yturbide Colony Grant protested such approval on the grounds that the Brown survey did not conform with the true western boundary of the Bracito Grant. As a result of their protest, a thorough investigation of the conflict was ordered by the Secretary of Interior on October 8, 1907, in order to determine whether or not the Leonard M. Brown Survey correctly retraced and located the west boundary of the Bracito Grant as surveyed in 1854 by Stephen Archer.[13] The court appointed William M. Tipton as a special investigator to study the problem. In his report dated June 30, 1908, Tipton stated that his investigation disclosed that the Brown survey did not follow the Archer survey or the riverbed of 1854. He also found that the Archer survey was so inaccurate that it was worthless as a guide to the correct location of the river of 1854. The Archer map of the Bracito Grant showed that its eastern boundary was 21,540 varas in length, and its western boundary was three leagues, or 15,000 varas, in length. According to the distances noted on the map, the east line should have been 43% longer than the west line, but it was, in fact, actually shorter. Based on a complete investigation of the area, he believed that the Turley survey of December, 1901 substantially followed the course of the old riverbed of 1854. Tipton's investigation indicated that in 1854 the river could not have made a horseshoe bend as surveyed by Leonard M. Brown. In order to have done so, the river would have to jump a five-foot bank near Brown's 45th survey station. The Department of Interior, in its decision dated March 20, 1909, rejected the Brown survey, and directed that a re-survey of the Bracito Grant be made in accordance with the findings set forth in Tipton's report.[14] The claimants of the Bracito Grant withdrew their request for a patent, stating that complete legal title to the grant had been conveyed to them by virtue of the Confirmation Act of June 21, 1860. They also objected to any further surveying of their claim. The Department of Interior acknowledged that a confirmed grant did not require the issuance of a patent where the boundaries of the tract had been clearly defined, but in cases where there were any questions concerning the location of the boundaries of a private land claim, an official survey of such a grant was necessary to segregate it properly from the public domain.[15]

The Bracito Grant was subsequently surveyed by Sidney E. Blout in September, 1909, in accordance with findings contained in Tipton's report. His survey disclosed that the grant contained only 14,808.075 acres. Blout's survey was approved by the Commissioner of the General Land Office on August 2, 1910.[16]

The approval of the Blout survey of the Bracito Grant finally established the boundaries of the grant, and settled the difficult boundary conflict betwen claimants of the Santo Tomás de Yturbide Colony Grant and the Bracito Grant.

REFERENCES

1 Juan Antonio García de Noriega's ancestors had long been prominent in the history of New Mexico. They were among the original settlers who retreated to El Paso del Norte with Governor Otermin after the Pueblo Revolt in 1680. He was a brother of Francisco García de Noriega, who owned the Santa Teresa Grant. Fray Angelico Chavez, *Origins of New Mexico Families*, (Santa Fe, 1954), 181.

2 Cessna v. United States (Mss., Court of Private Land Claims, Records of the Bureau of Land Management, Santa Fe, New Mexico), No. 59.

3 Juan Antonio García was survived by his six children: Francisco García y San Juan; Mariano García; Ramón García; Anastacio García Horcacitas; Nestora Bernal, wife of Tomás Bernal; and Josefa Córdoba, wife of José María Córdoba. *House Reports*, 36 Cong., 1st Sess., Report No. 321, 35 (1859).

4 *House Reports*, 36th Cong., 1st Sess., Report No. 321, 28 (1859).

5 After Hugh Stephenson acquired his interest in the Bracito Grant, it became known as the Hugh Stephenson Grant.

6 *House Reports,* 36th Cong., 1st Sess., Report No. 321, 44, 451 (1859).

7 *Ibid.*

8 *Deed Records* (Mss., Records of the Doña Ana County Clerk's Office, Las Cruces, New Mexico), B, 185, 187.

9 *House Reports,* 35th Cong., 1st Sess., Report No. 457, 24-34; *Land Claims Records* (Mss., Records of the Surveyor General's Office, Bureau of Land Management, Santa Fe, New Mexico), I, 203-208.

10 *House Executive Documents,* 46th Cong., 3rd Sess., Document No. 47, 944-945 (1881).

The Bracito tract was granted to García, as an individual, during the interim between April 11, 1823, when the Colonization Act of January 4, 1823 was repealed, and the date of the passage of the National Colonization Act of 1824. During this period, there was no law in Mexico which authorized any Mexican official to make a valid land grant to a colonist or individual. Due to the confusion which prevailed in Mexico during this period, Lieutenant Governor Ordas believed that the old Spanish laws governing the issuance of land grants were applicable. Under Spanish law, a governor, with the consent of the Provincial Deputation, had authority to make valid land grants to individuals. Lieutenant Governor Ordas apparently believed he had authority to make a valid grant to García in 1823. There is no evidence that the grant was presented to the Provincial Deputation of Chihuahua for its approval.

If Congress had not confirmed the Bracito Grant in 1860, the claim in all probability would have been subsequently rejected. In Pino v. Hatch, the Supreme Court of New Mexico held that the Governor *pro tem* of New Mexico, acting with the consent of the Provincial Deputation, did not have authority, on December 23, 1823, to make a land grant to an individual. The court held all power which Governors, Intendants, or other persons had to dispose of public domain by virtue of authority imparted by the King of Spain,, ceased upon the independence of Mexico. After Mexico gained its independence from Spain, the Governor of a province had no power, without express authority from the Mexican government, to grant any part of the public domain. Pino v. Hatch, 1 N.M. 125 (1855).

Based upon this decision, there is little question that the Bracito Grant was invalid, due to a complete lack of power by the granting authorities to issue the concession. The abandonment of the grant by the claimants between 1828 and 1851 would certainly weaken a presumption that Lieutenant Governor Ordas had authority to issue the grant to García. However, since Congress confirmed the claim, the United States is estopped from questioning the validity of the Bracito Grant.

11 Bracito Grant, Map File 6 (Mss., Records of the Cadastrial Engineer's Office, Santa Fe, New Mexico).

12 *Ibid.*

13 *Decisions of the Department of the Interior and the General Land Office* (Washington, D.C.), XXVI, 117-124.

14 *Ibid.,* XXXVIII, 509-512.

15 *Ibid.*

16 Bracito Grant, Report No. 6 (Mss., Records of the Surveyor General's Office, Bureau of Land Management, Santa Fe, New Mexico).

CHAPTER 13

The Canutillo Grant ৯

● THE EXTENSIVE INTEREST CREATED by the prospects of the development of the Mesilla Valley, which had been created by the issuance of the Heath Grant, prompted Juan María Ponce de León and twenty-nine other citizens of El Paso del Norte to petition the Ayuntamiento of that town for a land grant pursuant to the fourth article of the National Colonization Law of January 3, 1823. The petitioners requested that they be given one and a half leagues of farm land at the place known as El Canutillo,[1] which was located on the east bank of the Rio Grande, approximately sixteen miles northwest of El Paso del Norte.

The Ayuntamiento considered the petition on May 30, 1823 and granted the lands to the petitioners, subject to the conditions that they promptly settle and cultivate the tract or forfeit all their rights under the concession. A special commission, consisting of José Ynacio Marconi, Lorenzo Provencio, José María Vela, and Juan María Ponce de León, was appointed by the Ayuntamiento, ordered to survey the grant, and deliver legal possession of the land to the applicants. In response to the Ayuntamiento's order, the commission went to the El Canutillo *paraje* on June 3, 1823. This *paraje* was located on the Camino Real near the south end of an old crescent-shaped *playa* lake. Upon their arrival at the *paraje*, the commission appointed Geronimo Durán and Victor Fuentes as surveyors and furnished them with a *cordel*[2] which measured fifty varas of three geometrical feet each.

The surveyors commenced their survey at a cottonwood tree located on the south side of the lake, which point represented the central point or station of the survey. The surveyors ran a line thence north[3] 3,750 varas to a cottonwood tree opposite the Artesa Woods and the Sandijuela Marsh, which they marked. After completing the survey of the first line, the surveyors were forced to return to the central point, due to darkness. The next morning, at six o'clock, the surveyors resumed the survey by running the second line south 3,750 varas from the central point to a point at which they erected a stone mound around a mesquite tree located slightly north of the outlet of a salt lake into the Ancon de Borrego. The surveyors attempted to run the third line west from the central point to the river, but the river was flooding at the time and prevented the surveyors from actually measuring the distance. It was agreed that the west line was to extend from the central point to the east bank of the river. The final line was run east 3,750 varas from the central point to a point east of the foothills. While recognizing that the grantees had only requested the agricultural lands located between the river and the edge of the foothills, the commission deemed it advisable to also include the pasture lands located east of the foothills within the boundaries of the survey.

After the survey had been completed, the commission asked the grantees if they were satisfied with the results of the survey. They stated that they had no objections, but in view of the fact that their irrigation water would have to be taken out of the river some distance north of the grant and transported to their farms through an *acequia*, it would be imperative for them to also possess the land up to the mouth of their *acequia*. The commission thereupon declared that the grantees were entitled to draw water from the river above the grant, and held they should not be deprived of the use of such water in the event the vacant lands located north of their concession were subsequently granted to new colonists. Having fully satisfied the grantees on this point, the commission proceeded to place them in possession of the premises. The commission submitted a report to the Ayuntamiento on June 5, 1823 covering its proceedings. The Ayuntamiento approved the actions of the commission on June 6, 1823.[4]

The grantees established a small settlement on the grant in 1824, and continuously occupied and cultivated the lands until 1833, when they were driven off the land by the Apache Indians.[5] The grant remained unoccupied until James W. Magoffin settled upon a portion of such land in the spring of 1850. Believing the premises to be unappropriated, he proceeded to improve and cultivate them and constructed improvements thereon valued at two thousand dollars.

The owners of the Canutillo Grant realized that unless they acted promptly they would forfeit their claim. They appointed José Sánchez, Romulo Barelo, and Guadalupe Miranda as their attorneys in fact on September 1, 1852, with complete and unlimited authority to manage, control and sell the grant.[6] Shortly thereafter, Sánchez, Barelo, and Miranda, as attorneys in fact, reached an agreement with Magoffin whereby he agreed to secure recognition of the grant by Texas, and release his adverse claim. In consideration for Magoffin's covenants, Sánchez, Barelo, and Miranda agreed to convey an undivided one-third interest in the entire grant to him, upon the confirmation of the grant by Texas. Magoffin retained District Attorney Josiah F. Crosby to represent him in his efforts to secure recognition of the grant. Crosby was to receive one-half of Magoffin's interest as compensation for his legal services.[7]

The Act of February 8, 1850[8] had provided for the investigation of Spanish and Mexican land titles in the area between the Nueces and Rio Grande, but J. B. Miller and William B. Bourland, the Commissioners appointed pursuant to this law, did not conduct any investigations within

El Paso or Presidio Counties. As a result of the Miller-Bourland Commission's failure to investigate a large number of known Spanish and Mexican land titles in the area between the Nueces and Rio Grande, there was a great deal of pressure exerted on the Texas Legislature by property owners in that area to secure passage of an act creating a similar Board of Commissioners to investigate such titles. Magoffin and Crosby were especially interested in seeing the establishment of such a commission, for at that time there were no means by which they could secure recognition of the Canutillo Grant. In an effort to help secure passage of this desired legislation, Crosby successfully ran for the position of State Representative in the August, 1853 election, instead of seeking re-election as District Attorney for El Paso County.[9] Crosby was instrumental in securing passage of the Act of February 11, 1854 by the House of Representatives. This act created a Board of Commissioners, known as the Rio Grande Commission, which had authority to investigate and report on land titles in Kinney, Webb, Starr, Hidalgo, Cameron, Nueces, Presidio and El Paso Counties.[10]

Charles S. Taylor and Robert H. Lane, who were appointed by Governor E. M. Pease as the two commissioners of the Rio Grande Commission, made a tour through the counties enumerated in the act, investigating Spanish and Mexican land claims. Very little is known concerning the activities of the Rio Grande Commission, but it has been definitely established that it actually investigated land titles in El Paso County. When the commission arrived at Franklin, one of the first claims presented to it for consideration was the Canutillo Grant.

On July 28, 1855 Guadalupe Miranda, one of the attorneys in fact, appeared before the commission, presented a copy of the grant papers, and testified that to the best of his knowledge, the grant had not been forged or antedated, but was in all respects genuine.[11] In further support of his principals' claim, Miranda presented two witnesses, Juan Apodaca and José María Cordoba, who testified that the owners of the grant had occupied and cultivated the tract from 1824 until 1833, when they had been driven off the land by hostile Indians. They also stated that the grant had always been recognized by those living at El Paso del Norte.[12]

Early in November, 1855 the Rio Grande Commission submitted a detailed report to Governor Pease, together with all of the supporting evidence which had been collected. In its report, the Rio Grande Commission recommended confirmation of only a portion of the claims which had been submitted for investigation.[13] Governor Pease transmitted the report, on November 27, 1855, to the Texas Legislature for its information and action. A bill was introduced in the House of Representatives entitled "An Act to relinquish the rights of the State to certain lands therein named." The object of this was to release the right of the State to sixty different tracts of land situated in Nueces, Webb, El Paso, Kinney, Starr, Hidalgo and

Cameron Counties, Texas, covering an aggregate of 205 leagues, or approximately 900,000 acres of land. This bill was subsequently passed by both houses of the Legislature and forwarded to Governor Pease for approval. He vetoed it on August 23, 1856, because it included many tracts which had not been recommended for confirmation by the Rio Grande Commission. In conclusion, the governor stated that had this act only confirmed the small number of claims that the commission recommended for confirmation, he would have felt no hesitation in approving it.[14]

It would appear that the Canutillo Grant was listed among the grants which had been approved by the Rio Grande Commission.[15] Its claimants were undoubtedly encouraged by the above quoted pronouncement, and therefore promptly sought special relief legislation. On December 14, 1857 Senator Archibald C. Hyde introduced a bill in the Texas Senate which provided for confirmation of the Canutillo Grant and other grants located in El Paso County. After a favorable report by their Committees on Private Land Claims, the bill was passed by the Senate and House of Representatives. This bill, which was enacted into law on February 11, 1858, relinquished all of the right and interest of the State of Texas in one and a half leagues of land called El Canutillo to José Sánchez, Guadalupe Miranda, and Romulo Barelo.[16]

The second section of the Act of February 11, 1858 required the claimants to have their grants surveyed by the District or County Surveyor. The act specifically provided that the survey was to conform in all respects to the metes and bounds designated in the original grant. Upon receipt of the field notes of such a survey, the Commissioner of the General Land Office was required to plat the grant on the proper maps of his office and issue a patent on the grant.[17]

Pursuant to this provision, Sánchez, Miranda, and Barelo hired Anson Mills, District Surveyor for the El Paso and Presidio Land District, to make the required survey. They agreed to give Mills one hundred acres out of the grant in consideration for his services. Mills carefully studied the *testimonio* of the grant in connection with the provisions of the Relinquishment Act of 1858. He realized that there was a conflict between the original grant and the original Mexican field notes. The original grant purported to concede one and a half square leagues of land, but the original Mexican field notes embraced one and a half leagues square, or a total of two and a quarter leagues of land. This discrepancy apparently due to the fact that no professional mathematician or trained surveyor accompanied the commission. The commissioners evidently believed that in order for the grant to contain one and a half leagues of land, its boundary lines should extend three-quarters of a league in each direction from the central point. Mills also noted that the Relinquishment Act of 1858 stated that the grant covered one and a half leagues, but directed him to conform in all respects to the metes and bounds designated in the original grant. In attempting to reconcile these conflicts, Mills took into consideration the fact that when the commission made the original survey, it had extended the north and south lines on the east side of the grant over and across the sand hills, in spite of the fact that the grantees had requested only the cultivable valley lands. Mills believed that by mentioning the size of the grant in the Relinquishment Act of 1858, the Legislature had intended to limit its confirmation to one and a half leagues of land. He therefore concluded that limitation in size would prevail over the provision requiring him to execute the re-survey in strict conformity with the original metes and bounds. Once Mills had reached this decision, it was logical for him to decide that the three-quarter of a league in excess land should be eliminated from the east side of the grant.[18]

Upon arriving at the grant, Mills found that all of the original landmarks erected by the Mexican surveyors had been obliterated. In an effort to locate the boundaries of the grant, Mills re-established the central point of the grant at a stake which he set on the east bank of the Canutillo Lake. This stake was located north 16° east 500 varas from the old Canutillo ranch headquarters. Commencing his survey at this stake, Mills ran north 3,750 varas to a point on the north line of the grant and ran thence west 2,172 varas to the east bank of the Rio Grande, where he established the northwest corner of the grant. He ran thence east 2,967 varas to a stake and a mound for the northeast corner; thence south 7,500 varas to a stake and a mound for the southeast corner, thence west 4,294 varas to a stake set on the east bank of the river for the southwest corner; and thence up the river to the northwest corner. According to Mill's survey, the grant contained exactly one and a half leagues of land. The survey is known as Survey No. 173 of Section 1, and was made on August 9, 1860.[19]

Sánchez, Miranda, and Barelo were disappointed with the results of Mills' work, because they felt that Mills should have followed the footsteps of the original Mexican surveyors, instead of limiting his re-survey to the one and a half leagues specified in the *testimonio* and the Relinquishment Act of 1858. However, rather than jeopardize their title to the valuable valley lands by questioning the correctness of the survey, the record owners of the grant elected to abandon their claim to the three-quarters of a league of sandhill land which Mills had arbitrarily excluded.

The commencement of the Civil War temporarily terminated further attempts to perfect title to the grant. After the Confederate forces had withdrawn from the El Paso area, Joab Houghton, Judge of the Third Judicial District Court of the Territory of New Mexico, confiscated a great deal of West Texas properly belonging to prominent southern sympathizers. Among the lands so condemned was Judge Crosby's interest in the Canutillo Grant. Pursuant to an order by Judge Houghton, Abraham

Cutler, United States Marshall, sold Crosby's interest in the grant to W. W. Mills on December 18, 1865 for the meager sum of $110.[20] The "Prize Court" apparently overlooked James W. Magoffin's interest in the Canutillo Grant, for it failed to confiscate his undivided one-sixth interest therein when it seized his property at Magoffinsville. The Marshal's deed to Mills purportedly covered an undivided one-third interest in the grant.

Believing that he owned a valid interest in the grant, Mills and his attorney friend, John S. Watts, offered to purchase the remaining interests held by José Sánchez, Romulo Barelo, and Guadalupe Miranda. Sánchez, Barelo, and Miranda notified their principals of the offer, and all of them, save Juan Joé Sánchez and Juan José Olguín, who had previously acquired the interests of three of the original grantees, directed Sánchez, Barelo, and Miranda to sell their interests in the grant. On December 30, 1865 Sánchez, Barelo, and Miranda sold an undivided 17/30ths interest in the grant to W. W. Mills and John S. Watts for $1,849.50, subject to the undivided one hundred acre interest owned by Anson Mills. The remaining 1/10th interest in the grant was expressly reserved for the benefit of Sánchez and Olguín.[21]

In the meantime, Josiah F. Crosby appealed Judge Houghton's decision, which confiscated several lots of land in the Mills addition to the City of El Paso, Texas to the Supreme Court of the Territory of New Mexico. The New Mexico Supreme Court reversed the decision, on the grounds that the lower court did not have jurisdiction to confiscate real estate located in El Paso County. The government appealed the case to the United States Supreme Court, which affirmed the decision of the New Mexico Supreme Court on March 30, 1868.[22] Although this decision did not directly involve Crosby's interest in the Canutillo Grant, it unquestionably invalidated the United States Marshal's deed to W. W. Mills. Shortly after the decision, James W. Magoffin conveyed his interest in the grant to his son, Joseph Magoffin.[23]

In 1871 a number of locations were made in the area south of the Canutillo Grant for the San Antonio & Mexican Gulf Railroad Company by virtue of certain certificates granted to it by the State of Texas. Patents were subsequently issued by the State of Texas to the assignees of the railroad. It appeared that several of these tracts would conflict with the Canutillo Grant. Fearing that these surveys might adversely affect their interests, Joseph Magoffin and Josiah F. Crosby filed a petition in the 25th Judicial District Court of El Paso County, Texas, on November 4, 1873, requesting the court to partition the grant among its various owners.[24] The institution of this suit prompted Juan José Sánchez and Juan José Olguín to convey their interest to José Sánchez.

After hearing the evidence, Judge Charles H. Howard ordered the partitioning of the grant, and appointed a commission consisting of Benjamin

S. Dowell, A. C. Hyde, and Pedro Aguirre to make the division. The court instructed the commission to divide the one and one-half leagues of land embraced within the grant among the claimants in the following proportions:

1. To Anson Mills — a one hundred acre tract.
2. To Joseph Magoffin and Josiah F. Crosby — 1/3rd of the grant, after deducting the one hundred acres allotted to Anson Mills.
3. To John S. Watts and W. W. Mills — 9/10ths of the remainder, after deducting the lands allotted to Anson Mills, Joseph Magoffin, and Josiah F. Crosby.
4. To José Sánchez — 1/10th of the remainder, after deducting the lands allocated to Anson Mills, Joseph Magoffin, and Josiah F. Crosby.

The commission was further ordered to divide the grant in a manner which would give each owner his proportionate share of the valley lands and river frontage. The commission was authorized to employ a competent surveyor to assist it in the partitioning of the grant.[25]

Joseph Wilkin Tays, El Paso County Surveyor, was retained by the commissioner to re-survey and subdivide the grant in accordance with the court's decree. Tays surveyed the grant on August 26, 1874, and his work showed that the grant contained only 5,285 acres.[26] Having ascertained the exterior boundaries of the grant, Tays proceeded to subdivide it into four tracts. The first tract commenced at the northwest corner of the grant and contained one hundred acres. This tract was awarded to Anson Mills. Adjoining Mills' tract on the south was a 345-2/3 acre tract, which was allotted to José Sánchez. The third tract was located immediately south of Sánchez' tract, and contained 1,728-1/3 acres. This tract was allocated to Joseph Magoffin and Josiah F. Crosby. The south 3,111 acres of the grant were alloted to John S. Watts and W. W. Mills. The court approved Tays' survey and subdivision of the grant, together with the commission's formal report, on September 9, 1874.[27]

After the railroads had been completed into El Paso from each of the four cardinal directions, land values began to skyrocket. The increased value of their tracts prompted the owners of the grant to take the final steps necessary to perfect their title to the grant. Some twenty-five years after its execution, the claimants filed a copy of Anson Mills' survey and field notes in the General Land Office, and requested the State to issue a patent for the lands. The Commissioner of the General Land Office returned Mills' field notes, and requested the claimants to have the field notes corrected, in order to show the true course of the Rio Grande. The Mills survey was rejected because he had used the offset method while surveying the river, instead of actually surveying its meanders. The claimants hired John P. Randolph to make the corrected survey. Randolph re-surveyed the grant between the 9th and 13th of August, 1886. Randolph's survey covered 6,642.6 acres and was substantially the same as Mills'.[28]

When the Commissioner of the General Land Office, W. C. Walch, plotted the grant on his official county map, he discovered that it definitely conflicted with the metes and bounds descriptions contained in several of the San Antonio & Mexican Gulf Railroad Company surveys. However, in addition to the course and distance calls, the field notes for each of these conflicting surveys called for it to extend to and join the southern boundary line of the Canutillo Grant. Walch requested an opinion by Attorney General John D. Templeton as to whether he could issue a patent for the Canutillo Grant based on Randolph's corrected field notes, notwithstanding the conflict. In an opinion dated August 30, 1886, Templeton stated that the railroad surveys did not conflict with the grant. By calling for the railroad surveys to join the grant, the owners of the railroad surveys had excluded any lands embraced within the boundaries of the recognized but unpatented grant.[29] Relying upon Templeton's advise, Walch issued a patent on September 14, 1886 to José Sánchez, Guadalupe Miranda, and Romulo Barelo covering the grant in accordance with Randolph's corrected field notes.[30]

The partitioning and patenting of the tract, for all practical purposes, ended the history of the Canutillo Grant as a single unit. The grant, however, subsequently played an important role in the controversial Texas-New Mexico boundary dispute along the Rio Grande.

REFERENCES

[1] *Canutillo* is an Indian word meaning a bend in the river. Queen M. Gary, "Brief History of Lone Star School," (Mss., History Seminar Paper, Texas Western College, El Paso, Texas), I.

[2] A *cordel* is the Spanish term for a rope, usually waxed hemp, used in land surveying, which measures exactly fifty *varas* of three geometrical feet each in length when held taut. Due to the fact that the *cordel* had a tendency to stretch, it was checked every fifty times it was used.

[3] The original Mexican Field Notes state that the first line ran in an "eastern course, up stream. . . ." This statement is obviously erroneous, as the first line unquestionably ran in a northerly direction. The directions called for by the Commission in its Field Notes for the remaining boundary lines of the grant are also erroneous. The Commission apparently believed that north was east. All other courses were ninety degrees off. The true directions taken by the surveyors have been set out above, in order to avoid confusion. The errors in direction can be explained by the fact that the surveyors were not professional surveyors. Also, the river ran west to east at El Paso del Norte, while it ran north to south at El Canutillo, and the surveyors may have assumed that the river ran in the same direction as at El Paso del Norte. File No. Bexar 1-2212 (Mss., Records of the General Land Office, Austin, Texas.).

[4] *Deed Records* (Mss., Records of the El Paso County Clerk's Office, El Paso, Texas), "C" 3191325. This grant is note-worthy, in that it is the only surviving Spanish or

Mexican grant on the Rio Grande in present day Texas which specifically gives the grantee the right to withdraw water from the river for irrigation purposes.

5 *Ibid.*, "C" 315.   6 *Ibid.*, "C" 311.

7 Magoffin v. Mills (Mss., Records of the El Paso District Clerk's Office, El Paso, Texas), No. 157.

Crosby wrote Magoffin, advising him of his preliminary views on the validity of the Canutillo Grant. In his letter Crosby says:

"I have not yet had the Canutillo Grant thoroughly investigated, but the copy of the title is now in the hands of one of the most eminent members of this bar. From the examination which I have given the subject, I am inclined to the option that the title of the plaintiffs is one of that description known as 'Labor Grants,' if such be really the case, the grant is not worth a good chew of tobacco. If, on the other hand, it proves to be of the class of 'Eleven League Grants,' the matter may be mixed with more or less doubt, as the courts throughout the whole state have given evidence of great particularity for the claims of the last class in their late adjudications. The matter, however, will be fully investigated before I return." *Judge Josiah F. Crosby — Letters* (Mss., Records of the Texas Archives, Austin, Texas), Josiah F. Crosby to James W. Magoffin, December 21, 1852.

8 H. P. N. Gammel, *The Laws of Texas* (10 Vols. 1898), III, 582-587.

9 *State Gazette*, August 27, 1853.

10 H. P. N. Gammel, *The Laws of Texas*, III, 1533-1538.

11 *Deed Records* (Mss., Records of the El Paso County Clerk's Office, El Paso, Texas), C, 316.

12 *Ibid.*, C, 315.

13 *Records of the Executive Office, December 21, 1856-December 21, 1857, E. M. Pease* (Mss., Records of the Texas Archives, Austin, Texas), 520.

14 *Ibid.*, 521.

15 The Report of the Rio Grande Commission, and all of the evidence which it gathered, were lost sometime prior to January 27, 1858. The House of Representatives' Committee unsuccessfully attempted to locate a copy of this report in connection with its investigation of the Hyde Bill. *Journal of the House of Representatives of the State of Texas, Seventh Legislature* (Austin, 1858), 705-706. The statement in the report of the Senate's Committee on Private Land Claims that "all of the evidence outside the official report of said commission, sustained the conclusion" that the grant was valid, would indicate that the grant had not been confirmed by the Rio Grande Commission. *Journal of the Senate of the State of Texas, Seventh Legislature* (Austin, 1858), 358. However, the report by the House of Representatives' Committee on Private Land Claims states that the Rio Grande Commission reported on all of the titles set forth in the Hyde Bill, and "recommended that they be confirmed." *Journal of the House of Representatives, Seventh Legislature*, 706. It is difficult to reconcile the conflicting statements contained in these two reports. In view of the mysterious disappearance of the Rio Grande Commission's report, it is recognized that a very persuasive argument could be advanced that this unsupported statement might have been inserted in the committee report to insure against a possible veto of the act by the governor.

16 H. P. N. Gammel, *The Laws of Texas*, IV, 1027.

It is interesting to note that the Relinquishment Act of 1858 vested legal title to the grant in José Sánchez, Guadalupe Miranda, and Romulo Barelo in their individual capacities, instead of as attorneys in fact for the original grantees.

Under the decisions in the Cessna and Morris cases [Cessna v. United States, 169 U.S. 165 (1898); and Morris v. Canda, 80 F. 739 (1897)], it is now clear that the Ayuntamiento of El Paso del Norte had no authority to issue the Canutillo Grant to Juan María Ponce de León and his twenty-nine associates on May 30, 1823, because:

(1) The National Colonization Law of 1823 had been repealed prior to issuance of the grant; and

(2) The Ayuntamiento had no jurisdiction over lands located outside the limits of this town grant. The Canutillo Grant, which was located approximately sixteen miles from the Town of El Paso del Norte, was unquestionably outside the boundaries of the grant to that town.

17 *Ibid.*

18 It is now clear that Mills should have followed the footsteps of the original surveyors, instead of limiting his re-survey of the grant to the one and one-half leagues specified in the Relinquishment Act. The effect of the Relinquishment Act of 1858 was to recognize the title to the entire tract known as El Canutillo, and the special limitation as to quantity was of no consequence. Texas v. Indio Cattle Company, 154 S.W. 2d 308 (1941). However, since the owners of the grant secured the Mills survey and accepted a patent based thereon, they are now bound by such patent. Hamilton v. Texas, 152 S.W. 1117 (1913).

19 *Book of Field Notes* (Mss., Records of El Paso County Surveyor's Office, El Paso, Texas), A-1, 197 and 198.

20 *Deed Records* (Mss., Records of the El Paso County Clerk's Office, El Paso, Texas), C, 102.

21 *Ibid.*, I, 178.

22 United States v. Crosby, 73 S. Ct. Rep. 915 (1926).

23 *Deed Records* (Mss., Records of the El Paso County Clerk's Office, El Paso, Texas), C, 476.

24 Magoffin v. Mills (Mss., Records of the El Paso District Clerk's Office, El Paso, Texas), No. 157.

25 *Minute Book* (Mss., Records of the El Paso District Clerk's Office, El Paso, Texas), A, 182 and 183.

26 It is evident that the discrepancy between Anson Mills' and Joseph Wilkin Tays' surveys arose due to the fact that Mills' survey followed the east bank of the Rio Grande as it ran in 1860, and Tays' followed the river of 1874. It is known that the spring floods of 1862, 1863, 1865 and 1868 materially altered the course of the river.

27 *Deed Records* (Mss., Records of the El Paso County Clerk's Office, El Paso, Texas), E, 518-524.

28 File No. Bexar 1-2212 (Mss., Records of the General Land Office, Austin, Texas.

29 Letter File 199, 908 (Mss., Records of the General Land Office, Austin, Texas).

30 *Deed Records* (Mss., Records of the El Paso County Clerk's Office, El Paso, Texas), XXC, 3.

CHAPTER 14

The Ponce de León Grant

• THE HISTORY of the Ponce de León Grant is of particular interest, for the original townsite and the present downtown business district of El Paso, Texas is located on this famous Mexican land grant. The growth and expansion of this metropolitan city is intimately related to the development and improvement of the Ponce de León Grant.

Sometime during January, 1827 Juan María Ponce de León petitioned the Ayuntamiento of El Paso del Norte for a tract of vacant land on the north side of the Rio Grande and about one-half a league north of that town. The Ayuntamiento authorized Ponce de León to clear and cultivate the lands pending final decision of the Supreme Government of Chihuahua, to which his petition had been referred. On August 13, 1827 Luis Bustamante García, Secretary of the Supreme Government of Chihuahua, advised the Ayuntamiento that the lands which had been requested belonged to the Town of El Paso del Norte, and that they could be sold to the petitioner. In response to this decision, the Ayuntamiento appointed a committee, on August 23, 1827, to appraise the lands which were to be sold to the petitioner. The committee returned its appraisal of the tract on September 20, 1827. It estimated that the tract contained two *caballerías* of land, which it valued at eighty *pesos*. The Ayuntamiento, by a decree dated September 20, 1827, sold and conveyed the lands in question to Juan María Ponce de León, who promptly requested the Alcalde of El Paso del Norte to survey the grant and place him in legal possession of such lands.

On September 25, 1827 Alcalde Agapito Albo made the following survey of the grant:

The survey was commenced where the new acequia cuts the one excavated by Francisco Xavier Bernal, deceased, at the point of a hill, where I ordered a monument of lime and rock; taking a course of west to east along the north side a caballería was obtained, to which five hundred and thirty-five varas were added on account of the disproportionate triangular form of the land, because at its center it was only two hundred and twenty-seven varas wide. With this ended the survey of the first caballería; and the survey of the other continued, following the direction of west to east, on the north boundary, and on the edges of the hills, including all the land that could be cultivated; and on the south it is bounded by the river, and has seven hundred and fifty varas, with regard to having increased it two hnudred and forty varas, on account of the width which was lacking in the other caballería.

After completing the survey, the Alcalde placed Ponce de León in possession of the lands embraced within the boundaries of the survey.[1]

Ponce de León built an *adobe* home on his grant near the river, but it was washed away in 1830 during a violent spring flood. The flood waters also caused considerable damage to his fields and crops.[2]

Seeking compensation for the flood damage to his lands, Juan María Ponce de León petitioned the Ayuntamiento for an additional grant of land. The Ayuntamiento appointed another committee to investigate the merits of this second request. The committee recommended that only the sand bar lying between the old and new riverbeds be conceded to the petitioner. Based upon this report, on May 4, 1830, the Ayuntamiento granted Ponce de León the accretion lands lying north of the Rio Grande.[3] After Ponce de León's death on July 1, 1852, title to the grant passed to his wife and daughter. His estate was managed by his son-in-law, Mariano Varela, who had a lucrative freighting partnership with William T. Smith.

After the government established Fort Bliss at Magoffinsville, Smith realized the potential value of the grant, and requested Ponce de León's heirs to sell the tract to him for $10,000.[4] The heirs readily accepted, because the Ponce de León claim had not been recognized by the State of Texas, and the sizeable consideration offered by Smith for their inchoate interest was very attractive. In order to satisfy Smith's inquires concerning the extent and boundaries of the grant, Varela employed W. L. Diffenderfer, District Surveyor for the El Paso District, to survey the grant. The survey began at a stake set on the bank of the Rio Grande which bore north 67½° west 2,428 varas from the southwest corner of the Moses Hughes Survey No. 1, and ran thence east 1,104 varas to a stake and stone heap; thence north 53° east 1,861 varas to a stake and mound; thence south 26½° east 1,340 varas along a ridge of earth to the bank of the Rio Grande; and thence up the river with its meanders 3,903 varas to the place of beginning. Diffenderfer completed the survey on March 25, 1853. His survey showed the grant as containing slightly more than 599 acres of land.[5] On the same day, Dolores Zozaya Ponce de León, Josefa Ponce de León Varela, and Mariano Varela executed a deed conveying the grant to William T. Smith. This deed described the grant in accordance with the metes and bounds description contained in Diffenderfer's field notes.[6] Smith took immediate possession of the land, and used it primarily as a headquarters for his extensive commercial operations. From time to time Smith sold small unsurveyed tracts of land to persons who had settled upon the grant.

In the spring of 1852 Josiah F. Crrosby, who had just resigned his position as District Attorney in Austin, Texas due to ill health, met Smith in San Antonio. Upon learning of Crosby's plans to move to the El Paso area in hopes of regaining his health, Smith invited him to join his wagon train as a guest. Thereafter, Crosby became Smith's close friend, attorney, and financial adviser.[7]

Pursuant to the Act of February 11, 1854,[8] which created a special commission to investigate Spanish and Mexican land titles in certain west Texas counties, Governor E. M. Pease appointed Charles S. Taylor and Robert H. Lane commissioners.[9] They became known as the Rio Grande commission. William T. Smith presented his claim to the commission for its investigation while Taylor was in El Paso during the summer of 1855. It appears that the commission recommended confirmation of the Ponce de León Grant and that it was included in the Relinquishment Act passed by the Sixth Legislature. However, the act was vetoed by Governor Pease on the grounds that it included a large number of tracts which had not been recommended by the Rio Grande Commission. The governor expressly stated, however, that had it not been for the inclusion of those tracts, he would have approved the bill without hesitation.[10]

Encouraged by the governor's statement, Smith and a number of other El Paso County grant owners consulted their Senator, Archibald C. Hyde, who agreed to sponsor a special relief act which would recognize their claims. In accordance with his agreement, Hyde introduced a bill in the Texas Senate on December 14, 1857, to relinquish the rights of the state to those certain tracts of land known as El Pueblo Socorro, El Canutillo, El Rancho de Ponce, and El Rancho de Ascarate.[11]

In due time the bill was passed by both houses, following only a cursory investigation of the four claims by their respective Committees on Private Land Claims.[12] This act was approved[13] by Governor H. R. Runnels on February 11, 1858, and, in regard to the Ponce de León Grant, relinquished all of the right and interest of the State of Texas:

> To Juan María Ponce de León two caballerias of land, called "El Rancho de Ponce," now known as the town of Franklin.

It should be noted that this law did not describe the grants by metes and bounds, but merely made reference to the names by which they were generally known in the locality. However, the second section of the act required the claimants to have their lands surveyed by either the District or County Surveyor, and that the surveys should in all respects conform to the metes and bounds designated in the original grant.[14] After the grants were surveyed, the field notes were to be sent to the General Land Office in order that a patent could be issued.[15]

The confirmation of Smith's claim by the State of Texas naturally enhanced the potential value of the Ponce de León Grant. Smith soon realized that his overland freighting interests required his full attention, and that he did not have the time necessary to manage adequately the development of the rapidly growing settlement located upon the grant, which was then called Franklin. The new settlers were continuously requesting Smith to give them a deed to the lands upon which they had built their homes or businesses. Crosby advised Smith that if he continued his policy of indiscriminately conveying unsurveyed tracts of land, he would retard development of the town and depress land values on the grant. In order to be relieved of the complicated and technical real estate problems connected with the grant, Smith advised Crosby that he desired to sell his remaining interest in both the Ponce de León Grant and the Pierce Finley Survey, which was located immediately north of the grant.[16]

On January 30, 1859 Smith sold an undivided one-half interest in the two tracts to John S. and Henry S. Gillett; an undivided one-eighth interest to Josiah F. Crosby; and an Undivided one-eighth interest to William J. Morton. He also agreed to sell Vincent St. Vrain an undivided one-eighth interest at the same time, but the final conveyance was not consumated until December 29, 1859. The deed was then made to Vincent St. Vrain and his partner, Anthony B. Rohman. Smith decided to retain the remaining undivided one-eighth interest.[17]

The new owners of the grant immediately formed a syndicate known as The El Paso Company for the purpose of developing the lands surrounding the town of Franklin. In order to provide a convenient and orderly method of identifying its land for resale, the syndicate hired Anson Mills to subdivide approximately fifty acres surrounding the town of Franklin into a townsite. Smith's practice of conveying portions of the grant without any restrictions as to size or boundaries caused Mills a considerable amount of difficulty when he attempted to plat the subdivision. He found that settlers had built their homes at random, and that the existing streets were neither parallel nor at right angles to each other. This resulted in giving the heart of the townsite a very disjointed and irregular pattern. After submitting a number of proposals, Mills presented a plan on February 28, 1859, which subdivided the townsite in a manner acceptable to all of the interested parties. Realizing the inseparable relationship between the town and the famous mountain pass, the owners of the syndicate changed the name of the settlement from Franklin to El Paso.

The new owners of the grant also employed Mills to survey the entire grant in accordance with the provisions of the Relinquishment Act. After inspecting the lands and interviewing a number of witnesses who professed to know the true boundaries of the grant, Mills concluded that the grant included all of the land embraced within the Diffenderfer Survey. Mills reasoned that the survey commenced on the river and then ran back from the river one *caballeria*, or 1,104 varas. Then, in order to include all lands capable of bein cultivated, the course of the northern line would have to be deflected from its due east course to a course running in an approximately northeast direction. The line should run in that direction 1,104 varas, or one *caballeria*, plus the augmentation distances; thence the line should run in a southerly direction to the river; and thence up the river to the place of beginning. When Mills attempted to find Diffenderfer's beginning point, he discovered that the monument had been washed away; however, with Diffenderfer's assistance, he was able to locate a pile of stone which marked Diffenderfer's second corner, which was located near Dr. F. M. Giddings' grave.[18] Working back from this corner, Mills was able to establish the location of the initial corner, or beginning point, of the grant. The initial corner, as re-established by Mills, was located between two *acequias* at a point 2,428 varas north 67½° west of the southwest corner of the Moses Hughes Survey number one. The line then turned and ran thence north 53° east 1,861 varas to the northeast corner of the grant. The line took a course bearing thence south 261½°. After running 750 varas from the northeast corner, Mills came to what appeared to be an old riverbed, where he found an old monument of lime and stone. This apparently was the location of the river as it ran in 1827. Continuing, Mills crossed the old riverbed on the same course and measured 673½ varas to a stake and three large stones on the bank of the Rio Grande. He ran thence up the river to the place of beginning. The survey was completed on February 8, 1859, and showed that the grant contained 637.48 acres of land.[19]

The field notes of the Mills' survey of the grant were forwarded to the General Land Office, with a request that a patent be issued.[20] The State of Texas patented the land on May 4, 1887 to Juan María Ponce de León, his heirs and assigns.[21]

R E F E R E N C E S

[1] *Deed Records* (Mss., Records of the El Paso County Clerk's Office, El Paso, Texas), A, 324.

[2] *Appellee's Brief in Clark v. Hills* (Mss., Records of the Supreme Court of Texas, Austin, Texas), 24.

[3] *Deed Records* (Mss., Records of the El Paso County Clerk's Office, El Paso, Texas), A, 324.

[4] *Ibid.*, A, 472.

[5] *Record* (Mss., Records of the El Paso County Surveyor's Office, El Paso, Texas), A (Transcribed), 29.

[6] *Deed Records* (Mss., Records of the El Paso County Clerk's Office, El Paso, Texas), A, 472.

[7] Deposition of Josiah F. Crosby in Warder v. The Campbell Real Estate Company (Records of the U.S. Circuit Court for the Western District of Texas, El Paso, Texas), No. 277.

[8] H. P. N. Gammel, *The Laws of Texas* (10 Vols., Austin, 1898), III, 1533-1538.

[9] E. M. Pease to Charles S. Taylor, February 15, 1854, and May 8, 1854 (Mss., R. B. Blake Collection, *Letters and Papers of Charles S. Taylor*, Stephen F. Austin State Teachers College, Nacogdoches, Texas), I, 106-109, 127.

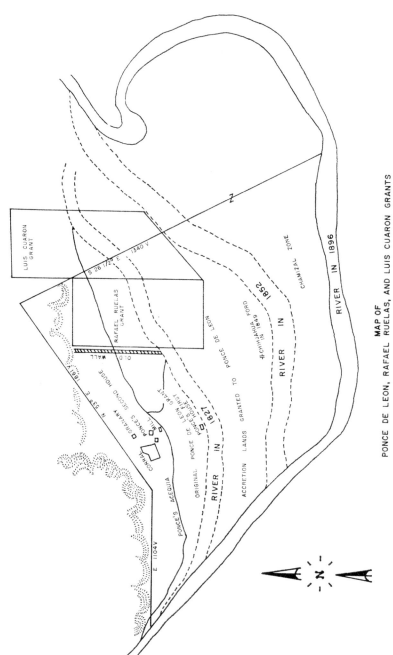

MAP OF
PONCE DE LEON, RAFAEL RUELAS, AND LUIS CUARON GRANTS

10 *Journal of the House of Representatives, Seventh Legislature* (Austin, 1858), 706.

11 *Ibid.*, 195.

12 *Ibid.*, 368; and *Journal of the House of Representatives of the State of Texas, Seventh Legislature* (Austin, 1858), 705, 791.

Josiah F. Crosby was a member of the House of Representatives at the time this bill was presented. He was very active in securing its passage by the House. Deposition of Josiah F. Crosby in Warder v. The Campbell Real Estate Company (Mss., Records of the United States Circuit Court for the Western District of Texas, El Paso, Texas), No. 277.

13 H. P. N. Gammel, *The Laws of Texas*, IV, 1027.

14 *Ibid.*

15 *Ibid.*

16 Deposition of Josiah F. Crosby in Warder v. The Campbell Real Estate Company (Mss., Records of the United States Circuit Court for the Western District of Texas, El Paso, Texas), No. 277.

17 *Deed Records* (Mss., Records of the El Paso County Clerk's Office, El Paso, Texas), B, 14, 15, 28 and 53.

18 Dr. Francis Marion Giddings was shot and killed on May 15, 1858 in a billiard saloon in El Paso by a gambler named Tom Smith. William T. Smith was also wounded in the leg during the fracas. The murderer escaped into Mexico. William A. Duffen, "Overland Via Jackass Mail," *Arizona and the West* (1960), II, 148; and Strickland, W. W. *Mills: Forty Years at El Paso* (El Paso, 1962), 181.

19 Testimony of Anson Mills in Clark v. Hill (Mss., Records of the Supreme Court of Texas, Austin, Texas), No. 5534; and *Record* (Mss., Records of the El Paso County Surveyor's Office, El Paso, Texas), A-1, 163.

20 File No. Bexar 1-1382 (Mss., Records of the General Land Office, Austin, Texas.

21 *Deed Records* (Records of El Paso County Clerk's Office, El Paso, Texas), XXV, 7. For a fuller account of this grant, see J. J. Bowden, The Ponce de León Grant (El Paso, Texas, 1969).

CHAPTER 15

The Rafael Ruelas Grant 🙌

● THE NATURAL DILATION of the population of El Paso del Norte had, by 1847, resulted in allocation and distribution of all the irrigable lands south of the Rio Grande. As a result, the Ayuntamiento of El Paso del Norte permitted a number of the more ambitious landless citizens of that town to establish a new colony on the *terrenos valdíos* which were located on the Texas side of the river northeast of El Paso del Norte. The settlement was known as the Colony of Aguapa, and Tomás Yrigoyen was the appointed Commissioner of Emigration.

Several months after Colonel Alexander W. Doniphan and his troops had departed from El Paso del Norte in 1847, Rafael Ruelas decided to immigrate from El Paso del Norte to the Colony of Aguapa. Soon after his arrival, Ruelas requested Commissioner Yrigoyen to grant him the *caballería* of land to which he was entitled as a colonist. Yrigoyen designated a plot of land north of the river and east of the Camino Real for his occupation and use; however, Ruelas did not receive legal title to the tract at this time. Ruelas, upon taking possession of the tract, constructed a two-room *jacal* and a corral, and commenced cultivating a small portion of the grant. For irrigation purposes, he constructed a lateral ditch which tied onto the acequia belonging to Ponce de León.

In order to protect his equitable interest in the lands, Ruelas petitioned Francisco Robles, Judge of Letters of El Paso del Norte, seeking confirmation of his claim. In his petition to Judge Robles, Ruelas described his *caballería* as a rectangular tract of land with a length of 1,104 varas and a width, or frontage on the river, of 552 varas. The tract was bounded on the north by the foothills; on the east by the lands of Alejandro Ramírez;[1] on the south by the river; and on the west by the public road. On January 4, 1848 Judge Robles entered a decree confirming the grant. Ruelas was placed in legal possession of the land by Judge Robles on January 26, 1848.[2] The grant was allegedly made in conformance with the State of Chihuahua's Colonization Law of 1828.[3]

The Ruelas family resided on the grant from 1847 until late in the summer of 1849. Each year they benefitted from the crops of corn, wheat, beans, and vegetables raised on the tract. In August, 1849, the Mescalero Indians raided the colony and killed at least fifteen men. As a consequence of this particular raid, Ruelas suddenly realized that he could no longer safely occupy the grant, and therefore, decided to move to Doña Ana, New Mexico, until the Indian hostilities subsided.

Ramón Ortiz, Commissioner of Emigration of Mexico, encouraged Ruelas to lead about sixty loyal Mexican families across the river on March 1, 1850, to establish the Colony of Mesilla. Thereupon, Don Rafael was appointed Alcalde of La Mesilla by the Commissioner. This settlement developed into the principal Mexican colony in the Mesilla Valley.[4]

Ruelas occasionally visited his grant up until 1866, when he moved to San Antonio, Texas. Upon returning to Mesilla in 1874, he authorized a number of Mexicans to farm the grant. The tenants encountered no opposition from the Texans, and Ruelas assumed everyone recognized his claim to the land.[5] Content with the belief that his claim was fully protected by the fifth article of the Treaty of Guadalupe Hidalgo, Ruelas saw no reason to take any further steps to perfect his title.

It was not until after the United States Circuit Court[6] had recognized the Ponce de León Grant, which was senior to and conflicted with a major portion of the Rafael Ruelas Grant, that Ruelas realized that he would steadfastly have to assert his claim to all of the lands embraced within the original boundaries of the grant. However, by this time he was over sixty-six years old and unable to withstand the strain of a hotly contested title suit. To avoid further involvement, Rafael Ruelas and his wife, Blasa Ruelas, sold the grant to their son-in-law, Alfred J. Buchoz, on January 4, 1883, for a cash consideration of $5,000.[7]

Buchoz publically asserted his claim, and indicated that a suit would shortly be instituted, in an effort to secure its recognition.[8] However, for some unexplained reason, Buchoz postponed filing the suit until March 10, 1890.[9] The action was against C. R. Morehead, Joseph Magoffin, El Paso Real Estate Company, and thirty-three other defendants, who claimed adverse interests in the lands covered by the Ruelas Grant.

Both sides waived a jury, and the trail opened with Ruelas personally taking the stand to recount the history of the grant. The defendants countered by pointing out that the grant had been issued after Texas had acquired its independence and subsequent to the actual conquest and occupation of the area by Colonel Doniphan during the Mexican War. The defendants asserted that the Ruelas Grant was obsolutely void, due to a complete lack of authority by the Mexican officials to make a valid concession covering lands which were, on the date of the issuance of the grant, unquestionably under the jurisdiction of the State of Texas. After hearing the evidence and arguments, the court acknowledged the validity of the defendants contentions, and decreed on April 3, 1895[10] that plaintiff take nothing. Buchoz did not appeal the decision, because he felt further action would be fruitless.

REFERENCES

1 The lands located east of the Rafael Ruelas Grant had been informally allotted to Luis Cuarón on October 8, 1847 by Alejandro Ramirez, Prefect of El Paso del Norte. It is strange that this grant should refer to such lands as being owned by Ramirez.

2 *Deed Records* (Mss., Records of the El Paso County Clerk's Office, El Paso, Texas), IV, 261.

3 The State of Chihuahua Colonization Law was dated May 25, 1825. The reference is undoubtedly to the Regulations for the Colonization of the Territories of the Republic dated November 28, 1828. The Regulations of 1828 only applied to lands in the Mexican Territories, and were never applicable in the State of Chihuahua.

4 George Griggs, *History of Mesilla Valley* (Mesilla, 1930), 95.

5 Buchoz v. The El Paso Real Estate Company (Mss., Records of the United States Circuit Court for the Western District of Texas, El Paso, Texas), No. 135.

6 Magoffin v. Campbell (Mss., Records of the United States Circuit Court for the Western District of Texas, Austin, Texas), No. 1290½.

7 *Deed Records* (Mss., Records of the El Paso County Clerk's Office, El Paso, Texas), IV, 263.

8 *Lone Star*, February 7, 1883.

9 Buchoz v. Morehead (Mss., Records of the United States Circuit Court for the Western District of Texas, El Paso, Texas), No. 101.

Buchoz filed a second suit in the same court against the El Paso Real Estate Company on April 22, 1891. These two suits were consolidated and tried together. The El Paso Real Estate Company acquired and developed the lands now known as the Magoffin Addition. This Addition is located about a mile southeast of the downtown section of El Paso. It covers a major portion of the Ruelas Grant, and embraces most of the land involved in the conflict between the Ponce de León Grant and the Manning Survey No. 4, located south of Magoffin's homestead tract. The El Paso Real Estate Company derived its title from the owners of the Ponce de León Grant and Joseph Magoffin. C. R. Morehead was President of the Company. Buchoz v. El Paso Real Estate Company. *Ibid.*, No. 135.

10 *Minute Book* (Mss., Records of the United States Circuit Court for the Western District of Texas, El Paso, Texas), I, 478.

CHAPTER 16

The Luis Cuarón Grant 🙌

● ON DECEMBER 27, 1847, Luis Cuarón petitioned Francisco Robles, Judge of Letters of El Paso del Norte, requesting that he be furnished a *testimonio* evidencing his title to the tract of land which had been granted to him on December 8, 1847 by the Prefect of El Paso del Norte, Alejandro Ramires. He stated that the tract contained a total of a *sitio* and *caballe-ría* of land, and was located on the north side of the Rio Grande at the Rincón de Alonzo. In order to determine the merits of the request, Judge Robles set the matter down for hearing on January 26, 1848 and directed that notice thereof be given to the adjoining land owners. At the hearing no one questioned Cuarón's right to the land or objected to the granting of his request. Therefore, Judge Robles confirmed the grant and appointed a special commission to survey the tract and place Cuarón in legal posses-sion of the land. The commission commenced the survey of the *caballería* at a little hill which marked the northeast corner of the Rafael Ruelas Grant and ran east 552 varas; thence south 1,104 varas along the boundary of the common wood lands to the river; thence west 552 varas with the meanders of the river to the southeast corner of the Ruelas Grant; thence north 1,104 varas along the east line of the Ruelas Grant to the point of beginning. The commission did not actually survey the *sitio* of land which had been granted to Cuarón as a pasture for his cattle, but merely stated that it was located north of the *caballería*. After the survey had been com-pleted, the Judge formally placed Cuarón in possession of the grant in the name of the Supreme Power of the Nation.[1]

The depredations of the Apache Indians forced Cuarón to move back to El Paso del Norte shortly after the grant had been issued. Thereafter, he made no effort to claim or occupy the land until April 2, 1883, when he sold the entire grant to Dr. Edward Alexander for two hundred fifty *pesos.*[2]

Dr. Alexander instituted a trespass to try title suit[3] in the 34th Judicial District Court in the spring of 1891, against C. R. Morehead, Frank B. Cotton, The East El Paso Town Company, Major B. H. Davis, Charles Davis, T. J. Beall, O. T. Bassett, and William Cameron, in an effort to secure judicial recognition of his claim. The defendants held title to the lands covered by the grant under patents issued by the State of Texas.

The case went to trial before Special Judge F. B. Sexton on January 30, 1895. The defendants' principal defense was that all Mexican grants located north and east of the Rio Grande, and made subsequent to December 19, 1836, were invalid. First, they pointed out that Article X of the Treaty of Guadalupe Hidalgo had been inserted in the treaty at the insistence of Mexico for the specific purpose of protecting Mexican land titles located within the State of Texas, but had been stricken therefrom by the United States Senate before its ratification. Next, they called the court's attention to the fact that the Eighth Article of the treaty, which expressly provided for the protection of Mexican property rights, applied only to the territories of California and New Mexico.[4] In support of their contentions, the defendants cited decisions by the Supreme Courts of both the United States and Texas.[5]

Judge Sexton, in a short opinion dated February 4, 1895, held that the Luis Cuarón Grant was invalid on the grounds that at the time of its issuance the lands covered thereby were within the jurisdiction of the State of Texas, and therefore, the Mexican authorities did not have the power to make the concession.[6]

REFERENCES

[1] *Deed Records* (Mss., Records of the El Paso County Clerk's Office, El Paso, Texas), XX, 145-147.

[2] *Ibid.,* XX, 147-149.

[3] Alexander v. Morehead (Mss., Records of the El Paso District Clerk's Office, El Paso, Texas), No. 1504.

[4] *El Paso Daily Herald,* January 31, 1895.

[5] McKinney v. Saviego, 18 How. (59 U.S.) 235 (1856); and Texas v. Cardinas, 47 Tex. 250 (1877).

[6] *Minute Book* (Mss., Records of the El Paso District Clerk's Office, El Paso, Texas), VIII, 135.

CHAPTER 17

The Ascarate Grant ?

● THE EARLY HISTORY of the Ascarate Grant is the most obscure of all of the recognized Spanish and Mexican land grants in the territory covered by the Chihuahuan acquisition. There is no known documentary evidence supporting the validity of this concession. Perhaps the first known record reference to the Ascarate Grant is found in a bill[1] introduced in the Texas Senate by Archibald C. Hyde on December 14, 1857, which provided for the relinquishment of all of the State's rights to four tracts of land located in El Paso County, Texas, and known as El Pueblo Socorro, El Canutillo, El Rancho de Ponce, and El Rancho de Ascarate. This bill was read for the first and second time, and then referred to the Senate's Committee on Private Land Claims.[2]

James M. Burroughs, a member of said committee, submitted the following report[3] concerning the Hyde Bill to the Senate on January 20, 1858:

The Committee on Private Land Claims has considered a bill to relinquish the rights of the State to certain lands herein named, and a majority of this committee instructs me to recommend the passage of the bill for the following reasons:

1. That the lands were titled by the Spanish Government for more than a century ago, and have ever since been held in possession by the original grantees, their descendants or assigns; and upon which are two towns of great antiquity.

2. These claims were presented to the Commissioners appointed to examine land titles west of the Pecos River; and all the evidence outside of the official report of said Commissioners sustains the conclusions that they were approved and favorably reported.

On motion of Senator Hyde, the rule was suspended, and the bill was taken up, read and ordered to be engrossed. The rule was further suspended on the motion of Senator Burroughs, and the bill was read a third time and passed.[4]

The Hyde Bill was transmitted to the House of Representatives for its further action on January 21, 1858. After having been read a first and second time, the bill was referred to the House of Representatives' Committee on Private Land Claims. This Committee, on January 27, 1857, submitted the following report:[5]

The Committee on Private Land Claims, to whom was referred the bill from the Senate, to be entitled "An Act to relinquish the rights of the State to certain lands therein named, have had the same under consideration, and find that one of the Commissioners appointed under and by virtue of the Act of the Legislature, approved 11th February, 1854, to investigate land titles between the Nueces and Rio Grande Rivers, reported the titles set forth in the bill, and recommended that they be confirmed. Said report was before the last Legislature, and a bill was passed confirming the titles in question, together with many others, which was vetoed by the Governor, because said bill embraced many other lands titles besides those recommended by the Commission appointed by virtue of the act aforesaid. In his veto message, the Governor stated that he would have approved the bill had it contained no other lands than those favorably recommended by the Commissioners appointed for that purpose.

Since the adjournment of the last Legislature, the report of said Commission has not been seen, nor can it be found, notwithstanding the most diligent search which has been made for it in every place where such a document should be found.

Although said report has been lost, mislaid or abstracted from the archives of this house and no copy thereof was ever made, so far as your committee can ascertain from the evidence before them, they have no doubt, whatsoever, as to the fact that each and every claim specified in the bill was recommended by Commissioner Charles S. Taylor for confirmation. In addition to these facts, the committee is satisfied that the lands in question have been long occupied by the claimants under an imperfect title, and that they are meritorious in character.

In consideration of the foregoing facts and circumstances, they instruct me to report the bill back to the House and recommend its passage.

C. W. Buckley, Chairman

This highly favorable report undoubtedly influenced the members of the House of Representatives. On the motion of Mr. Hall, the rule was suspended on February 5, 1858. The Hyde Bill was thereupon taken up, read, and passed to a third reading. The rule was then immediately further suspended, in order to read the bill a third time. Following this action, the bill was voted upon and passed by a vote of fifty-five yeas to eight nays.[6] The bill was signed into law by Governor Hardin R. Runnels on February 11, 1858. This act relinquished to Juan and Jacinto Ascarate[7] all of the right and interest of the State of Texas in and to that certain three-league tract of land located in El Paso County, Texas, called El Rancho de Ascarate. The second section of the act required the claimants to have their lands surveyed by either the District or County Surveyor. The survey was to conform in all respects to the metes and bounds designated in the original grant. Upon completion of the survey, the field notes were to be sent to the Commissioner of the General Land Office, in order that a patent could be issued. The third section of the act expressly provided that the confirmation of the grant would in no way be construed so as to interfere with the rights of any third party which accrued prior to the passage of the act.[8]

The ink was handly dry on the Relinquishment Act of February 11, 1858 before one of its staunchest supporters, Josiah F. Crosby, acquired a substantial interest in the Ascarate Grant. By warranty deed dated December 13, 1858, Juan and Jacinto Ascarate sold an undivided two leagues out of the Ascarate Grant to Josiah F. Crosby and Horace F. Stephenson for a stated consideration of $5,000. The deed was witnessed by J. F. Cassino, George Lyles and Fred A. Percy. Juan and Jacinto Ascarate, who purportedly were wealthy and highly educated, executed this instrument by their respective marks.[9]

On January 24, 1859, Anson Mills, Deputy Surveyor of El Paso and Presidio District, set out with a pack burro and two Mexican chain carriers, Juan Apodaca and Feliz Armadares, to make Survey No. 144 for the owners of the Ascarate Grant, in compliance with the second section of the Act of February 11, 1858.[10] Mills' survey called for a three-league tract of land situated in Section One of El Paso County, Texas, on the north bank of the Rio Viejo, a branch of the Rio Grande about five miles below the town of El Paso. The beginning point of the Mills survey was located at a cottonwood post five inches in diameter set at the lower or southeast corner of Survey No. 12 made for J. W. McGoffin (sic), assignee of Elijah Bennett. From this point, Mills ran down the north bank of the Rio Viejo, with its meanders, to a post six inches in diameter set at the southeast corner of the Thos. H. Duggan Survey No. 12. He ran thence north 5,782 varas to a stake and mound set for the northeast corner of this survey. He then turned northwesterly and ran a distance of 15,360 varas along a course of north 62° west to a stake and mound established for the northwest corner. The last line ran thence south a distance of 6,376 varas to the point of beginning. Rufus Doane, District Surveyor for the El Paso and Presidio District, found the survey correct, and recorded it in his records on January 25, 1859.[11]

A copy of the Mills survey was forwarded to the General Land Office, where it was filed by Commissioner Stephen Crosby on July 18, 1859. However, the Mills survey was rejected, since the General Land Office required an accurate survey of the courses and distances of the meanders of the river, instead of merely a generalized survey of the river, as reflected by the offset method utilized by Mills.[12]

Also, a glance at the office General Land Office Map of El Paso County shows that the Mills survey of the Ascarate Grant includes all or a portion of five tracts of land, which had been appropriated by third parties prior to the passage of the Relinquishment Act of February 11, 1858. These tracts are the G. M. Collingsworth Surveys Nos. 13 and 14, the D. P. Cummings Survey No. 9, the Thos. H. Duggan No. 12, and a portion of the Ysleta Grant.

George M. Collingsworth was issued Bounty Warrant No. 1785 for 320 acres by the Secretary of War Bernard E. Bee, on January 12, 1838. Collingsworth sold this certificate to Charles McCormick, who in turn sold same to James Buchanan in San Antonio on December 1, 1857, for $115.

On December 27, 1857 Buchanan filed an application with the District Surveyor for the El Paso District, requesting that two contiguous surveys of 160 acres each be made for him, by virtue of Bounty Warrant No. 1785. He further requested that the surveys be located on the north bank of the Rio Grande in El Paso County and just east of the Elijah Bennett Survey No. 12, which had been made for James M. Magoffin. District Surveyor Stephen Archer made Surveys 13 and 14 in Section 1 for James Buchanan on May 7, 1858. Although both of these surveys conflicted with the Ascarate Grant, Buchanan prevailed, since his entry of December 27, 1857 served to withdraw the lands covered by the two surveys from the unappropriated public domain[13] prior to passage of the Relinquishment Act of February 11, 1858. Patents covering the two George M. Collingsworth surveys were issued to James Buchanan on April 12, 1861.[14]

The heirs of David P. Cummings received Donation Certificate No. 535 by virtue of an Act dated December 21, 1837,[15] which granted 640 acres of land to all persons who fell at the Alamo. Robert B. Hays, Deputy Surveyor for the Bexar Land District, located this certificate on October 4, 1849 as Survey No. 9 in Section 15 of the Bexar Land District. It is situated in El Paso County on the north bank of the Rio Viejo, about eight miles east of the City of El Paso, Texas. The field notes pertaining to this survey were filed in the General Land Office on August 17, 1853, and a patent was issued on November 10, 1858.[16]

On October 4, 1849 Survey No. 12 in Section 15 of the Bexar County Land District was made by Robert B. Hays by virtue of third class Headright Certificate No. 38, which had been issued to Thos. H. Duggan. While a patent was issued to Duggan on January 24, 1856, covering 640 acres embraced within this survey, only 200.53 acres situated in the northern portion of the tract has been recognized. Title to all of the land located in and south of the north line of the Ysleta Grant has failed, since such land had been appropriated prior to the location of the Duggan certificate. Although the northern part of the Thos. H. Duggan Survey No. 12 conflicts with the Ascarate Grant, that portion of the survey has been recognized, since it was patented prior to passage of the Relinquishment Act of February 11, 1858.

The Relinquishment Act of February 1, 1854[17] confirmed the claim of the inhabitants of the Town of Ysleta to the 8,147.5 acres of land contained in the portion of the Ysleta Grant located north of the Rio Grande. The portion of the Ysleta Grant in conflict with the Ascarate Grant has prevailed over the Ascarate Grant, since the former grant was relinquished by the state prior to the latter. The Ysleta Grant was patented on May 22, 1873.[18]

J. R. Owens, Deputy Surveyor for El Paso County, Texas, was employed by the owners of the Ascarate Grant to resurvey the grant. He conducted his survey on the 18th, 19th, and 25th days of December, 1885. The Owens survey was rejected by the General Land Office, because it did not close by a large error.[19] On January 4, 1886 another survey of the grant was made by J. R. Randolph, County Surveyor of El Paso County, Texas. The Randolph survey was accepted by the General Land Office, and on September 14, 1886, nearly twenty-nine years after passage of the Relinquishment Act, a patent[20] was issued by the State of Texas to Juan and Jacinto Ascarate, their heirs and assigns, covering the 12,399.7 acres embraced within the following boundaries:

Beginning at a cottonwood post set on the North bank of the Rio Viejo 545 varas South from the Northeast corner of the G. M. Collingsworth Survey No. 14; thence down the Rio Viejo with its meanders to a stake for the Southwest corner of the D. P. Cummings Survey No. 9; thence North 3,686 varas to a stake; thence East 950 varas to a stake; thence South 4,106 varas to a stake on the bank of the Rio Viejo; thence down the Rio Viejo with its meanders to a stake set on the North bank of the Rio Viejo and also on the West line of the Ysleta Grant; thence North 16° East 3,390 varas to a stake for the Northwest corner of the Ysleta Grant from which the crest of a high sand hill known as La Loma Tigua bears due East 300 varas; thence South 42½° East 1,120 varas to a stake on the West line of the Thos. H. Duggan Survey No. 12; thence North 652 varas; thence East 1,332 varas; thence North 3,807 varas; thence North 65° West 13,445 varas to a pile of rock from which the Southwest corner of Section 19, Block 81, Tsp. 2, T&P Ry. Co. Survey bears due West 337 varas; thence South 5,129 varas to the Northwest corner of G. M. Collingsworth Survey No. 13; thence East 950 varas to a pile of rocks for the Northeast corner of the G. M. Collingsworth Survey No. 14; and thence South 545 varas to the place of Beginning.

Once a patent had been issued to the owners of the Ascarate Grant, they were vested with title to the lands embraced within its boundaries good against everyone's except those who could show a superior pre-existing right.[21] However, shortly after Randolph had completed his resurvey of the Ascarate Grant, it was discovered that the Ysleta Grant was actually located approximately 4¾ miles west of the location it occupied on the then current General Land Office Map of El Paso County. This placed the Thos. H. Duggan Survey No. 12 over 1,100 varas east of the west line of the Ysleta Grant, instead of some 4¾ miles west of the northwest corner of that grant. It was therefore obvious that the portion of the Senecú Grant lying north of the Rio Viejo conflicted with the Ascarate Grant. This immediately raised the question as to whether or not the land embraced within the portion of the Senecú Grant lying north of the river belonged to the owners of the Ascarate Grant or to the inhabitants of the town of Ysleta.

The inhabitants of the town of Ysleta contended that the patent issued to them pursuant to the Relinquishment Act of January 31, 1854, as amended by the Act of February 15, 1858, embraced the lands in conflict, notwithstanding the call for the north line of their tract to run down the

Rio Viejo to the southeast corner of the Thos. H. Duggan Survey No. 12. This claim was based on the assumption that the Legislature had intended to relinquish to the inhabitants of Ysleta all of the land embraced within the Senecú Grant north of the Rio Viejo, together with all of the land between the Rio Grande and Rio Viejo Rivers lying west of the Senecú Grant. This assumption is supported by the fact that the official maps of the General Land Office in use in 1854 and 1858 placed the Thos. H. Duggan Survey No. 12 immediately west of the Senecú Grant, and that the Legislature unquestionably believed it was so located when it enacted such Relinquishment Acts. To require the north line of the tract relinquished to the inhabitants of the Town of Ysleta to run down the Rio Viejo to the southeast corner of the Thos. H. Duggan Survey No. 12 would create a latent ambiguity, and would be absolutely meaningless. There is a presumption that the Legislature intended to accomplish some useful purpose by referring to such corner, and this purpose may be realized only by limiting the call for the north line of the relinquishment tract to run down the north bank of the Rio Viejo from the point of separation of the Rio Viejo and Rio Grande to the point where the Legislature believed the southeast corner of the Thos. H. Duggan Survey No. 12 was located. If this were true, then the reference to the southeast corner of the Thos. H. Duggan Survey No. 12 would yield to the Legislature's "footsteps," and the north line of the tract which had been relinquished to the Ysletans would run down the north bank of the Rio Viejo from the point where it separated from the Rio Grande to the west line of the Senecú Grant; thence north with the west line of the Senecú Grant to its northwest corner; and thence east along the north line of the Senecú Grant to the northwest corner of the Ysleta Grant.[22]

The owners of the Ascarate Grant took the position that the Relinquishment Act of January 31, 1854, as amended by the Act of February 15, 1858, did not give the inhabitants of Ysleta any land north of the north bank of the Rio Viejo between the point where the Rio Viejo departed from the Rio Grande and the point where the west line of the Ysleta Grant intersected the north bank of the Rio Viejo. Should this position triumph, then the Ascarate Grant would embrace all of that portion of the Senecú Grant lying north of the Rio Viejo except the land contained in the D. P. Cummings Survey No. 9.

On July 28, 1887 Josiah F. Crosby, as the owner of an undivided interest[23] in the Ascarate Grant, filed a trespass to try title suit in the District Court of El Paso County against Richard Di Palma and thirty other defendants, in order to remove the cloud cast upon their interests by the claims of the defendants under Tays' Survey and his interpretation of the Relinquishment Act of January 31, 1854, as amended by the Act of February 15, 1858.[24] Each of the defendants claimed one or more separate tracts of land located within that portion of the Senecú Grant lying north of the Rio Viejo under titles emanating through the town of Ysleta.

Since neither side pressed for an early setting of the case, the suit remained dormant until 1907, when Crosby resumed the active prosecution of the action. Numerous new parties had to be added or substituted as a result of their having acquired interests by the purchase, devise or descent from a number of the original parties. When the action finally went to trial there were 15 plaintiffs and 157 defendants. The plaintiffs obtained default judgments against many of the defendants, and other defendants disclaimed any interest in the controversy. At the request of a number of the defendants, the suit was severed into 16 separate actions.

The court, in order to better acquaint itself with the issues involved in these cases, appointed J. W. Eubank, Surveyor of El Paso County, to survey the lands involved in the alleged conflict between the Ascarate Grant and the Ysleta lands. Eubank discovered a number of errors in the calls along the Rio Viejo contained in the original patent to the Ascarate Grant. However, Eubank was able to relocate the course of the old river. Wherever there was an apparent conflict between the calls in the patent and natural objects, he adhered to the latter. In other words, he relocated the Rio Viejo by following its banks or the trees which unquestionably grew along its course.[25]

The plaintiffs dismissed their action as to each defendant who had filed an answer in the suit, and sought a default judgment against all the rest. During the hearing on this action, the plaintiffs introduced their complete chain of title and argued that the patent issued to the Inhabitants of the Town of Ysleta, pursuant to the Relinquishment Act of January 31, 1854, as amended by the Act of February 15, 1858, did not embrace any land located in the Senecú Grant lying north of the Rio Viejo. Since none of the remaining defendants had answered, the court had no alternative but to enter a judgment for the plaintiffs. This decision was dated June 23, 1909.[26]

In the early part of 1910 Richard Di Palma filed a suit in the Thirty-Fourth District Court, El Paso County, Texas, to set aside the judgment of June 23, 1909. Di Palma was the owner of a number of tracts emanating under Corporate Deeds issued by the Town Council of Ysleta, and which were located within the portion of the Senecú Grant lying north of the Rio Viejo. The tracts owned by Di Palma consisted of a number of Valley Surveys containing 119 acres and seven Hill Surveys.[27] Di Palma held such land in trust for the Society of Jesus. He contended that said judgment should be vacated on the grounds that (a) he had not been properly served; (b) by reason of the plaintiffs' failure to diligently prosecute the suit, it had been abandoned, and therefore the court had lost jurisdiction over the suit; and (c) the judgment had been rendered through fraud, accident or mistake. It appears that Di Palma had been personally cited in 1887, and that his attorney, J. P. Hague, had filed two separate answers on his behalf. Di Palma moved to New Mexico in June, 1890. At that time, Hague assured him that he would keep him informed of any further action taken in the case by the plaintiffs. No one notified Di Palma of the trial of the case until 1910. Meanwhile, both Hague and the plaintiffs' attorney, B. H. Davis, had died, and all of the original papers in the suit had been lost. When the plaintiffs substituted parties in 1907, they had Di Palma recited by publication. He called the court's attention to the fact that as a result of no negligence on his part he had not been given an opportunity to assert his meritorious defenses. Upon the trial of Di Palma's action, the court issued pre-emptory instructions to the jury to render a verdict in his favor. The court then rendered its judgment in favor of Di Palma, based upon such instructed verdict.

The plaintiffs in the original case appealed this decision. They contended that Di Palma had been properly cited by publication, and had been afforded his day in court during the trial of the base case, but had failed to timely protect his interests. The Court of Civil Appeals at El Paso affirmed the lower court's decision and held that a delay of twenty years in the production of a suit, during which time the attorneys on both sides had died, and nothing evidencing an intention to prosecute except the filing of a motion to substitute a lost petition and service of process on a few defendants, operates as a discontinuance. A judgment rendered after a cause is discontinued can be attacked and set aside, because the court loses jurisdiction over the subject matter and the parties once the case is discontinued.[28] Since Di Palma, or those claiming under him, had held actual possession of the lands in question for at least twenty-five years prior to the decision in the base case, and had probably perfected a limitation title thereto, even though the Ysleta Corporate Deeds may not have conveyed a legal title, the plaintiffs did not take further action against him seeking to clear their title. Therefore, this case did not definitely settle the question as to which grant covered the lands in the disputed area.

Meanwhile, the plaintiffs had carefully analyzed each of the segregated cases. They apparently realized that many of the defendants had perfected good limitation titles, even though they may not have acquired a good title from the Town of Ysleta. Therefore, they dismissed seven of the several cases. However, they proceeded to trial in the remaining eight cases, but lost six of them. The defendants in the cases which were lost were able to prove that they had perfected limitation titles. The only case which the plaintiffs clearly won covered one small tract located on the edge of the sandhills.

The action against the El Paso Dairy Company was probably the most important of all of the cases which went to trial. In this case, the dairy, in addition to claiming title to an undivided 214 acres under the Ascarate Grant, also claimed title to ten parcels of land which emanated under deeds from the Town Council of Ysleta. Nine of these parcels were located in the portion of the Senecú Grant lying between the Rio Viejo and the edge of the sand hills. The tenth parcel embraced forty of the Hill Surveys. On September 5, 1910 the court held that all ten parcels involved in this suit comprised a portion of the Ascarate Grant, but that the dairy was entitled to retain all nine of the valley parcels, together with the south 80 acres of Hill Surveys numbered 1 through 15, inclusive. The dairy had actually occupied and used these parcels in the operation of its business for more than five years prior to the institution of said suit. The dairy was able to establish a limitation title under its deeds emanating from the Town of Ysleta to the lands awarded to it, and therefore was not claiming title to such land as a joint tenant with the plaintiffs under its title emanating under the Ascarate Grant.[29]

This case clearly indicates that the Relinquishment Act of January 31, 1854, as amended by the Act of February 15, 1858, did not relinquish that portion of the Senecú Grant lying north of the Rio Viejo to the Inhabitants of the Town of Ysleta. The decision in Cause No. 832(b) is supported by a decision rendered on March 15, 1914, wherein the El Paso County Court of Civil Appeals held[30] that:

the north bank of the Rio Viejo is the dividing line between the Ascarate Grant and the Ysleta Grant eastward or downward from the junction of the new and old rivers, and, in case of conflict between the course and distance calls in the south line of the Ascarate patent and the Rio Viejo, the latter wil prevail.

While these court decisions indicate that the owners of the Ascarate Grant were entitled to the lands covered by that portion of the Senecú Grant lying north of the Rio Viejo, a number of parties, other than the defendants mentioned above, claimed certain lands in that portion of the Senecú Grant lying between the Rio Viejo and the edge of the sand hills, under deeds issued by the Town Council of Ysleta. These parties had perfected good limitation titles to such lands. As a matter of fact, the owners of the Ascarate Grant either lost by court decisions or voluntarily recognized the conflicting claims of the Ysletans to all of the land in the Senecú Grant lying between the Rio Viejo and the edge of the sand hills. In addition to the valley lands, they also lost two tracts north of the sand hills. These two tracts are the 80-acre tract out of Hill Surveys 1 through 15, which was awarded to the El Paso Dairy, and Hill Survey No. 40, which was originally owned by T. V. de Espalin. Since the decision in the El Paso Dairy Company case, all the land south of the edge of the sand hills in the Senecú Grant has been considered to be a portion of the Ysleta Grant, and the Ysleta titles north of the sand hills in the first 100 Wood Grants have been disregarded.

The El Paso Dairy Company case is particularly important, because it determined and fixed the various interests of each owner in the Ascarate Grant. It also shows that there is an excess of 1,678.8 acres over and above the number of acres called for in the patent.

While a portion of Sections 31, 39, 40, and 41, Block 80, Township 2, Texas & Pacific Railway Company Survey, are shown on the General Land Office Map of El Paso County as conflicting with the Ascarate Grant, it is recognized that the land involved in these overlapping areas is covered by the Ascarate Grant.

In order to assist the El Paso County Tax Collector in assessing and collecting county and state ad valorem taxes, the Commissioner's Court of El Paso County awarded a contract to R. B. De Witt on April 22, 1927, to compile an abstract covering all property possessed, unknown or un-rendered in the upper and lower El Paso Valley. The Commissioner's Court also employed Sid A. Coldwell to prepare plats covering such ab-stracted lands. On December 12, 1932 the abstracts and plats were ac-cepted by the Commissioner's Court.[31]

The El Paso County Tax Collector, on the basis of this information, revised his tax rolls and commenced assessing the taxes in accordance with the ownership and land descriptions reflected by the plats and abstracts.

Once the Ascarate Grant was subdivided into blocks and tracts, its grandeur and compactness were forever lost. These smaller parcels have had a tendency to become merely statistical data in the overall county land picture. This is especially true now that the original tracts are continuously being further divided after subdivision after subdivision are constructed upon the grant. Deeds and other instruments pertaining to the lands em-braced within the Ascarate Grant are being filed daily as the metropolitan El Paso mushrooms east ward. The legal descriptions contained in such conveyances rarely refer to the Ascarate Grant, but merely describe a particular lot in one of the numerous subdivisions now located within its boundaries. Thus, it appears that the logical date for terminating the His-tories of the Ascarate Grant is December 12, 1932—the date El Paso County Commissioners approved the official county plats of the Ascarate Grant.

R E F E R E N C E S

[1] *Journal of the Senate of the State of Texas, Seventh Legislature* (Austin, 1858), 195.

[2] *Ibid.*

[3] *Ibid.*, 367. The Reference to the Commissioners appointed to examine land titles west of the Pecos River is undoubtedly to the Commission created under the act of February 11, 1854 [H.P.N. Gammel, *The Laws of Texas* (10 Vols., Austin, 1898), III, 1533], and

generally known as the Rio Grande Commission. Charles S. Taylor, of Nacogdoches County, and R. H. Lane, of Fannin County, were appointed by Governor E. M. Pease as the two Commissioners of the Rio Grande Commission. This Commission investigated land titles in El Paso County during the summer of 1855. After the Commission completed its investigation, it prepared and submitted to Governor Pease a detailed report, supported with a large amount of evidence which had been gathered. In this report, the Commissioners recommended that only a portion of titles which it had investigated be confirmed. The report and supporting data were transmitted by Governor Pease to the Texas Legislature on November 27, 1855. The Sixth Legislature of the State of Texas passed an act which would have relinquished all of the State's rights to sixty tracts which embraced approximately 205 leagues of land. This act, in addition to relinquishing title to the claims which the Rio Grande Committee had recommended for confirmation, released all of the State's rights in a number of tracts which had not been recommended for confirmation, and also a number of tracts which had not been presented to the Commission. As a matter of fact, the claims which the Commission recommended for confirmation constituted only a very small portion of the lands covered by the act. Governor Pease, in a message dated August 23, 1856, and addressed to both Houses of the Texas Legislature, stated that he had vetoed the act because it embraced many land titles besides those recommended for approval by the Rio Grande Commission. *State Gazette,* August 30, 1856. At the conclusion of his veto message, the Governor stated that if the act had confirmed only the small number of claims which the Commission had recommended for confirmation, he would have approved it. The report and data submitted by the Rio Grande Commission were lost or destroyed sometime prior to January 27, 1858.

While not conclusive, the reference contained in the second paragraph of James M. Burroughs' report that "all of the evidence outside the official report" of the Rio Grande Commission would indicate that title to the Ascarate Grant was examined by the Rio Grande Commission and found to be invalid. However, in this connection, it is noted that the Senate's Committee on Private Land Claims conflicts with the report submitted by the House of Representatives' Committee on Private Land Claims, and which is hereinafter set out.

At this point, it is appropriate to point out that the Burroughs Report contains several erroneous statements which show that the Senate's Committee on Private Land Claims had not adequately investigated the four claims covered by the Hyde Bill. Such statements undoubtedly influenced the passage of the bill by the Senate. The report stated that the lands to be relinquished had been "titled" by the Spanish Government more than a century prior to the date of the presentation of the Hyde Bill. However, it is well known that the Canutillo and Ponce de León Grants were Mexican concessions, and were at that time less than thirty-one years old. There is even some question as to whether Juan and Jacinto Ascarate had ever received a grant covering the tract known as El Rancho Ascarate. Juan María Gonzáles, a life-long resident of Ysleta, who was born in October, 1825, stated in an affidavit dated March 16, 1886, that he had been intimately acquainted with Juan and Jacinto Ascarate since he was sixteen. He was well acquainted with the boundaries of the Ysleta and Senecú Grants, and also the lands owned by the Ascarates. He stated that all of the lands owned by the Ascarates were located south of the Rio Grande near San Lorenzo. He had never heard of Juan or Jacinto Ascarate claiming or owning any lands north of the river. He recalled that, prior to 1854, the Ascarate family had used the portion of the Senecú Grant located north of the river as a pasturage for their livestock with the consent and permission of the inhabitants of the Pueblo de Senecú, and that the Ascarates were prohibited from using such lands by the inhabitants of Ysleta after 1854. In conclusion, he stated that he had never heard of the Ascarate Grant until about 1855, when it was first asserted by Horace Stephenson and Josiah F. Crosby. This was several years after the death of both Juan and Jacinto Ascarate. Juan María Gonzáles was a prominent political figure in El Paso County, and appears to be a creditable disinterested party. He held the positions of Justice of the Peace, Mayor of Ysleta, County Commissioner, and County Judge.

Juan Serveriano Gonzáles, the Cacique of the Tigua Indians, and a resident of Ysleta since his birth in 1804, gave an affidavit concerning the Ascarate Grant on March 19, 1886. He likewise was well acquainted with the Ascarate family and their lands. He stated that Juan and Jacinto Ascarate resided in Mexico about one mile from the San Lorenzo Church, and never owned any land north of the river. He acknowledged that they had used the northern portion of the Senecú Grant, but stated that such use was made with the express consent and approval of the officials of the Pueblo de Senecú. The Ascarates had a corral north of the river and about four miles from their home, and pastured their livestock on such land, but had never cultivated any of it. He recalled that on one ocassion he had cut some fire wood near the Ascarate corral and was carrying it home, when Ignacio Ascarate, son of Juan Ascarate, stopped him and asked where he got it. After he had furnished his explanation, Ignacio Ascarate told him not to cut any more wood on the Senecú Grant, since the Ascarates had permission from the Senecús "to use and take care of the lands."

Juan Padillo, who was born in 1815, and was a resident of Senecú, in an affidavit dated March 13, 1886, swore that Juan and Jacinto Ascarate "never had title nor grant from the State of Chihuahua nor from the General Government" to the lands of Senecú that are now in the possession of Ysleta.

Gabriel Cordero, who was born in 1804, and was a resident of Senecú, gave a similar affidavit on March 13, 1886, in which he stated that Juan and Jacinto Ascarate had "never presented or shown any document or authority showing possession in favor of the Ascarates." He concluded by saying that he was satisfied that the Ascarate Grant was "null and that they never had any grant. . . ."

All four of these affidavits may be found in Letter File 194001½ (Mss., Records of the General Land Office, Austin, Texas). The statement in the Burroughs Report that the lands covered by the four grants had been held in the possession of the original grantees, since they were titled, is also untrue. It is known that shortly after the close of the Mexican War the lands embraced within the Canutillo and Ascarate Grants were unoccupied. While the Pueblo de Socorro qualifies as a town of "great antiquity," there was no second ancient town upon any of the four grants, as alleged in the Burroughs Report. The only other settlement located on any of the grants was the Town of Franklin, which was originally founded by Ponce de León in 1827.

4 *Journal of the Senate of the State of Texas, Seventh Legislature,* 368.

5 *Journal of the House of Representatives, Seventh Legislature* (Austin, 1858), 705-706.

6 *Ibid.,* 791.

7 Juan Ascarate was born in Spain in 1776. At an early age, he embarked on a military career. Later, he was transferred to America. Upon retirement, he settled upon a forty-acre tract of land which had been awarded to him by the Spanish government in consideration for his services in the army. This forty-acre grant was located on the south side of the Rio Grande, approximately four miles east of the church in El Paso del Norte, and one mile west of the San Lorenzo church. Juan Ascarate became a prominent stock raiser and one of the wealthiest and most influential citizens of the El Paso area. He died intestate at his hacienda, which was located on his forty-acre grant, in 1851, at the age of seventy-five. He was survived by his five sons and one daughter — Jacinto, Ygnacio, Anastacio, Cristobal, Geronimo and Juana. *An Illustrated History of New Mexico*

(Chicago, 1895), 473. *Caveat:* Anecious Ascarate is the name given in the biographical sketch of S. P. Ascarate found on Page 473 of *An Illustrated History of New Mexico*, but this is undoubtedly an error or another of Juan Ascarate's names, for it is well known that Juan Ascarate had six children — five boys and one girl — one of which was Anastacio Ascarate, the father of S. P. Ascarate.

Jacinto Ascarate and his brother, Cristobal, owned extensive cattle ranches and silver mining interests at Janos and Casas Grandes in the State of Chihuahua, Mexico. Jacinto Ascarate was killed by lightning at El Paso del Norte a few years after the death of his father. He was survived by his wife, Dolores Carbajal, and two children, María Ascarate de Bermudez and Manuel Ascarate. *Ibid.; El Paso Times*, July 3 and 10, 1949; and Affidavits of José María Gonzáles and Juan Serveriano, contained in Crosby v. Cadwallader and Bros. (Records of the El Paso District Clerk's Office, El Paso, Texas), No. 832.

8 H. P. N. Gammel, *The Laws of Texas*, IV, 1027.

9 *Deed Records* (Mss., Records of the County Clerk's Office, El Paso, Texas), "A" 527. This instrument is highly suspect for two reasons. First, it seems improbable that Juan and Jacinto Ascarate were illiterate, as suggested by the deed. If the affidavit executed by Juan María Gonzáles is to be believed, then neither Juan nor Jacinto Ascarate could have executed this instrument. It will be recalled that Gonzáles stated that Juan Ascarate had died in 1851, and his son Jacinto had been killed a few years later by lightning in El Paso del Norte. *Letter File 194001½* (Mss., Records of the General Land Office, Austin, Texas).

10 Bexar 1-1390 (Mss., Records of the General Land Office, Austin, Texas).

11 *Book of Field Notes* (Mss., Records of El Paso County Surveyor's Office, El Paso, Texas), A-1, 160.

12 Bexar 1-1390 (Mss., Records of the General Land Office, Austin, Texas).

13 Wylie v. Wynne, 26 Tex. 43 (1861).

14 Bexar B-1350 (Records of the General Land Office, Austin, Texas.

15 H. P. N. Gammel, *The Laws of Texas*, I, 1450.

16 Bexar D-1034 (Mss., Records of the General Land Office, Austin, Texas).

17 H. P. N. Gammel, *The Laws of Texas*, IV, 53.

18 Bexar 1-1499 (Mss., Records of the General Land Office, Austin, Texas).

19 Bexar 1-1390 (Mss., Records of the General Land Office, Austin, Texas).

20 *Deed Records* (Mss., Records of the El Paso County Clerk's Office, El Paso, Texas), XXV, 6. It is noted that the most easterly line of Randolph's survey of the Ascarate Grant is located 382 varas east of the projected east line of the Thos. H. Duggan Survey No. 12. Mills had located the east line of the Ascarate Grant along and north of the east line of said Duggan Survey No. 12.

21 Dunn v. Wing, 128 S.W. 108 (1910).

22 New York & Texas Land Co., Limited v. Thomson, 17 S.W. 920 (1891). This case holds that a call contained in an office survey for a natural or artificial object must yield to the surveyor's intention when it is clearly shown that he was mistaken as to true location of such object. It is also well established that a call for a line or corner of another survey, made under a misapprehension as to the true location of such survey, will not control as to the location of the survey calling for such corner or line. Hamilton v. Texas, 152 S.W. 1117 (1913). The contention urged by the inhabitants of the Town of Ysleta is very convincing if the direction of the calls contained in the Relinquishment Act of January 21, 1854, as amended by the Act of February 15, 1858, are reversed. By reversing the calls in the opposite direction, the boundaries of the tract relinquished by these

Acts would run north from the point where the west line of the Ysleta Grant intersects the north bank of the Rio Grande to the northwest corner of the Ysleta Grant; thence west along the north line of the Senecú Grant to the supposed east line of the Thos H. Duggan Survey No. 12; thence south with the west line of the Senecú Grant and the presumed location of the east line of the Thos. H. Duggan Survey No. 12 to the north bank of the Rio Viejo; and thence up the Rio Viejo to its junction with the Rio Grande; and thence down the Rio Grande to the point of beginning. The United States Supreme Court has recognized the reversing of calls when by so doing, the true boundaries of a tract can be better ascertained. New York & Texas Land Co., Limited v. Votaw, 150 U.S. 22 (1893).

23 Josiah F. Crosby and Horace F. Stephenson acquired an undivided two-thirds interest in the grant from Juan and Jacinto Ascarate by Warranty Deed dated December 13, 1858. *Deed Records* (Mss., Records of the El Paso County Clerk's Office, El Paso, Texas), A, 527.

24 Crosby v. Cadwallader and Bros., (Mss., Records of the District Clerk's Office, El Paso, Texas), No. 832.

25 *Ibid.*

26 *Ibid.*

27 The Tays subdivision of the Ysleta lands embraced two classes of surveys. The surveys lying between the Rio Grande and the edge of the sandhills were called "Valley Surveys." The portion of the Ysleta lands lying north of the foothills were referred to as the "Hill Surveys" of "Wood Grants." There were 110 Hill Surveys in the Senecú Grant and a like number in the Ysleta Grant. Each Hill Survey contained less than 24 acres, and was along a narrow strip of land approximately 1/16th of a mile wide and half a mile long. As a general rule, each person who received a Valley Survey also received a Hill Survey. The Hill Surveys were primarily used for the purpose of gathering mesquite roots for firewood

28 Crosby v. Di Palma, 141 S.W. 321 (1911).

29 *Minute Book* (Records of the District Clerk's Office, El Paso, Texas), XX, 203.

30 Stevens v. Crosby, 166 S.W. 62 (1914). It is noted that the lands involved in this suit were located west of the Senecú Grant, and the issue in the case involved only the true location of the Rio Viejo with reference to the lands in controversy.

31 *Minutes of the Commissioner's Court* (Mss., Records of the El Paso County Clerk's Office, El Paso, Texas), XIV, 6, 14.

CHAPTER 18

The Senecú Grant ॐ

• To ACCOMMODATE the Piro and Tompiro Indians, who had remained
loyal during the Pueblo Revolt of 1680 the Pueblo de Senecú[1] was formed
in 1682 by Governor Antonio de Otermín. It was originally located two
leagues east of El Paso del Norte, but was moved a league further east
when the El Paso Valley settlements were re-organized by Governor
Jironza Petriz de Cruzate in 1684. The valley soon developed into the
garden spot of the Southwest as a result of the perfection of an efficient
irrigation system that permitted the tilling of the soil independent of the
limited rainfall of that semi-desert region. Except for an avulsive south-
ward change in the course of the Rio Grande in 1831 or 1832, which placed
Senecú north of the river, few changes occurred in living conditions at the
pueblo prior to the coming of the railroad. Its sedentary inhabitants naturally were close and loved the rich land which provided their livelihood.

It would appear that the Spanish government had made a grant prior
to 1754 to the Pueblo de Senecú, since Father Trigo stated, on July 23,
1754, that the Indians of Senecú all had their vineyards.[2] While no Spanish
document is now in existence evidencing the original grant to the inhabitants of the Pueblo de Senecú, tradition says that such a grant did
exist. According to this tradition, the grant consisted of all the lands lying
within the area of one league in each of the four cardinal directions from
the door of the church, or a total of four square leagues of land. The only
condition which was allegedly imposed upon the grant was that the pueblo
could not sell or dispose of its lands without the consent of the sovereign.[3]
Such a grant would have been made in accordance with the Royal cédulas
dated June 4, 1687 and October 15, 1713.[4]

Several Mexican documents tend to substantiate the tradition that an
authentic Spanish grant had been made in favor of the inhabitants of the
Pueblo de Senecú. On February 18, 1823, the Ayuntamiento of the Pueblo
of San Lorenzo del Real petitioned the Provincial Deputation of New
Mexico, and requested that it be granted certain lands belonging to the
Pueblo de Senecú, which were surplus and abandoned.[5] While this instrument does not describe the lands in question, nor is there any evidence
that any action was taken on the petition, it indicates that the local Mexican
officials recognized that the Pueblo de Senecú owned the lands surrounding the Mission of San Antonio de Senecú. Less than two years later, the
boundaries of the Pueblo of Ysleta were surveyed by the Alcalde of El

Paso del Norte, Felix Pasos, and Father Sebastián Alvarez, in compliance with a Decree by the *ad interim* Governor of the State of Chihuahua, and in accordance with the instructions given by the Consulting Committee of Colonization, dated August 24, 1824. The survey[6] of the common boundary between Ysleta and Senecú was commenced on February 7, 1825, at:

a point called Loma del Negro, a terminal point known in antiquity that divides the towns, and all parties having agreed to take the measure, they commenced said measurement from South to North . . . from the Cerrito Colorado and passing the place of Loma del Apodaca, Loma del Negro, and crossing the river opposite the Loma del Tigua, where this Loma is 300 varas below where the measurement terminated being 9,900 varas, leaving the Pueblo of Senecú on the west side.

The Ysleta-Senecú boundary line was re-established and monumented as a straight line extending between a point 300 varas west of the Loma del Tigua and Cerrito Colorado on February 13, 1839, by the Alcaldes of both pueblos. The officials of both towns also agreed that the inhabitants of Ysleta, who had acquired land within the limits of the Pueblo de Senecú, by inheritance or purchase, would not lose their status as residents of the Pueblo of Ysleta by living upon such lands.[7] Although the boundary between the Pueblos of Ysleta and Senecú had been carefully located and monumented, the inhabitants of the Pueblo de Ysleta frequently challenged the correctness of the resurvey of 1829. To finally settle the controversy, Colonel José María Elías Gonzáles, Prefect of the District of El Paso, pursuant to Article 77 of the Act of March 20, 1837,[8] called a hearing on June 21, 1841, and ordered both villages to present their title papers, in order that he might establish their true common boundary line. The citizens of Ysleta presented their *testimonio,* while the inhabitants of Senecú produced a certified copy of their grant papers. One of the documents included among the Pueblo de Senecú grant papers was the field notes of a survey of the Senecú Grant which was made on November 1, 1828 by Alcalde Felix Pasos and Father Sebastián Alvarez, which described its eastern boundary as an easterly curved line running between Cerrito Colorado and a point 300 varas west of the Loma del Tigua. The Ysletans contended that the boundary commenced at a small red hill located a short distance west of Cerrito Colorado and ran north in a straight line to the point west of the Loma del Tigua. After a great deal of debate, the representatives of both pueblos compromised their differences and agreed that the southern corner of their common boundary line should be located on an intermediate hill between the two in question. Once the southern terminus had been agreed upon, Colonel Gonzáles caused a smoke signal to be raised at the northeast corner of the Senecú Grant, 300 varas west of the Loma del Tigua. Then, using a transit, he surveyed and marked the boundary line running between these two points.[9] If the Pueblo de Senecú had not received a formal grant from either the Spanish or Mexican governments, it would appear that these repeated acts of recognition would create an incipient or equitable title,[10] which deserved recognition. The *testimonio* and certified copy of the grant or grants to the Pueblo de Senecú were allegedly lost sometime prior to 1868, but it was believed that Antonio Miguel Lobato, of Bernalillo County, New Mexico, had somehow obtained possession thereof following the Civil War.[11]

Prior to the sudden change in the course of the Rio Grande, which occurred in 1831 or 1832, a majority of the Senecú lands were situated on the south side of the river. Only a small portion of the grant, which consisted of rolling sand hills and was used primarily as a pasturage and to gather mesquite roots for firewood, was located north of the river. The shifting of the river divided the grant into approximately equal parts and even threatened to destroy the Pueblo de Senecú. Shortly thereafter, the town was moved to a more favorable location about one thousand yards south of its original site.[12]

Following the flood which occurred in the early 1830's, the Rio Grande flowed primarily through its new channel; however, the old riverbed, or the Rio Viejo, carried a large amount of water when the river rose to flood stage. Therefore, a large portion of the north half of the Senecú Grant was located on the eastern portion of the twenty-mile long island lying between the Rio Viejo and Rio Grande. Shortly after the spring flood of 1849 abated, water ceased flowing through the Rio Viejo, thus leaving the island attached to Texas. The International Boundary Commission formally established the boundary between the United States and Mexico in the middle of the principal stream of the Rio Grande in 1852, pursuant to the terms of the Treaty of Guadalupe Hidalgo.

Since there were no Mexican settlements immediately east of the Pueblo de Senecú, Mexico placed all of the residents and lands formerly belonging to the Pueblos de Ysleta and Socorro, together with those of the Presidio de San Elizario, under the jurisdiction of the Pueblo de Senecú. Notwithstanding acquisition of such additional lands, the inhabitants of the Pueblo de Senecú continued to claim and use its grant land lying north of the river.

In retaliation for the granting of its lands lying in Mexico to the Pueblo de Senecú, the inhabitants of the Pueblo de Ysleta seized the portion of the Senecú Grant lying between the Rio Viejo and the Rio Grande. The Pueblo de Senecú promptly filed a trespass to try title suit in the District Court of El Paso County, Texas, to regain possession of all of its lands located in Texas.[13] The Pueblo de Senecú undoubtedly contended that title to its lands which were located within the State of Texas was protected by the Treaty of Guadalupe Hidalgo. In order to determine the extent and location of the lands in question, the District Court, on September 29,

1852, directed W. L. Diffenderfer, District Surveyor for the El Paso District, to survey same. Acting pursuant to this order, Diffenderfer made the following survey on January 10, 1853 of the one league, 15 labors, and 204.5 acres — or a total of 7,289.8 acres of land — covering that portion of the Senecú Grant lying north of the river:

Beginning at a stake on the bank of the Rio Grande about 1,500 varas due south of the western edge of the town of Isleta (sic.), said stake bears south 54¾° east 17,960 varas from the lower corner of Survey No. 1 as made by Robert B. Hayes; thence north 16° east 7,290 varas to a stake and stone heap from which a very high sand hill bears east 300 varas; thence north 54½° west 8,270 varas to a high sand hill known by the name of Loma Granado, on which there is a stone and mesquite tree; thence south 9½° west 3,970 varas to a stake set on the bank of the Rio Grande; thence down the Rio Grande with its meanders 10,993 varas to the place of beginning.

This survey was designated as Survey No. 39 in Section 1 of El Paso County, Texas.[14]

Fearing that the District Court might recognize the Pueblo de Senecú's title, the Ysletans caused a petition to be presented to the Fifth Legislature of the State of Texas by their Senator, Rufus Doane, on November 10, 1853, requesting the State to relinquish to them a certain tract of land adjoining the Ysleta Town Tract.[15]

The petition was referred to the Senate's Committee on Public Lands. This committee recommended passage of the bill, which provided for the relinquishment ". . . to the inhabitants of Ysleta a certain tract of land adjoining the town tract and how held and owned by said inhabitants."[16] The bill was referred to the House of Representatives on December 14, 1853,[17] where it was sponsored by Josiah F. Crosby, Representative for El Paso and Presidio Counties.[18] The House passed the bill, and it was signed by Governor E. M. Pease on January 31, 1854. This Special Act[19] relinquished to the inhabitants of the Town of Ysleta all rights vested in the State to the following described tract of land:

Commencing at the northwest corner of the town tract of Ysleta on the Rio Grande; thence up said river with its meanders to the point where the Rio Grande and the Rio Viejo separate; thence down the east bank of the Rio Viejo, to the southwest corner of survey number twelve, located in the name of T. H. Duggan; thence north with the east line of said survey to where it crosses the north line of the Cinecú tract; thence east with the north line of the Cinecú tract to the northwest corner of the Ysleta tract; thence along said line to the place of beginning, supposed to contain about two leagues.

This act expressly recognized that the citizens of the Town of Ysleta had been deprived of a large portion of the land granted to them by Spain. Thus, it may be assumed that the act was passed in order to compensate the Ysletans for such loss. The act directed the Commissioner of the

General Land Office to issue a patent covering said land to the Inhabitants of Ysleta; provided, however, it was not to be construed as adversely affecting any vested rights within the tract belonging to any individual. Texas took the position that since it had not been a Mexican territory within the meaning of the Treaty of Guadalupe Hidalgo,[20] it could not ignore the Senecú Grant and assume complete control over the disposition of the unappropriated portions thereof located within its borders.[21]

The Texas Supreme Court, in passing upon the eleven-league tract which had been granted to the inhabitants of the Mission of San José on November 18, 1766 by the Viceroy of New Spain, with the consent of the Royal Audiencia, had held that a grant to Mission Indians which could not be sold or alienated without the consent of the government, created only a tenancy at will. Such a grant was merely a usufruct, which could be terminated at the prerogative of the sovereign.[22]

After passage of the Act of January 31, 1854, the suit instituted by the inhabitants of the Pueblo de Senecú was apparently dismissed.

Since the Texas Legislature had relinquished all of the State's interest in the two leagues described in the Act of January 31, 1854 and had instructed the Commissioner of the General Land Office to issue a patent to such land, the inhabitants of Ysleta were not required to furnish an accurate survey of the tract. The General Land Office apparently caught the erroneous call for the southwest corner of the T. H. Duggan Survey No. 12 contained in description set out in the act and postponed the patenting of the tract, pending the correction of the mistake. On February 15, 1858 an act rectified this minor error.[23] Two days later Governor H. R. Runnels issued a patent to the Inhabitants of Ysleta covering the land described in the amendatory act.[24]

The Inhabitants of the Pueblo de Senecú filed a second suit against the Ysletans in the District Court of El Paso County, Texas during the month of September, 1859. By the suit, they sought to have the patent dated February 17, 1858 recalled, to secure recognition of their claim, and to obtain an injunction restraining the citizens of Ysleta from molesting or anywise interfering with their use of the lands covered by the Senecú Grant situated north of the Rio Grande.[25] The defendants apparently filed an answer to the plaintiffs' petition, but no further action was taken in the controversy due to the outbreak of the Civil War. After the war was over, the suit was dismissed for want of prosecution.

On January 13, 1870 the Pueblo de Senecú filed a claim for damages against the United States before the Joint Commission of the United States and Mexico under the Treaty of July 4, 1868.[26] In this action, the claimant alleged that, as a corporate body under the laws of the Republic of Mexico, it had sustained damages to the extent of $68,560 as a result of the State of Texas having illegally deprived it of its lands by issuing the patent dated

February 17, 1858. The damages represented the two leagues of land which had been taken, plus the timber located thereon. The land allegedly was worth $3 an acre, or $34,500, and the timber was value at $34,060.

The principal issue considered by the Joint Commission was whether or not the damages resulting from the granting of the land to the inhabitants of Ysleta was an injury which would entitle the claimant to redress through the diplomatic negotiations under the convention. In its opinion dated July 13, 1870, the Joint Commission held that the inhabitants of Ysleta had acquired the land under color of title, but that the patent conveyed only the interest owned by the state; and therefore, the Pueblo de Senecú had not been divested of any rights which were protected by the Treaty of Guadalupe Hidalgo, or the concepts of International Law. The Joint Commission further pointed out that the Pueblo de Senecú could establish its claim or right to damages, if any, in the appropriate courts of Texas.[27]

Following the Joint Commission's advice, the Pueblo de Senecú instituted a new trespass to try title suit against the Corporation of Ysleta[28] in the District Court of El Paso County, Texas, on October 2, 1871.[29] The defendant answered by alleging that it had acquired title to the land in question by limitation. The jury found for the defendant, and confirmed the Town of Ysleta's title as patented.[30]

Once title had been finally cleared of the cloud cast by the Pueblo de Senecú claim, the inhabitants of Ysleta clamored for issuance of title to their respective tracts, pursuant to the twenty-fourth section of the Act of May 9, 1871. This section[31] provided:

the town council shall have the power . . . to grant or sell portions of real estate, the property of said town Ysleta, to any of the following person or persons, and to no other: First, to actual settlers on said land who are citizens of the Town of Ysleta; second, to any person or company for the erection of building to be used for mechanical or manufacturing purposes, or for the building of railroad depots or workshops; provided, that the land granted or sold shall not exceed the quantity to be actually covered by the erection of said buildings; third, to any person or persons who may desire to become citizens of Ysleta, and who shall become actual settlers on the land sold or granted.

The twenty-fifth section of said Act required any qualified person who desired to purchase or obtain a grant of land within the corporate limits of the Town of Ysleta[32] to file an application with the town council in the following form:[33]

To the town council of the Town of Ysleta, Texas:

Your petitioner (or petitioners) respectfully pray that the following described tract of land, situated within the corporate limits of Ysleta, be sold (or granted) to him by your honorable body.

(Here must follow a correct description of the land.)
Your petitioner desires to use said land for the following purposes:
(Here follows the purposes for which the petitioners desire the lands.)

(Signed)

In order to assist its inhabitants in making their applications, the town council of the town of Ysleta retained County Surveyor Joseph Wilkin Tays to survey the boundaries of the lands owned by the town of Ysleta and locate the individual tracts located therein which were then used and occupied by its inhabitants. Tays first surveyed the exterior boundaries to the two tracts relinquished to the Inhabitants of the Town of Ysleta in 1854. The Tays survey[34] was made during the summer of 1873, and covered the following described lands located in El Paso County, Texas:

Beginning on the bank of the Rio Grande where the boundary lines of the towns of Socorro and Ysleta intersect said river; thence North 21¾° East 2,670 varas; thence North 48½° East 1,450 varas; thence North 37½° East 3,020 varas; thence North 70¾° East 940 varas; thence North 42½° West 8,590 varas; thence North 54½° West 8,270 varas to Loma Granado; thence South 9½° West to the North bank of the Rio Viejo; thence up the Rio Viejo to its junction with the Rio Grande; thence down the Rio Grande to the place of Beginning.

By running his initial line in a northeasterly direction from the beginning point, instead of up the Rio Grande, Tays was able to avoid the ambiguous call contained in the Relinquishment Act of January 31, 1854, as amended by the Act of February 15, 1858, to the southeast corner of the T. H. Duggan Survey No. 12. It is obvious that Tays made his survey in this manner in order to include that portion of the Senecú Grant lying north of the Rio Viejo within the tract relinquished to the Inhabitants of the Town of Ysleta by Patent of February 17, 1858. However, by doing so, he created a conflict between his survey and the Ascarate Grant.

The Tays survey effected a merger of the two tracts owned by the Inhabitants of the Town of Ysleta into a single unit thereafter known as the Public Lands of Ysleta. The execution of the Tays survey, for all practical purposes, marks the end of the history of the Senecú Grant. The subsequent history of the lands covered thereby is continued as a part of the Ysleta lands. However, it should be pointed out that the portion of the Senecú Grant lying north of the Rio Viejo generally has been treated as being a portion of the Ascarate Grant.

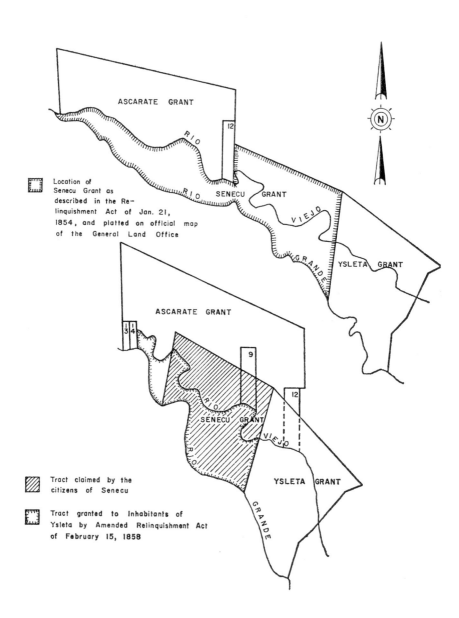

REFERENCES

1 The Pueblo de Senecú is sometimes called Senecú del Sur. Senecú is also sometimes spelled Cinecú, Cenecú, Zinecú and Sinecú.

2 Charles Wilson Hackett, *Historical Documents Relating to New Mexico, Nueva Vizcaya and Approaches Thereto, to 1773,* (3 Vols., Washington, D.C., 1937), III, 460. Prior to the conquest of the Southwest, the Pueblo Indians developed a system of land tenure which was accepted and respected by the Spaniards. Therefore, these settlements were neither religious nor civil pueblos. They were unique Indian Pueblos. Under the Indian Pueblo system of land tenure, the interest of a pueblo in its land grant amounts to little more than the right to distribute tracts among its inhabitants, all undistributed lands being held in trust by the pueblos for the benefit of its inhabitants. William M. McKinney, *Texas Jurisprudence,* (45 Vols., San Francisco, 1934), XXXIV, 311-312.

3 Petition by the Pueblo de Cenecú in the case *Pueblo de Cenecú v. United States, Cause No. 120, before the Joint Commission of the United States and Mexico under the Treaty of July 4, 1868,* (Mss., Records of the General Services Administration, Washington, D.C.), Record Group 76.

4 Marqués de Falcés, Viceroy of New Spain, issued an ordinance on May 24, 1567, by which he ordered that each Indian Pueblo be given a grant of land consisting of all the lands within an area of five hundred varas in each direction from the pueblo's church or public house. By Royal Cédula dated June 4, 1687, King Carlos II increased the size of pueblo grants. The boundaries under this decree were to be located six hundred varas from the last house in each of the cardinal directions of the settlement, instead of from the church. Ralph Emerson Twitchell, *The Spanish Archives of New Mexico* (2 Vols., Cedar Rapids, 1914), I, 475-477.

On October 15, 1713 King Philip V issued a decree, directing the Viceroy of New Spain to protect the civil liberties of the Pueblo Indians and to provide them "sufficient water, land and timber entrances and exits; for cultivation, be given to the settlements and towns (pueblos) of Indians which may be formed; and a common of one league, where they can pasture their cattle, without their being mixed with those of the Spaniards." *House Executive Documents,* 34th Cong., 3rd Sess., Document No. 1, 519-520. This plan for the establishment of Pueblos became Law 8, Title 3, Book 6, of the *Recopilación de Leyes de los Reynos las Indias.* The amount of land to be given to pueblos under this law is not clear, but it is generally interpreted to mean a league in each direction. After Mexico gained its independence, it adopted the Spanish Pueblo Plan.

The courts originally held that once legally formed, each town and pueblo automatically became entitled to four square leagues of land. Stevenson v. Bennett, 35 Cal. 424 (1868); and San Francisco v. LeRoy, 138 U.S. 656 (1891). Based upon these decisions, four square leagues became the accepted size of town and pueblo grants. However, in 1896, the United States Supreme Court — in United States v. Santa Fe, 165 U.S. 675 (1897) — held that "the Spanish law did not, *proprio vigore,* confer upon every Spanish villa or town a grant of four leagues of land, to be measured from the center of the plaza of such town." It is, therefore, important to recognize that there is a legal distinction between pueblos established for Christianized Indians and towns founded primarily for Spaniards.

5 Archives of New Mexico (Mss., Records of the New Mexico Museum, Santa Fe, New Mexico), Document No. 253. This statement is undoubtedly true, for the population of this pueblo had shrunk from 646 persons in 1760 to approximately 80 persons in 1850.

Eleanor B. Adams, *Bishop Tamarón's Visitation of New Mexico, 1760* (Albuquerque, 1954), 38; and John Russell Bartlett, *Personal Narrative* (2 Vols., London, 1854), I, 149.

6 *Deed Records* (Mss., Records of the County Clerk's Office, El Paso, Texas), B, 24.

7 *Ibid.* This instrument would indicate that portions of Senecú Grant had been distributed among its inhabitants. It is well settled that the officers of a pueblo had authority to distribute pueblo lands for building and agricultural purposes. Pence v. Cobb, 155 S.W. 608 (1913). The following statement by George Frederick Ruxton also indicates that the lands between El Paso del Norte and San Elizario had been distributed. He states that the entire valley was "A continued line of adobe houses, with their plots of garden and vineyard. The farms seldom contain more than twenty ocres, each family having a separate house and plot of land." George F. Ruxton, *Adventures in Mexico and the Rocky Mountains* (New York, 1848), 170-171.

8 This article provides that Prefects shall regulate administratively the distribution of the common lands in towns of the districts. Mathew G. Reynolds, *Spanish and Mexican Land Laws* (St. Louis, 1895), 221.

9 *Deed Records* (Mss., Records of the El Paso County Clerk's Records, El Paso, Texas), D, 392. The reference in this instrument to the field notes of November 1, 1828 would tend to indicate that a confirmation grant may have been issued to the Pueblo de Senecú on or about November 1, 1828.

10 Town of Refugio v. Byrne, 25 Tex. 193 (1860). It is clear from the tenor of Spanish and Mexican Laws that Indians were entitled, in equity and good conscience, and even according to the strict vigor of the Laws, to all of the lands which they held for cultivation, pasture or habitation, when such domain could be ascertained to have had any tolerably well defined boundaries. Frederic Hall, *The Laws of Mexico* (San Francisco, 1895), 61-62.

11 *Petition by the Pueblo de Cenecú in the case Pueblo de Cenecú v. United States, Cause No. 120, before the Joint Commission of the United States and Mexico under the Treaty of July 4, 1868* (Mss., Records of the General Services Administration, Washington, D.C.), Record Group 76.

12 *Ibid.*

13 All of the records of the District Court of El Paso County, Texas for the period prior to the Civil War have been lost. Therefore, none of the papers filed in connection with this suit are now available.

14 *Transcribed Records* (Mss., Records of the El Paso County Surveyor's Office, El Paso, Texas), A-31.

15 *Journal of the Senate of the State of Texas, Fifth Legislature* (Austin, 1854), 32.

16 *Ibid.*, 148.

17 *Journal of the House of Representatives of the State of Texas, Fifth Legislature* (Austin, 1854), 235.

18 *Ibid.*, 290.

19 H. P. N. Gammel, *The Laws of Texas* (10 Vols., Austin, 1898), IV, 42-43. The initial call for the northwest corner of the Ysleta Town Tract on the Rio Grande is obviously erroneous, and should call for the survey to commence at either the point where the west line of the Ysleta Town Tract intersects the Rio Grande River, or the southwest corner of the Ysleta Town Tract. The call for the "southwest corner" of the T. H. Duggan Survey No. 12 is also obviously a typographical error, and should have read "southeast corner." This error was corrected by an act passed by the Seventh Legislature on February 15, 1858, by amending the description of the concession, in order to call

for the "southeast corner" of the T. H. Duggan Survey No. 12. *Ibid.*, IV, 1094. However, even with this change, the description of the lands covered by this Legislative grant is defective. The Legislature apparently believed that the east line of the T. H. Duggan Survey No. 12 and the northern portion of the west line of the Senecú Grant were common. This misconception was depicted on maps of El Paso County as late as 1879. *House Executive Documents*, 45th Cong., 2nd Sess., Doc. No. 93, Appendix F, No. 3. The T. H. Duggan Survey No. 12 is located east of the northwest corner of the Ysleta Grant. *El Paso County, General Land Office, June, 1921* (Mss., Official County Maps of the General Land Office, Austin, Texas).

20 McKinney v. Saviego, 18 How. (59 U.S.), 235 (1856).

21 Board of School Trustees of the City of San Antonio v. G.H.&S.A. Ry. Co., 67 S.W. 147 (1902).

22 McMullen v. Hodge, 5 Tex. 33 (1849).

23 H. P. N. Gammel, *The Laws of Texas*, IV, 1094.

24 *Deed Records*, (Mss., Records of the El Paso County Clerk's Office, El Paso, Texas), B, 22.

25 Pueblo de Senecú v. The Inhabitants of Ysleta (Mss., Records of the District Clerk's Office, El Paso, Texas), No. 46. The papers filed in connection with this suit have been lost, but a copy of the order of dismissal may be found in the papers pertaining to Pueblo de Senecú v. The Inhabitants of Ysleta (Mss., Records of the District Clerk's Office, El Paso, Texas), No. 99.

26 The Pueblo de Senecú v. The United States, No. 120, before the Joint Commission of the United States and Mexico under the Treaty of July 4, 1868 (Mss., Records of the General Services Administration, Washington, D.C.), Record Group 76.

27 *Ibid.*

28 The Pueblo de Ysleta was incorporated as a body corporate under the name of the Town of Ysleta by an Act of the Texas Legislature dated May 9, 1871. H. P. N. Gammel, *The Laws of Texas*, VI, 1435.

29 Pueblo de Senecú v. Corporation of Ysleta (Mss., Records of the District Clerk's Office, El Paso, Texas), No. 99.

30 *Minute Book* (Mss., Records of the District Clerk's Office, El Paso, Texas), A-2, 72.

31 H. P. N. Gammel, *The Laws of Texas*, VI, 1435.

32 The corporate limits of the Town of Ysleta were defined in the Act of May 9, 1871 as: Commencing at the northwest corner of the Socorro Grant, on the Rio Grande; thence up the Rio Grande with its meanderings, to the point where the Rio Grande and River Viejo separate; thence down the east bank of the River Viejo, with its meanderings, to the southeast corner of Survey No. 12; thence north with the east line of Survey No. 12 to where it crosses the northern line of the Senecú Tract; thence southeast along the line of hills to the northeast corner of the Socorro Grant; thence along the northern boundary of the Socorro Grant to the place of beginning. *Ibid.* The description of the corporate limits will not close, since Survey No. 12 was actually located east of the east line of the Senecú Tract. However, at the time of the passage of this Act, it was generally believed that the Senecú Tract was situated immediately east of said Survey No. 12.

33 *Ibid.*

34 *Deed Records* (Mss., Records of the County Clerk's Office, El Paso, Texas), B-3, 67.

CHAPTER 19

The Ysleta Grant ᏋᏇ

• THE PROMINENCE of the Pueblo de Ysleta as the oldest permanent settlement in the State of Texas causes its land grant to be particularly interesting. It was founded by Governor Antonio de Otermín in the spring of 1682 as a refuge for the three hundred and five Tigua Indians from Isleta, New Mexico, who returned with him following his unsuccessful expedition into New Mexico in 1681-1682. Early records indicate that the Pueblo de Ysleta was originally located one league south of the Rio Grande and about three and a half leagues east of El Paso del Norte, but was moved a half league further east in 1684, when the El Paso District was re-organized by Governor Otermín's successor, Don Domingo Jironza Petriz de Cruzate.[1]

Records concerning the Pueblo de Ysleta during the first half of the Eighteenth Century are vague and sketchy; however, they reflect the development of a sedentary society centered around the Mission of San Antonio de Ysleta.[2]

In 1749 Fray Andrés Varo sent a secret report to the Viceroy which was extremely critical of the civil government of New Mexico. This report was so violent that the Viceroy sent Juan Antonio de Ordenal to New Mexico to investigate and report on conditions in that province. Ordenal's report, in turn, was very critical of the local religious authorities, and recommended secularization of the missions.[3]

One of his principal charges was that the Indians bitterly complained that they were forced to labor for the missionaries and to plant and cultivate fields far in excess of that which was required for their support. He also pointed out that the friars frequently searched the homes of the Indians and seized any grain which they had stored there for their personal use. He recommended that the Indians be relieved of the yoke of excessive planting and be allowed to acquire grain, sheep, and other personal property.[4]

In 1750 Fray José Jimeno, Reverend Father Provincial of the Province of El Santo Evangelio, denied Ordenal's allegation that the Indians were being exploited, and, among other things, called the Viceroy's attention to the industriousness of the inhabitants of the four Indian missions in the El Paso Valley. He proudly noted the agricultural development of that area, and is probably the first official to mention the birth of the famous wine industry in the El Paso Valley. Jimeno especially calls attention to

the fact that the native parishioners of the pueblos had been fully domesti-
cated and were inclined to speak Spanish. The portion of his report concerning the description of living conditions in the frontier missions is
especially interesting. He states:

The missionary religious, since they entered those provinces, not only
have labored and are laboring in teaching and instructing the Indians in
our holy Catholic faith and the spiritual life, but also in things for main-
taining corporal life, teaching them to cultivate the land, to plant fruits,
and to harvest their crops, the religious going so far as to take the plough
in their own hands, so that the Indians may learn more easily. Since those
early times, the Indians have observed the custom of planting a field which
they call the father's, which they took upon themselves voluntarily, and
which was very useful and advantageous to the Indians themselves, for
unless they had made this planting they would not have done their own,
as their indolence and little or no inclination for work will lead them to
perish of their own will, and it seems that the one planting accustoms,
disposes, and prepares them for the other. For that which they do for the
missionary religious, the Indians have the recompense of not having to pay
any charges on account of their administration, and the poor missionary
religious, unless he had, not an over-supply of corn and wheat, as the in-
formant says, but only what is necessary, and a small flock of lambs, would
not have the minimum indispensable for his support. From this, much
good results to the Indians, in spiritual matters as well as in corporal; in
the first, because, being diverted by work, they are removed from idleness
and the many sins that they would commit or vices to which they would
abandon themselves, for that same idleness is the mother of all, and experience has shown that when the Indians are without work to divert them,
they go to the mountains to hunt, a place where the common enemy re-
minds them of their former life.[5]

The quarrel between the religious and civil authorities, together with the
demands by the Pueblo Indians for reforms, undoubtedly influenced King
Ferdinand VI in reaching his decision to grant "a league of land"[6] to the
inhabitants of the Pueblo de Ysleta on March 3, 1751.[7]

The Ysletans jealously guarded their lands from continuous encroach-
ments by their neighbors. Since the pueblos in the El Paso Valley were
located so close to one another, there was little unappropriated agricultural
land available to accomodate natural expansion of the population of such
settlements.[8] Therefore, serious boundary disputes arose whenever the
spring freshets destroyed the monuments, demarking the common boundary lines between the Pueblos of Senecú, Ysleta, and Socorro. To alleviate
tensions which had built up between the Ysletans and their neighbors, the
ad interim Governor of the State of Chihuahua confirmed the Ysleta Grant,
and directed Felix Pasos, Alcalde of El Paso del Norte, and Father Sebastián Alvarez, priest for the Pueblos of Ysleta, Senecú, and Socorro, to re-
survey the boundaries of the Ysleta Grant in accordance with the instructions given them by the Committee of Colonization, dated August 24, 1824.

On February 6 ,1825 Pasos and Alvarez, together with the Umpires for the Pueblo de Ysleta and Socorro and several of the oldest citizens of said villages, assembled at a point near the Hermitage de San Miguel, which was the only point known and accepted without dispute to be on the common boundary between the two settlements. From this point, the surveying party proceeded to a little hill called Los Valencias, which was located north of both the Hermitage de San Miguel and the river. Los Valencias was located at the point of the Rincón de Antonio Marques and was close to the Cañada de Juan Antonio and the junction of the old and new rivers. All parties accepted this hill as being the northeast corner of the Ysleta Grant. The survey ran south from Los Valencias 10,111 varas to a clay hill called Loma del Barra, which was located on the edge of the glen called Cañada de Suma Muerto and close to the corner of the Rincón de Sopita. After completing the survey of this line, the Umpire of the Pueblo de Socorro protested on the grounds that the survey placed that certain willow grove known as El Sausal, which had belonged to the Pueblo de Socorro since time immemorial, within the boundaries of the Ysleta Grant. The Umpire for the Pueblo of Ysleta agreed that the willow grove should be excluded from their grant. Subject to this agreement, the survey of the eastern boundary of the Ysleta Grant was accepted by all of the interested parties. Turning west, the surveying party proceeded to survey the southern boundary of the Ysleta Grant. This line ran from Loma del Barra along the skirts of the foothills 4,070 varas to a hill known as Cerrito Colorado, which was near Salamayuca Spring. On the next day Alcalde Pasos and Father Alvarez met with the Umpires and representatives of the Pueblo de Ysleta and Senecú. The interested parties all agreed that the boundary line between the Pueblos de Ysleta and Senecú ran north from the Cerrito Colorado past Loma del Apodaca, Loma del Negro and the river, to a little hill located near the hill known as Loma del Tigua. In accordance with this understanding, the surveyors ran their third line in a northerly direction from Cerrito Colorado 9,900 varas to said hill, which was located 300 varas west of the Loma del Tigua. The final, or north line of the Ysleta Grant, was surveyed on the 8th of February. It ran east from the hill west of Loma del Tigua 10,592 varas along the edge of the desert to the point of beginning.[9]

In response to the *ad interim* governor's request, Pasos investigated the character and quality of the lands covered by the Ysleta Grant, and the extent of private ownership thereof. He reported that the land once had been good, but was then nearly worthless, on account of the numerous gullies which had been made by the frequent inundations of the river and the heavy impregnation of the soil with alkali. He also found that most of the land within the grant was privately owned, but that few of the inhabitants had received documents evidencing their titles. However, the boundaries of these individual tracts were well known. He reported that there were only three small pieces of unappropriated land within the grant, and there were no *ejidos* or common timber groves on the grant. Pasos concluded his report with a census of the pueblo, which showed that there were 55 Indian families, or a total of 226 Indians, and 72 Mexican citizens residing on the grant.[10]

On November 1, 1828 the common boundary between the Senecú and Ysleta Grants was re-surveyed by Alcalde Pasos and Father Alvarez as an easterly curved line extending between the Cerrito Colorado and a hill 300 varas west of Loma del Tigua. The inhabitants of the Pueblo de Ysleta contested this action. In an effort to settle the dispute, the line was re-established and monumented on February 13, 1829 as a straight line extending between the two recognized terminal points. However, even this re-survey did not end the controversy, and the inhabitants of the Pueblo de Ysleta continuously claimed that the boundary should have been located even farther west.

The persistency of this problem prompted Colonel José María Elías Gonzáles, Prefect of El Paso del Norte, to call a hearing on June 21, 1841, to determine the true location of the disputed boundary. The inhabitants of the Pueblo de Ysleta presented the *testimonio* evidencing their grant, and asserted that the boundary should be a straight line running between a red hill located west of the Cerrito Colorado and the hill 300 varas west of Loma del Tigua. After an extended argument, the interested parties compromised their differences by agreeing that the southern corner of their mutual boundary line should be located at an intermediate site. Once the southern terminus was agreed upon, the common boundary was surveyed and marked as a straight line connecting the new mutually accepted southern corner with the northern corner over which there was no dispute.[11]

The 1825 survey of the Ysleta Grant, as supplemented by the re-survey of 1841, temporarily settled the Pueblo de Ysleta's boundary problems; however, it was not long until the location of its southern boundary took on an international aspect. Since the Rio Grande had changed its course in 1831 or 1832, the Pueblos de Ysleta and Socorro and the Presidio de San Elizario were generally located north of the river. However, during the early 1850's, whenever the river rose, its waters would run in both its new and old channels, thereby forming a 20 mile long island, upon which those three ancient settlements were situated.[12] Pursuant to the terms of the Treaty of Guadalupe Hidalgo, the International Boundary between the United States and Mexico in the El Paso Valley was located in the middle of the principal stream of the Rio Grande. This portion of the International Boundary was separately surveyed in 1852 by M. Van Hippel for the United States, and Agustín Díaz for Mexico. Since there were minor variations in the surveys submitted by the two surveying parties resulting from slight shifts in the location of the river — the surveys having been made approximately six months apart — the Boundary Commission agreed to adopt the Díaz survey as the one which depicted the true location of the International Boundary.[13] The establishment of the International Boundary had a direct and substantial bearing on the history of the Ysleta Grant, for, as a result thereof, the grant was bisected almost in half, with only the northern portion being placed under the jurisdiction of Texas.

Shortly after establishment of the International Boundary, Mexico expropriated the portion of the Ysleta Grant lying south of the Rio Grande for the benefit of the inhabitants of the Pueblo de Senecú. The Ysletans in turn petitioned the Texas Legislature for confirmation of the remaining portion of their grant, and also for the relinquishment to them of the lands covered by the Senecú Grant lying north of the river, as compensation for the loss of the southern portion of their grant.[14] On November 10, 1853 Senator Rufus Doane presented the memorial of the Inhabitants of the Pueblo de Ysleta to the Senate.

The memorial was referred to the Senate's Committee on Private Land Claims,[15] which drafted two bills for the benefit of the citizens of the Town of Ysleta. The first was entitled "An Act for the relief of the inhabitants of the town of Ysleta, in the County of El Paso." This bill was designed to recognize and confirm the portion of the Ysleta Grant lying north of the river. The second was captioned "An Act to relinquish to the inhabitants of Ysleta in El Paso County, a certain tract of land adjoining the town tract now held and owned by said inhabitants." The purpose of this bill was to compensate the Ysletans for the portion of their lands which had been expropriated by Mexico. The Committee recommended passage of both bills.[16] Both bills passed the Senate and were forwarded to the House of Representatives on December 14, 1853.[17] They were referred to the House Committee on Private Land Claims. On January 21, 1854 it recommended passage of the bill which would relinquish to the Ysletans the tract which adjoined their town tract, but proposed an Amendment[18] to the Relief Act which would strike therefrom the third section, which read. "This act shall not be construed so as to affect any vested right now held to said tract by any person whatsoever."

This amendment was designed to defeat the claim of any former inhabitants of the Pueblo de Ysleta who had chosen to live south of the river to any of the lands covered by the Relief Act. The Relinquishment Act[19] passed the House of Representatives, and was signed by Governor E. M. Pease on January 31, 1854. It granted to the inhabitants of the Town of Ysleta:

all the right which is now vested in the State to the tract of land lying on the east side of the Rio Grande, above the town tract of Ysleta, which formerly belonged to the said inhabitants of Cenecú (sic.) commencing at the northwest corner of the town tract of Ysleta on the Rio Grande; thence up said river with its meanders to the point where the Rio Grande and the Rio Viejo separate; thence down the east bank of the Rio Viejo, to the southwest corner of survey number twelve, located in the name of T. H. Duggan; thence north with the east line of said survey to where it crosses the north line of the Cenecúe tract, to the northwest corner of the Ysleta tract; thence along said line to the place of beginning; supposed to contain about two leagues.

This tract is generally known as the "Inhabitants of Ysleta Grant." A few days later the Relief Act, as amended pursuant to the recommendation of the House's Committee on Private Land Claims, was passed by the House of Representatives. The amended bill was then referred back to the Senate, where it was engrossed. It was then referred to the Governor, who signed this Act on February 1, 1854. This Act[20] confirmed the Ysletans' title to the following described tract of land, which became known as the "Ysleta Town Tract":

Commencing on the Rio Grande, at a point where the established line of division between the towns of Socorro and Ysleta strikes the said river, for the southern boundary, and following said line to a point where it strikes the hills bordering on the east bank of the Rio Viejo; thence running northwest along said hills up the Rio Viejo to the southeast corner of the tract of land known as the Cenecú Tract; thence in a southwesterly direction along the line of said Cenecú tract to the Rio Grande; thence down the Rio Grande, to the place of beginning, containing one league, twenty-one labors, and ninety-one acres.

The Inhabitants of Ysleta Grant was patented to the Inhabitants of Ysleta on February 17, 1858, two days after the description of the lands granted by the Act of January 31, 1854 had been amended by a Special Act.[21]

Life in the El Paso Valley settlements retained much of its colorful Latin flavor until after the end of the Civil War. When the southern sympathizers withdrew from West Texas following the defeat of General H. H. Sibley in 1862, an economic and political depression was created in the El Paso area. Progress was not restored until March 3, 1871, when the Texas and Pacific Railroad Company was authorized by the United States Congress to construct a transcontinental railroad through the famous Paso del Norte.[22] During the next decade railroad construction brought numerous sudden and abrupt changes to the formerly isolated settlements huddled about the Pass. Perhaps the two most pronounced changes were an increase in land values and a demand for marketable land titles.

Ysleta came out of this financial doldrum in the early 1870's. On May 31, 1873 an Act was passed by the Texas Legislature, which provided that the permanent location of the County Seat of El Paso County should be determined by the qualified voters of the county.[23] An election was held on December 7, 1873, and by vote of 259 to 222, the County Seat was moved from San Elizario to Ysleta.[24] Thereafter, Ysleta steadily increased in size and importance. By 1880, it was the largest community in El Paso County, with a population of 1,453 persons.[25]

Since Ysleta was an incorporated village, the lands which had been granted to its inhabitants under the Acts of January 31 and February 1, 1854 could not be distributed among its occupants. To remedy this defect in their individual titles, the citizens of Ysleta procured passage of an Act by the Texas Legislature on May 9, 1871, incorporating their town under the name of "The Town of Ysleta."[26] Sections 24 and 26 of this Act authorized the Town Council to grant land to its inhabitants and issued valid deeds covering any lands so conveyed.[27]

To convey good title to the individual tracts of land occupied by its residents, it was obvious that the town should obtain a patent to the Ysleta Town Tract. Therefore, the Town Council requested the Commissioner of the General Land Office to issue a patent to such lands pursuant to the provisions of the second paragraph of the Act of February 1, 1854. It is not known why the Ysletans postponed their request for a patent to the Ysleta Town Tract for such a long period. In response to this request, a patent[28] was issued by Governor Edmond J. Davis to the Inhabitants of the Town of Ysleta on May 28, 1873, covering the following described land located in El Paso County, Texas:

Beginning at a point where the established line of division between the towns of Socorro and Ysleta strikes the said river for the southern boundary, and following said line as follows: N. 21½' E. 2,670 vrs; thence N. 48½° E. 1,450 vrs; thence N. 37° E. 3,020 vrs; thence N. 70¾° E. 940 vrs to a point where it strikes the hills bordering on the east bank of the Rio Viejo; thence running northwest along said hills up the Rio Viejo to the northeast corner of the tract known as the Cenecú tract; thence in a southwesterly direction along the line of said Cenecú tract to the Rio Grande; thence down the Rio Grande to the place of beginning.

After issuance of the patent to the Ysleta Town Tract, the citizens of Ysleta commenced petitioning the Town Council for the Individual tracts of land which they were claiming and occupying. Since the descriptions contained in such applications were generally written in vague terms, the Town Council recognized that an accurate survey of the exterior boundaries of Ysleta lands and the interior occupation lines was desirable. Therefore, the Town Council employed Joseph Wilkin Tays to conduct such a survey.

During the summer of 1873 Tays was busy surveying the Ysleta lands. His first step was to survey the boundaries of the two tracts granted to the inhabitants of the Town of Ysleta. His field notes[29] of the survey read as follows:

Beginning on the bank of the Rio Grande where the boundary line of the towns of Soccorro and Ysleta intersects said river; thence N. 21¾° E. 2,670 varas; thence N. 48½° E. 1,450 varas; thence N. 37½° E. 3,020 varas; thence N. 70½° E. 940 varas; thence N. 42½° W. 8,590 varas; thence N. 54½° W. 8,270 varas, Loma Granada; thence S. 9½° W. to the north bank of the Rio Viejo; thence up the Rio Viejo to its junction with the Rio Grande; and thence down the Rio Grande to the place of beginning.

Next he proceeded to survey the 220 occupied tracts of valley land located within the Ysleta lands. These tracts are called the "Valley Surveys." Tays concluded his work on August 21, 1873, after having subdivided all of the Ysleta lands situated north of the edge of the sand hills into 220 separate tracts called the "Hill Surveys." Each applicant was awarded the Valley Survey which he occupied, together with the correspondingly numbered Hill Survey.[30]

Since many of the deeds issued by the Towns of Ysleta, Socorro and San Elizario had been made without the strict compliance of all of the formalities specified in their respective charters, many title examiners questioned the validity of such conveyances. In order to cure such defects, the Texas Legislature passed a Special Relief Act on April 2, 1889, which validated all such instruments.[31]

The subdivision of the Ysleta lands would ordinarily be the logical place to terminate an historical account of the Ysleta Grant. However, there is one additional aspect of its history which should be discussed. This facet is the boundary dispute between the Ysleta Lands and the Ascarate Grant. The Ascarate Grant, as patented on September 14, 1886, conflicted with the northwestern portion of the Ysleta Lands, as surveyed by Joseph Wilkin Tays. Tays had interpreted the Relinquishment Act of January 31, 1854, as amended by the Act of February 15, 1858, as covering, among other lands, all of the Senecú Grant lying north of the Rio Viejo. In order for this interpretation to be calid, the call in the Relinquishment Act, as amended, for the southeast corner of the Thos. W. Duggan Survey No. 12 would have to be disregarded. The dispute was settled[32] when the El Paso Court of Civil Appeals held "that the east or north bank of the Rio Viejo is the dividing line between the Ascarate and Ysleta Grants eastward or downward from the junction of the new and old rivers."

The result of this judicial interpretation of boundaries of the two adjoining grants was that the Act of January 31, 1854, as amended, had not relinquished to the Inhabitants of the Town of Ysleta any of the lands formerly embraced within the Senecú Grant lying north of the Rio Viejo. However, since practically all of the land embraced within the portion of the Senecú Grant situated between the edge of the sand hills and the Rio Viejo had been adversely possessed for more than twenty-five years by a

number of Ysletans, the owners of the Ascarate Grant recognized the titles
which they had perfected by limitation. Thereafter, such lands have been
considered to be a portion of the Ysleta Lands.

Settlement of its northwestern boundary finally quieted title to the Ysleta
Lands, which are composed of portions of two of the three oldest continuously occupied tracts of land located in the State of Texas.

R E F E R E N C E S

1 Anne E. Hughes, *The Beginnings of Spanish Settlement in the El Paso District*, (El
Paso, 1935), 320-330; 366-368.

2 Fray Juan Alvarez, on January 12, 1706, states:
   In the Mission of San Antonio de la Ysleta, composed of Indians of the Tigua nation
who left this kingdom in the year 1680, Father Fray Juan de la Peña ministers. There
are many people. It has a church and a bell; the ornament is old and mended, and
there is an old missal — one of the very old ones. Charles Wilson Hackett, *Historical
Documents Relating to New Mexico, Nueva Vizcaya, and Approaches Thereto, to 1773*
(3 Vols., Washington, D.C., 1937), III, 377.
   On May 10, 1744 Fray Miguel de Menchero reports that:
   The Mission of San Antonio de la Isleta is one hundred and sixty leagues south (of
Santa Fe); it has ninety families, and is situated one league from the Rio del Norte. Its
mission is administered by a father who is building, by his own efforts, a very capacious
church which I do not doubt his faithful industry will bring to a conclusion. *Ibid.*,
III, 406.

3 *Ibid.*, III, 450. The only change which would have resulted from secularization of the
missions would have been the substitution of parish priests for the Franciscans. It must
be remembered that the New Mexican missions were radically different from those of
East Texas and California. The padres of New Mexico managed no mission estates.
Henry W. Kelly, "Franciscan Missions of New Mexico, 1740-1760," *New Mexico
Historical Review* (1940), XV, 364-365. The missions in the El Paso Valley followed
the New Mexico pueblo pattern of administration. Dr. Myra Ellen Jenkins to J.J.B.,
September 7, 1970. The El Paso Valley missions remained under the jurisdiction of
the Franciscans until 1817, when they were transferred to the secular authorities under
the Bishop of Durango. *Patentes* IX and *Accounts* LXXXII (Mss., Archives of the
Archdiocese of Santa Fe, New Mexico).

4 Charles Wilson Hackett, *Historical Documents Relating to New Mexico, Nueva Vizcaya, and Approaches Thereto, to 1773*, III, 446-448.

5 *Ibid.*, III, 446-447; 453.

6 The term "a league of land" as used in Spanish Pueblo Grants is a 4-league tract,
instead of a square league. Such grants were generally measured one league in each
direction from the church entrance. Herbert O. Brayer, *Pueblo Indian Land Grants of
the "Rio Abajo," New Mexico*, (Albuquerque, 1938), 13.

7 H. P. N. Gammel, *The Laws of Texas* (10 Vols., Austin, 1898), IV, 53; and *Deed
Records* (Mss., Records of the El Paso County Clerk's Office, El Paso, Texas), B, 24.
Caveat: While there is a tradition that the King of Spain granted a community grant
of four square leagues of land to the inhabitants of the Pueblo de Ysleta in 1751, nothing
is known about the whereabouts of papers evidencing the grant. The General Land
Office file on the grant (Bexar 1-1499) contains only a copy of the Act of February 1,
1854. However, this tradition is supported by reference to the grant in some of the
earliest titles in the El Paso Valley.

8 The huddling of the missions so closely together resulted in 1684 when Governor Cruzate relocated Real de San Lorenzo and the three Christianized Indian Pueblos, in order to afford greater protection for the residents of such villages against the forays of the hostile Apaches. While elbow room, fertile soil and water were considerations to be taken into account in determining the site for a Spanish settlement, features offering protection against Indian raids were even more important. As a result of the re-organization of the El Paso District, the three Indian Pueblos were located approximately three miles apart, with the Pueblo of Ysleta in the middle. In 1760 the Pueblo de Ysleta had a population of 85 families of Piro Indians and 18 Spanish families, or a total population of 560 persons. Eleanor B. Adams, *Bishop Tamarón's Visitation of New Mexico*, 1760 (Albuquerque, 1954), 38.

Since the grant was located on both sides of the river but most of the inhabitants of the Pueblo de Ysleta resided on the south side of the river between 1751 and 1831, the portion of the grant lying north of the river was probably used as the *ejidos*, and the land lying south of the river surrounding the mission was probably divided into *suertes*. Each family was probably allotted one *solares*, 2 *suertes* of irrigatable land, and 2 *suertes* of dry land, or a total of approximately 23 acres of land. Irving Berdine Richman, *California Under Spain and Mexico*, (New York, 1911), 126. Even though the population of the El Paso Valley had greatly increased by 1846, this supposition is supported by Geroge Ruxton's statement that each family in the El Paso Valley had a separate house and plot of land, and that each such tract seldom contained more than 20 acres. LeRoy R. Hafen, *Ruxton of the Rockies*, (Norman, 1950), 161.

9 *Deed Records* (Mss., Records of the El Paso County Clerk's Office, El Paso, Texas), B, 24.

In connection with the 1853 litigation between the Pueblos of Senecú and Ysleta, the court ordered District Surveyor W. L. Diffenderfer to survey the Ysleta Grant. This survey commenced at a stake and mound on the east bank of the Rio Grande set for the southeast corner of the Senecú Grant and ran thence N. 16⁰ E. 7,290 varas to a pile of stone; thence S. 42½⁰ E. 8,590 varas to a point on a sand hill; thence S. 70¾⁰ W. 940 varas to a point on the sand hill called Loma de la Cruz de Juan Antonio; thence S. 37½⁰ W. 3,020 varas to the bank of an acequia; thence S. 48½⁰ W. 1,450 varas; thence S. 21¾⁰ W. 2,670 varas to the bank of the Rio Grande; and thence up the Rio Grande to the place of beginning. Diffenderfer's survey shows that the portion of the Ysleta Grant north of the Rio Grande contained one league and 21 labors, or 8,148.34 acres. This survey undoubtedly was used to prepare the description in the Act of February 1, 1854, which confirmed the Ysleta Grant. However, it now appears that he did not locate correctly the boundaries of the grant. A subsequent survey indicates that the Ysleta-Senecú line should be further southwest, and the Ysleta-Socorro line should be further east. This error probably resulted from Diffenderfer's mistaking Loma de la Cruz de Juan Antonio for Loma de los Valencias and his failure to locate the natural objects called for in the 1825 survey that were south of the Rio Grande. Lipan Apache Tribe v. United States (Mss., Records of the Indian Claims Commission), No. 22-C.

10 *Ibid.*

11 *Ibid.*, D, 392.

12 John Russell Bartlett, *Personal Narrative*, I, 193. This island commenced at a point about 4 miles east of the downtown area of El Paso, Texas, and extended down the river to a point 2½ miles southwest of Tornillo, Texas. It frequently has been presumed that Ysleta took its name from the Spanish word "isleta," which means "little island," on account of its location on this island. However, this is not true. The town was named by Governor Cruzate in 1682 after the Pueblo of Isleta, New Mexico, since most of its inhabitants came from that village. To distinguish the lower settlement from its pre-

decessor, it frequently was referred to as the Pueblo de Ysleta del Sur. Roscoe P. and Margaret B. Conkling, *The Butterfield Overland Mail* (3 Vols., Glendale, 1947), II, 55.

[13] *Chamizal Arbitration, Appendix to the Case of the United States* (2 Vols., Washington, 1911), I, 109-110; and John Russell Bartlett, *Personal Narrative*, II, 547.

[14] H. P. N. Gammel, *The Laws of Texas* (10 Vols., Austin, 1898), IV, 42-43.

[15] *Journal of the Senate of the State of Texas, Fifth Legislature* (Austin, 1854), 32.

[16] *Ibid.*, 148.

[17] *Journal of the House of Representatives of the State of Texas, Fifth Legislature*, (Austin, 1854), 135.

[18] *Ibid.*, 226.

[19] H. P. N. Gammel, *The Laws of Texas*, IV, 43. A check of the official General Land Office map for El Paso County, which was in use in 1854, shows that the Legislature undoubtedly believed that the T. H. Duggan Survey No. 12 was located west of and adjacent to the Senecú Grant. This supposition is supported by the Act of February 15, 1858, which amended the description of the tract covered by the Relief Act, in order to call for the southeast, instead of the southwest, corner of the Duggan Survey. *Ibid.*, IV, 222. The Relief Act, as amended, would therefore appear to cover all of the Senecú Grant lying north of the Rio Grande, together with the tract lying between the Rio Grande and Rio Viejo Rivers west of the Senecú Grant.

[20] *Ibid.*, IV, 53.

[21] *Ibid.*, IV, 222; and *Deed Records* (Mss., Records of the El Paso County Clerk's Office, El Paso, Texas), B, 22.

[22] *United States Statutes at Large*, XVI, 673-679 (1871).

[23] H. P. N. Gammel, *The Laws of Texas*, VII, 1433.

[24] Nancy Lee Hammons, *A History of El Paso County, Texas to 1900* (Mss., Master's Thesis, Texas Western College, El Paso, Texas), 105.

[25] Grace Long, *The Anglo-American Occupation of the El Paso District* (Mss., Master's Thesis, University of Texas, Austin, Texas), 145.

[26] H. P. N. Gammel, *The Laws of Texas*, VI, 1435.

[27] The Tigua Indian Community of Ysleta, Texas has asserted a claim before the Indian Claims Commission, seeking substantial damages from the United States. The Tribe alleges that prior to 1850 Ysleta was a recognized Indian Pueblo, that it had been granted a tract of land, and, under the doctrine of the Sandoval case [United States v. Sandoval, 231 U.S. 28 (1913)], the government, as its guardian, was obligated to protect its property rights. However, notwithstanding this solemn obligation, the United States transferred jurisdiction over the area in which the grant was located to Texas, under the Compromise of 1850, without adequately protecting the Tribe's interest, and as a result thereof, non-Indians were permitted to acquire most of the lands covered by the grant. Lipan Apache Tribe v. United States (Mss., Records of the Indian Claims Commission), No. 22-C.

[28] *Deed Records* (Mss., Records of the County Clerk's Office, El Paso, Texas), I, 184.

[29] *Ibid.*, B-3, 67; and *Ysleta Grant Survey Book* (Mss., Records of the El Paso County Surveyor's Office, El Paso, Texas).

[30] *Ysleta Grant Survey Book* (Mss., Records of the El Paso County Surveyor's Office, El Paso, Texas).

[31] H. P. N. Gammel, *The Laws of Texas*, IX, 1371.

[32] Stevens v. Crosby, 166 S.W. 62 (1914).

CHAPTER 20

The Socorro Grant ॐ

● THE PUEBLO OF SOCORRO was established in the spring of 1682 for the Piro, Tano, and Jemez Indians, who had joined Governor de Otermín during the Pueblo Revolt. It was originally located about twelve leagues east of El Paso del Norte, but was moved to a point about one league east of the Pueblo of Ysleta in 1684. As long as there was vacant land between the two agrarian communities, few land disputes arose. However, as the El Paso Valley developed and the intervening lands were appropriated, serious jurisdictional quarrels arose between Ysleta and Socorro. In order to protect the interests of its inhabitants, the Pueblo of Socorro allegedly petitioned the Spanish government for a grant of four leagues of land surrounding its church. There is a tradition that King Ferdinand VI personally granted the requested lands to the inhabitants of the pueblo on March 13, 1751.[1]

Mexico, an offspring of revolution and unencumbered by treaty obligations, could have ignored all Spanish land grants located within its borders.[2] However, it elected to follow the established principles of International Law and to recognize all valid grants issued by the former sovereign. Therefore, the change of sovereignty had no prejudicial effect upon private land claims in Mexico. Notwithstanding this tacit recognition of the grant to inhabitants of the Pueblo de Socorro, there is a tradition that the Mexican government actually confirmed said grant on June 21, 1832.[3]

While the original and confirmation papers have apparently been lost or destroyed, several collateral documents tend to support the existence of a grant to the Inhabitants of the Pueblo de Socorro. The most pertinent document on this point is the Field Notes of a re-survey of the Ysleta Grant conducted in February, 1825.[4] This instrument shows that the Alcalde of the Pueblo de Socorro, with the "title papers of Socorro," witnessed the execution of the survey of the common boundary line between the Pueblos de Ysleta and Socorro. Another document is a letter by Juan María Ponce de León, Secretary of the Ayuntamiento of El Paso del Norte, to the Provincial Deputation of New Mexico concerning the boundaries of settlements under its supervision. This official report states that the lands of the settlements under the jurisdiction of the Ayuntamiento extended in an easterly direction as far as the garrison of San Elizario.[5] Since the towns of Socorro and San Elizario were adjacent to one another, it would appear that this line ran along their common bonudary. The probative force of this meager documentary evidence, coupled with the adverse, exclusive and uninterrupted possession of the lands claimed by inhabitants of the Pueblo de Socorro for one and three-quarters centuries, created a presumption that a valid grant had been made, even though instruments of record thereof could not be found.[6] This presumption required all the forums of the State of Texas to defend the ancient and equitable rights of the inhabitants of the Pueblo de Socorro. When the Texas Legislature was called upon to confirm such rights, it promptly passed an act which recognized the full integrity of that portion of the Socorro Grant lying north of the Rio Grande. This act was enacted on February 11, 1858, and relinquished all the state's right and interest: To the people of the town of Socorro, one league of land called "El Pueblo de Socorro."[7]

In an effort to satisfy the second paragraph of the Act of February 11, 1858, which required an accurate survey of the land prior to its patenting, the inhabitants of the Pueblo de Socorro retained George Villars, Deputy Surveyor of El Paso County, in 1862, to survey the portion of the Socorro Grant lying north of the river. W. L. Diffenderfer, District Surveyor for El Paso County, had previously surveyed this tract, but the inhabitants of the Pueblo de Socorro could not use this survey to satisfy the survey requirement of said act, since it did not contain a description of the meanders of the river. However, it was utilized by Villars, for it purported to conform in all respects to the metes and bounds designated in the original grant.[8] Diffenderfer's Survey[9] had been made on July 14, 1853, and showed that the Socorro town tract contained two leagues, fourteen labors, and one hundred square varas, or approximately 11,357.5 acres, instead of just the one league of land mentioned in the Relinquishment Act of February 11, 1858. The survey commenced at a stake on the north bank of the Rio Grande at the point where the eastern, or lower, boundary line of the Ysleta Grant intersected said river and ran:

Thence N. 21¾° E. 2,870 varas to a stake and mound on the western edge of the town of Socorro; Thence N. 48½° E. 1,450 varas to a stake and mound on the banks of an acequia; Thence N. 37° E. 3,020 varas to a sand hill called La Loma de la Cruz de Juan Antonio, situated on the northern border of the Valley of the River; Thence N. 70¾° E. 940 varas to a stake and mound; Thence S. 30° E. 10,810 varas along the sand hills 140 varas from the border of the Valley; Thence S. 73½° W. 7,740 varas to a stake and mound on the banks of the Rio Grande; and Thence up the river with its meanders to the place of beginning.

The difference between Diffenderfer's Survey and Villars' Survey was that the latter contained a detailed description of the meanders of the river and increased the area covered by the tract by a total of four hundred square varas.[10]

Between April and December, 1862, Villars surveyed fifty-seven individual tracts located within the Socorro Grant, which were occupied by
twenty-nine of the inhabitants of the Pueblo de Socorro. These surveys
cover approximately 1,060 acres of land.[11] Meanwhile, the inhabitants of
the Pueblo de Socorro had treated the tracts which they occupied as if
they owned them in severalty. Since 1854 such tracts had been inherited,
devised and sold, without any regard being given to the fact that the
original occupants had not received any legal title thereto.[12] Approximately
one-half of the lands covered by the grant were actually occupied and
utilized by the individual inhabitants of the Pueblo de Socorro as if they
had fee simple title to the tracts of land which they occupied. Whatever
interest the inhabitants themselves may have had in such tracts, it certainly
was not such an interest as would authorize them to dispose of or convey
portions thereof in severalty.[13]

Before the Pueblo de Socorro could be incorporated or a patent issued
to the inhabitants of the Pueblo de Socorro, the Civil War disrupted efficient
governmental operations in Texas. Interest in the perfection of individual
land claims or the patenting of the Socorro lands was not revived until the
prospects of constructing a railroad through the pass at El Paso created a
land boom in the area during the 1870's.

By an act dated April 26, 1871,[14] the Town of Socorro was incorporated,
with corporate limits coincident with its land grant. Control over its corporate affairs, including the disposition of the town lands, was vested in a
town conucil, composed of a mayor and nine aldermen.[15]

Judge Charles H. Howard was retained sometime in the mid 1870's by
the Town Council to secure a patent to the Socorro Grant and assist it in
distributing the occupied tracts located therein among residents of the
Town of Socorro. In the summer of 1877 Howard, in the name of his father-
in-law, George B. Zimpleman, located land certificates upon the remaining
unappropriated Guadalupe Salt Lakes, which were being used by the
Mexicans in the El Paso Valley. This action strained his relations with the
town council of Socorro to the breaking point. Thereafter, little progress
was made in clearing the Socorro land title until after Howard's violent
death at San Elizario, Texas on December 17, 1877 during the notorious
Salt War. However, the grant had been re-surveyed by Ward B. Blanchard,
Deputy Surveyor of El Paso County, on November 12, 1877. This survey
was practically identical to the Villars Survey of 1862. When the Blanchard
Survey was submitted to the General Land Office for approval, together
with a petition requesting issuance of a patent to the inhabitants of the
town of Socorro, Howard's father-in-law and associate, George B. Zimpleman, filed a protest against the patenting of the Socorro Grant. It seems
that Howard was to receive a portion of the grant as compensation for his
services. The town council had repudiated the contract on the grounds

that it was personal and had terminated upon Howard's death.[16] Notwithstanding said protest, a patent was issued to the inhabitants of the town of Socorro on September 23, 1878, covering the two leagues, fourteen labors, and five hundred square varas of land described in the Blanchard Survey.[17]

The inhabitants of Socorro ignored the special charter of 1871, and organized under the State's general incorporation laws. On January 26, 1886 an order was entered in the Minutes of the Commissioners' Court of El Paso County, declaring the inhabitants thereof incorporated under the name of the Town of Socorro. In order to assist them in managing the town lands, the town officials retained A. H. Parker to survey the occupied tracts within the Socorro Grant in 1877. He surveyed and wrote field notes on two hundred sixty-seven small individual tracts. As consideration for his services, Parker was given four hundred acres of land out of the grant.[18] The town of Socorro conveyed these small tracts by informal deeds to hundreds of persons who occupied, improved and cultivated same in good faith, believing they had acquired good title to their individual tracts. In order to validate such titles, the Texas Legislature passed two special acts. The first[19] was dated April 2, 1889, and was designed to quiet land titles in the towns of Socorro, Ysleta and San Elizario. It provided:

That all genuine deeds made by the towns of Socorro, Ysleta and San Elizario to lands lying in their respective corporate limits, whether the same be in form or attended with the formalities prescribed by charters, are hereby declared valid and operative as fully as if all the forms and formalities required had been complied with, saving the rights of any third parties.

The purpose of the other act[20] was to validate deeds made by the Town of Socorro while acting under the General Incorporation Laws.

The heirs of many of the original grantees still have possession of the Socorro Grant lands which their ancestors had occupied and cultivated for centuries. The growth, which the railroad could have brought, failed when the Galveston, Harrisburg and San Antonio Railway Company bypassed the town. The state and national highways which were subsequently built through the El Paso Valley practically parallelled the railroad. Only a narrow, winding, farm-to-market road links the town of Socorro with its neighbors to the east and west. Despite today's thin power lines, television antennae, and noisy chugging tractors, the quaint adobe houses of the town of Socorro — set among lush green fields and interlaced by sluggishly flowing acequias — appear much the same as they did centuries ago. As one of the two oldest continuously occupied settlements in Texas, Socorro truly deserves a place of distinction in Texas history.

REFERENCES

1 *Deed Records* (Mss., Records of the El Paso County Clerk's Office, El Paso, Texas), XX, 107-109; and *Biennial Report of the Commissioner of the General Land Office* (Austin, 1908), 7. *Caveat:* A search of the Archivo General de Indias, located in Sevilla, Spain, failed to disclose any evidence of the alleged Royal Decree dated March 13, 1751. José Antonio Garcia Noblijas, El Director General de Archivos y Bibliotecas to J.J.B., June 15, 1959.

2 The Treaty of Cordova, which ended the Mexican War for Independence, did not contain an express provision requiring Mexico to recognize valid Spanish land titles. Hubert Howe Bancroft, *History of Mexico* (66 Vols., San Francisco, 1885), IV, 728-729. However, there is a well established principle of International Law which obligates a succeeding sovereign to recognize valid private land claims emanating through its predecessor. William Mack, *Corpus Juris* (76 Vols., New York, 1930), L, 1206-1207; and Harris v. O'Connor, 185 S.W. 2d 993 (1944).

3 *Appendices to the Brief of the Appellants* (Mss., Records of Clerk of the Court of Civil Appeals, San Antonio, Texas; Texas v. Valmont Plantations, No. 13,583), 142. *Caveat: The Appendices to the Brief of the Appellant* cites File Bexar 1-1447 of the Records of the General Land Office as authority for the above statement; however, a check of said file failed to reveal any mention of said confirmation.

4 *Deed Records* (Mss., Records of the County Clerk's Office, El Paso, Texas), B, 24.

5 *Archive No. 1290* (Mss., Records of the Museum of New Mexico, Santa Fe, New Mexico).

6 United States v. Chaves, 175 U.S. 509 (1899).

7 H. P. N. Gammel, *The Laws of Texas*, (10 Vols., Austin, 1898), IV, 1027.

8 There is some doubt as to whether or not Diffenderfer examined the grant papers to the Pueblo de Socorro Grant. This question is raised as a result of the statement that his survey was made by virtue of a grant made to the town by the King of Spain in 1690. It is generally believed that the Socorro Grant was made in 1751. To avoid this objection, the subsequent surveys of the Socorro Grant omitted this reference.

9 *Transcribed Records* (Mss., Records of the El Paso County Surveyor's Office, El Paso, Texas), A, 33.

10 Bexar 1-1447 (Mss., Records of the General Land Office, Austin, Texas).

11 *Private Land Surveys* (Mss., Records of the El Paso County Surveyor's Office, El Paso, Texas).

12 Pence v. Cobb, 155 S.W. 608 (1913).

13 *Ibid.*

14 H. P. N. Gammel, *The Laws of Texas*, VI, 1314.

15 Pence v. Cobb, 155 S.W. 608 (1913).

16 Bexar 1-1447 (Mss., Records of the General Land Office, Austin, Texas).

17 *Deed Records* (Mss., Records of the El Paso County Clerk's Office, El Paso, Texas), G, 90.

18 *Ibid.*, VIII, 264; and *Field Book No. 74* (Mss., Records of the El Paso County Surveyor's Office, El Paso, Texas).

19 H. P. N. Gammel, *The Laws of Texas*, IX, 1371.

20 *Ibid.*, X, 234.

CHAPTER 21

The San Elizario Grant ᕽ

● MISMANAGEMENT and Indian depredations created such an urgent
need for reliable information concerning conditions on the northern frontiers of New Spain that Carlos III ordered a general inspection of the
presidios from California to Louisiana. Marqués de Rubí was commis-
sioned to make the tedious and dangerous 7,000 mile inspection tour. He
found that, because of its economic stability and size, El Paso del Norte
could be defended through the organization of a militia. Therefore, he
recommended that the presidio located there be moved to Carrizal; he
further recommended that new presidios be established at Robledo, Agua
Nueva, and San Bernardo, El Sauz or Valle de San Elzeario.[1] The establishment of these presidios would not only reduce the hazards of travel upon
the Camino Real, but would also tend to protect the El Paso valley settlements from surprise Indian attacks. Rubí also made sweeping recommen-
dations concerning improvement of equipment, supplies and living conditions at the frontier garrisons. The principal features of Rubí's report
were incorporated in the Royal Regulations of September 10, 1772.[2]

Hugh O'Connor was appointed Commander-Inspector in 1772 to carry
out the royal regulations. He reorganized the entire presidial system.[3] The
Presidio de Nuestra Señora del Pilar del Paso del Rio del Norte was moved
to the Pueblo de Carrizal, and the Presidio Nuestra Señora de las Caldas,
which had been located at the Pueblo de Guajaquilla,[4] was transferred in
1774 to a site at the lower end of the Valle de Elzeario, about fifty-four
miles southeast of El Paso del Norte. Its ruins are still visible just west of
the present City of El Porvenir, Mexico. The presidio was re-named Presidio de San Elceario.[5] The presidio did not remain at this location very
long. On February 14, 1780 Lieutenant Governor Francisco Xavier Uranga
ordered it transferred to a site near the Hacienda de los Tiburcios.[6]

There is a tradition that the inhabitants of the substantial civil settlement which had developed around the presidio received a grant covering
at least four leagues of land in 1790. The exact description of the lands
covered by the grant is not now known, for the papers evidencing same
were allegedly destroyed by the American troops in 1846, but it was
purportedly surveyed and monumented pursuant to instructions given by
the Field Marshall of Spain in a letter dated March 30, 1789.[7]

After Mexico gained its independence, the Presidio de San Elizario
continued to play an important role in the defense of the El Paso area.[8]

Prior to 1823, the Presidio de San Elizario was under the jurisdiction of Nueva Vizcaya, while El Paso del Norte, San Lorenzo, Senecú, Ysleta, and Socorro were under the jurisdiction of New Mexico. After the State of Chihuahua was created on July 19, 1823, all six of the settlements in the El Paso District were placed under its control.[9]

The meager records now available indicate that the Ayuntamiento de El Paso del Norte, on September 7, 1823, either confirmed the alleged Spanish grant of 1790 or made a new grant to the inhabitants of the Presidio de San Elizario covering eight and one-half leagues of land located on the Rio Grande immediately east of the Socorro Grant.[10] The field notes[11] of this conveyance describe the following tract of land:

The survey was commenced where the lower line of the Socorro Town tract touches the River where a monument of stone was made, and taking a course from west to east eight thousand varas were measured to the most eastern corner of the Socorro Town tract. The parties interested wishing the foothills for their boundary it was agreed to. And thirty thousand varas were measured to a corner on a sand hill opposite the junction of the Rio Viejo and Rio Bravo del Norte. And four thousand varas from said junction. In which terms the survey was concluded — the Rio Bravo del Norte being the other boundary, and in consequence of its having insufficient width, it contains only eight and one-half leagues.

On December 30, 1846, just three days after Colonel Alexander W. Doniphan's triumphant entry into El Paso del Norte following his Christmas Day victory over the Mexican forces at Bracito, a detachment of United States Cavalry, under Major William Gilpin and Captain John W. Reid, reconnoitered the Presidio de San Elizario. They found the garrison deserted, but it was apparent that a large force had recently been stationed there. A large number of bloody bandages were discovered, indicating that the Mexicans who had been wounded at the Battle of Bracito received medical attention at the post. Several wagonloads of ammunition and one cannon were found cached or buried in the sand.[12]

The State of Texas organized El Paso County in 1850. The county seat was established at San Elizario, the largest town in the county.[13] Many reputable Spanish families and a few Americans resided in the settlement which surrounded the presidio.

A company of United States Infantry was stationed at the old Spanish presidio in December, 1849, but was withdrawn about a year later. Once the American troops were transferred, the public buildings at San Elizario were allowed to deteriorate rapidly. The presidio and church were described in April, 1851 as being in a ruined condition.[14] It is possible that the inhabitants of San Elizario dismantled the presidial walls and even damaged the public buildings, in order to obtain adobe for use in construction or improvement of their private residences. In an effort to save the historic buildings at San Elizario from total destruction, the Texas Legislature passed an Act on December 13, 1851, which relinquished to the County of El Paso, for county purposes, that certain tract of land in the town of San Elizario upon which were located the presidio, corral, and other buildings and out houses which had been occupied by the United States troops.[15]

Pursuant to Article V of the Treaty of Guadalupe Hidalgo, Major William H. Emory and José Salazar y Larrequi surveyed the location of the principal stream of the Rio Grande as it ran through the El Paso Valley in 1852.[16] The Emory-Salazar Surveys of the International Boundary fixed the southeastern boundary of the portion of the San Elizario Grant located within the State of Texas.[17]

When the Bourland-Miller Commission failed to investigate the validity of Spanish and Mexican land titles in El Paso County, the residents of San Elizario looked to the Texas Legislature for relief. On January 18, 1853 the representative for El Paso and Presidio Counties, E. M. Browder, introduced a bill for the relief of the inhabitants of the Town of San Elizario.[18] The Browder Bill was passed on February 5, 1853,[19] and relinquished all of the State's title to the inhabitants of San Elizario in and to the following described tract of land located in El Paso County, Texas:

Commencing on the Rio Grande at a point where the established line of division between the towns of Socorro and San Elizario strikes said river for the northern boundary, and following said line to the hills bordering on the eastern bank of the River Viejo; thence running southeast along with said hills down the River Viejo, to a point at which said Rio Viejo empties into the Rio Grande; thence up said Rio Grande from the mouth of the Rio Viejo to the place of beginning, containing four leagues, more or less.

The tract of land described in the Relinquishment Act of February 5, 1853 was patented to the inhabitants of the town of Presidio de San Elizario on March 8, 1853.[20] However, the land continued to be held in common for the benefit of all of the inhabitants of the town. Since the Presidio de San Elizario was unincorporated, it did not have the power to allot the occupied tracts among its residents. On April 5, 1871 an act was passed by the Texas Legislature, incorporating the town of San Elizario. The corporate boundaries were the same as those described in the patent. Among other things, this act gave the town council of San Elizario the power to grant or sell portions of the town's property to its citizens.[21] The town council did not exercise its prerogative for nearly eleven years. By that time, the town had disregarded its special charter, and had incorporated under the state's general incorporation laws. Meanwhile, each family which inhabited the grant selected, occupied and cultivated the amount of land needed for its subsistence. Such possession and labor were the only evidence of its ownership of such plots; however, pending delivery of legal title, the community recognized the natural rights of the occupant.

Since the boundaries of the grant had not been surveyed following its relinquishment to the inhabitants of the Presidio de San Elizario, and in view of the appropriation of certain lands adjacent to the grant by the Texas and Pacific Railway Company, the town council retained A. Q. Wingo, Surveyor of El Paso County, Texas, to re-survey the grant. An abbreviated description of his survey is as follows:

Commencing at a stake and the northeast corner of the Socorro Grant 140 varas from the edge of the sand hills; Thence S. 35° E. 15,540 varas with the crest of the hills bordering on the Rio Viejo to a pile of stone; Thence S. 1° E. 1,920 varas to a corner; Thence S. 43° E. 14,000 varas to a pile of small stones; Thence S. 60° W. 4,200 varas to a corner at the mouth of the old river from which the northwest corner of the Ralph Wright Survey No. 44 bears in a southeasterly direction 1,006 varas; Thence up the channel of the Rio Grande as it ran in 1852 with its meanders to the point where the common line between the Socorro and San Elizario Grants intersect the Rio Grande; and Thence N. 73½° E. 7,740 varas to the point of beginning.

The survey[22] was completed on October 21, 1879, and disclosed that the grant contained a total of 40,869 acres, and included the tract commonly known as the San Elizario Island.[23]

After the Galveston, Harrisburg and San Antonio Railway Company had completed construction of its line through the San Elizario Grant, land values in the El Paso lower valley rapidly increased. This prompted the inhabitants of the town of San Elizario to demand a distribution of the lands which were being occupied and used. A total of six hundred sixty-eight separate tracts located in the grant were surveyed for and conveyed to the inhabitants of the grant.[24] Since many of these deeds were not executed on the form or with the formalities prescribed in the town's charter, a special act[25] was passed by the Legislature on April 2, 1889, which validated such deeds. The defect created by San Elizario's attempted incorporation under the General Incorporation Laws was remedied by a special act[26] passed on March 17, 1891.

While the Wingo survey of the grant solved a number of internal problems for the inhabitants of the town of San Elizario, it created two serious boundary conflicts which ultimately had to be settled in the court house. The first of these suits involved the western, or upper, line of the San Elizario Grant. According to the Wingo survey, this line was located six hundred sixty-five feet northwest of lower boundary of the Socorro Grant. This created a nine hundred twelve acre overlap between the Socorro and San Elizario Grants. If the Wingo survey correctly located the division line between the two grants, then the inhabitants of the town of San Elizario

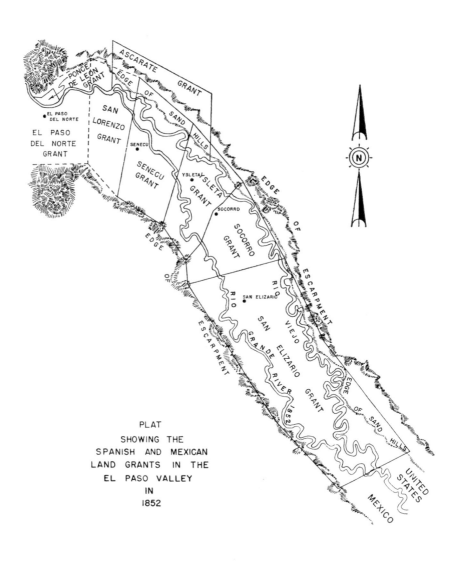

PLAT
SHOWING THE
SPANISH AND MEXICAN
LAND GRANTS IN THE
EL PASO VALLEY
IN
1852

would prevail, since their grant had been patented first. To protect its interests, the town of Socorro filed a trespass to try title suit against the town
of San Elizario in the district court of El Paso County in March, 1882.[27]
The plaintiff alleged that the defendant had illegally dispossessed it, encouraged and permitted its inhabitants to cut timber from the strip of
land in question, and issued quitclaim deeds covering portions of such
land. In its answer, the defendant alleged that its grant covered the disputed tract. It contented that, while its grant papers had been lost or destroyed, the common boundary between the Socorro and San Elizario
Grants always had been recognized as being located in the position designated in the Wingo Survey. Continuing, it asserted that the Spanish
and Mexican governments had never recognized the Socorro Grant as
extending beyond one league below the old location of the Mission de la
Purísima Concepción del Socorro. The pleas of the Corporation of the
Town of San Elizario went unheeded, and judgment was rendered for the
plaintiff. In 1883 the boundary between the two grants was re-surveyed
and marked by Sam H. Wade along the line described in the Blanchard
survey of the Socorro grant.[28]

The second case involved the location of the northern boundary of the
San Elizario grant. The Mexican field notes of the grant and the patent to
the inhabitants of the Presidio de San Elizario established its northern
boundary as slightly concaved line running from the northeastern corner
of the Socorro Grant southeasterly along the sand hills to a point on the
sand hills north of the junction of the Rio Viejo and Rio Grande. The Wingo
survey located this boundary as an almost straight line running along the
crest of the same hills. Sections 1 through 9, Block L, University Lands,
which were located along the north bank of the Rio Viejo, conflicted with
the northeastern portion of the grant. The State of Texas filed suit in the
district court of Travis County, Texas against Michael Meecham and others
who had acquired lands from the town of San Elizario, which were situated
between the foot of the sand hills and the grant's north line as surveyed
by Wingo. The State sought to have the ambiguous clause "along the
sand hills" defined as meaning along the foot or edge, instead of their
crest.[29] On December 6, 1902 the court held that the boundary was a
sinuous line following the edge of the sand hills.[30]

The subdivision of the San Elizario Grant into numerous small tracts as
a result of issuance of the multitude of corporate deeds and the settlement
of the disputes involving the grant's boundaries marks the end of the
history of the San Elizario Grant as a separate and distinct entity. Thereafter, its history becomes highly technical, and deals with the improvement
of these individual tracts. Since the turn of the century, the grant has
played an important role in the agricultural history of the El Paso Valley.
Otherwise, the grant, and its principal city, San Elizario have been over-
shadowed by the activities centered around the El Paso metropolis.

REFERENCES

1 The Valle de San Elzeario begins just above the present town of San Elizario, Texas, and extends southeastwardly down the river almost to the present town of Fort Hancock, Texas.

2 Carlos E. Castañeda, *Our Catholic Heritage in Texas* (7 Vols., Austin, 1939), IV, 242-247.

3 Alfred Barnaby Thomas, *Teodoro de Croix and the Northern Frontier of New Spain, 1776-1783* (Norman, 1941), 16; and Bernard E. Bobb, *The Viceregency of Antonio Bucareli* (Austin, 1962), 132-140.

4 The Pueblo de Guajaquilla was located upon the site of the present town of Jimenez, Chihuahua.

5 Due to the difficulty Americans had in pronouncing San Elceario, the name was anglicized to San Elizario. The latter name will be used hereafter.

6 Eugene O. Porter, "The Founding of San Elizario," *Password*, IX, 96-97. The Hacienda de los Tiburcios was located on the south bank of the river about twenty miles southeast of El Paso del Norte. It is not known when the Hacienda de los Tiburcios was originally founded, but in 1744 six Spanish families were living there. It was attached to the Pueblo de Socorro for jurisdictional purposes. Sixty-five Spanish families were living there in 1765. Walter Prescott Webb, *The Handbook of Texas* (2 Vols., Austin, 1952), II, 292; Alfred Barnaby Thomas, *Forgotten Frontiers* (Norman, 1932), 109; and Rex E. Gerald, *Spanish Presidios of the Late Eighteenth Century in Northern New Spain* (Santa Fe, 1968), 25-27.

7 H. P. N. Gammel, *The Laws of Texas* (10 Vols., Austin, 1898), III, 1362; and The Corporation of the Town of Socorro v. The Corporation of the Town of San Elizario, No. 332 (Mss., Records of the El Paso District Clerk's Office, El Paso, Texas). The District Court apparently refused to receive an alleged copy of this letter. Such refusal was probably on the grounds that its authenticity had not been properly verified. This tradition may be in error as to the date of issuance of the alleged grant. If such a grant had been made, it would appear that it would have been dated after March 22, 1791, for on that date, Pedro de Nava, *ad interum* Intendente of Guadalajara, issued a decree which formulated a new plan for establishment of civil settlements around presidios. This plan provided that the boundaries of such settlements should be measured two leagues in every direction from the center of the presidio square. This would authorize the granting of a total of sixteen leagues of land to presidial towns. It also authorized the captains of the presidios to distribute land among the inhabitants and soldiers of such presidio. Frederic Hall, *The Laws of New Mexico* (San Francisco, 1895), 42.

8 In 1833 the Presidio de San Elizario had a complement of one Captain, one Lieutenant, one First Class Second Lieutenant, one Second Class Second Lieutenant, one Chaplain, one Amourer, three Sergeants, one Bugler, six Corporals, and eighty soldiers. J. A. de Escudero, *Noticias Estadisticas del Estado de Chihuahua* (Mexico, 1834), 57.

9 Hubert Howe Bancroft, *History of the North Mexican States and Texas* (2 Vols., San Francisco, 1886), II, 586.

10 The records of the General Land Office contain a translated copy of the field notes of the grant to the Inhabitants of Presidio de San Elizario. This instrument was certified on June 4, 1873 by T. Rush Spencer, Surveyor General of New Mexico, to be a true and correct translation of the field notes contained in the *testimonio* of the title issued to the Inhabitants of Presidio de San Elizario by the Ayuntamiento of Paso del Norte on the 7th day of September, 1823, recorded in Volume B, pages 164 and 165, of the records of his office. File No. Bexar 1-1007 (Mss., Records of the General Land Office,

Austin, Texas). Volume B of the *Kearny Registers of Land Transfers in New Mexico* disappeared from the Surveyor General's Office in June, 1880, and is believed to have been stolen. Jane F. Smith to J.J.B., September 24, 1959; and Myra Ellen Jenkins to J.J.B., July 25, 1963.

11 Bexar 1-1007 (Mss., Records of the General Land Office, Austin, Texas). The correctness of these field notes is somewhat questionable, since it is known that the Rio Bravo del Norte ran in the stream bed now known as Rio Viejo up until 1831 or 1832. The initial call for a monument on the river located eight thousand varas west of the southeastern corner of the Socorro Grant, and the call for the junction of the Rio Viejo and Rio Bravo del Norte indicates that this survey was made subsequent to change of the course of the river, and not in 1823, as purported.

12 William Elsey Connelly, *Doniphan's Expedition* (Topeka, 1907), 384.

13 Grace Long, *The Anglo-American Occupation of the El Paso District* (Master's Thesis, University of Texas, 1931), 59.

14 Bartlett, *Personal Narrative*, I, 193.

15 H. P. N. Gammel, *The Laws of Texas*, III, 889.

16 *Proceedings of the International (Water) Boundary Commission, United States and Mexico, Treaties of 1884 and 1889, Equitable Distribution of the Waters of the Rio Grande* (2 Vols., Washington, 1903), I, 103-106.

17 The Rio Grande made an abrupt northeastwardly change in its course in 1857 or 1858. Some thirteen thousand acres of land contained in the San Elizario Grant and located within the State of Texas were left south of the river following the change. This tract became known as the Island of San Elizario. In order to determine whether the Island of San Elizario belonged to the United States or Mexico, the Mexican Commissioner, on November 4, 1895, presented the case to the International Boundary Commission for its adjudication under the Treaties of 1884 and 1889. The International Boundary Commission found that the Rio Grande abandoned its old channel in 1857 or 1858 as a result of an avulsive change, and opened up a new one in the vicinity of the bed of the river as it was located in 1896. In its decision dated August 10, 1896, the Commission held that the true boundary remained in the original bed of the river as marked on the Emory-Salazar maps. The decision was approved by both governments. *Chamizal Arbitration, The Counter-Case of the United States of America* (Washington, 1911), 15-17.

18 *Journal of the House of Representatives of the State of Texas, Fourth Legislature, Extra Session* (Austin, 1853), 110.

19 Gammel, *The Laws of Texas*, III, 1362.

20 *Deed Records* (Records of the El Paso County Clerk's Office, El Paso, Texas), F. 492.

21 Gammel, *The Laws of Texas*, VI, 1221.

22 *Transcribed Records* (Mss., Records of the El Paso County Surveyor's Office, El Paso, Texas), B, 248-255.

23 On November 4, 1895 the Mexican Commissioner presented the San Elizario Island Case to the International Boundary Commission for its adjudication under Article II of the Treaty of 1884. Testimony by two witnesses and maps prepared by the Commission's engineers indicated that in 1857 or 1858 the Rio Grande River made a sudden avulsive northward change in its course. Thereafter, the river ran down the northern channel. As a result of this change, some 13,000 acres of land, which theretofore had been included in the San Elizario Grant, were located south of the river. The Commission held that the International Boundary should remain in the center of the old river-

bed. The boundary was marked with twenty-one monuments in the old channel. This decision was approved by both the United States and Mexico. *Proceedings of the International (Water) Boundary Commission, United States and Mexico* (2 Vols., Washington, D.C., 1903), I, 1-1-107. Since the International Boundary remained in the center of the old river channel, the shift in the course of the Rio Grande did not deprive the inhabitants of the Presidio de San Elizario of the land located on the island.

24 *Field Note Book No. 70* (Mss., Records of the El Paso County Surveyor's Office, El Paso, Texas).

25 Gammel, *The Laws of Texas*, IX, 1371.

26 *Ibid.*, X, 235.

27 The Corporation of the Town of Socorro v. The Corporation of the Town of San Elizario (Mss., Records of the District Clerk's Office, El Paso, Texas), No. 332.

28 Katherine H. White, *The Pueblo de Socorro Grant* (Mss., Master's Thesis, Texas Western College, El Paso, Texas, 1958), 125-126.

29 Texas v. Meecham (Mss., Records of the District Clerk's Office, Austin, Texas), No. 16,282.

30 *Minute Book* (Mss., Records of the Travis County District Clerk's Office, Austin, Texas), X, 63.

CHAPTER 22

The Fray Joachín de Hinojosa Grant ৵

● THE OLDEST but least known grant in the area covered by the Chihuahuan Acquisition is the Fray Joachín de Hinojosa Grant.[1] Its inception was over two and three-quarter centuries ago when Governor Diego de Vargas was preparing to launch his reconquest of New Mexico. On May 16, 1692, he announced his plans to tour the missions in the El Paso Valley which were under Hinojosa's custody. This afforded Hinojosa the opportunity to petition for *autos* of possession in his name covering church property at the Pueblos of San Lorenzo, Senecú, Ysleta and Socorro, together with sufficient land for the support of their Indian inhabitants. He asserted that the Franciscans were responsible for both the spiritual and temporal welfare of the natives. Vargas gave him an *auto* of possession for each of the churches and convents, together with enough land to support the padre at each mission, but he carefully omitted any reference to land for use by the Indians. Thereupon, Hinojosa specifically requested that the Indians be assigned individual farm tracts. On the following day, Vargas advised Hinojosa that the Indians were not the sole responsibility of the Franciscans, for the Spaniards and Indians were living peacefully side by side, and neither could exist without the other.[2] Two days later, Vargas proceeded to inspect the church and convent at the Pueblo de Ysleta, together with their fixtures and ornaments. At the conclusion of the inspection, Vargas granted real, civil, and judicial possession of the mission to Fray Joachín Hinojosa, for himself and as a representative of his holy religion. The adjacent fields, being the tillable land necessary to raise four *fanegas* of wheat and one of corn, together with sufficient land to grow an appropriate amount of staple crops like beans and squash, were also included in the award. Upon completion of the visit to Ysleta, Vargas proceeded to the Pueblo of Socorro. After inspecting the religious facilities there, on May 20, 1692, he awarded them to Hinojosa, for himself and as head of the holy jurisdiction. Four and a half *fanegas* of land for wheat, one *fanega* of land for corn, plus such additional lands for cultivation of vegetable gardens and other staples, were pointed out by the governor and given to the petitioner. A similar award was made to Hinojosa, for himself, and as head of that holy jurisdiction, and in the name of his holy religion, on the following day covering the ecclesiastical improvements at the Pueblo of Senecú. In addition to four *fanegas* of wheat land, one *fanega* for corn, and a sufficient amount of land for gardens, the award at Senecú specifically included irrigation rights.[3]

On May 30, 1692, Hinojosa again petitioned Vargas for a mission grant. Notwithstanding a threat of excommunication, Vargas continued to refuse to allow the Pueblo Indians to be placed under the mission system. Because of his firmness, Vargas prevailed. However, in order to prevent the recurrence of the dispute at a later date, he wrote the Viceroy and reminded him that the conflict between civil and religious authorities was responsible in part for the loss of New Mexico in 1680. He stated that it would be bad to revive old trouble when all was tranquil and everyone was laboring to recover the kingdom. In closing, he requested the Viceroy's approval of his action. After the triumphant reconquest of New Mexico, Hinojosa dropped the matter.[4]

There is no evidence that Fray Hinojosa ever asserted any personal claim to the churches and lands covered by the grant. However, on June 21, 1794, more than a century after its issuance, Juan José de Ynojosa Ballí[5] petitioned the Lieutenant Chief Justice of the Town of Reynosa, Juan Antonio Ballí, for confirmation of the grant. In his petition, Ballí alleged that he was the legitimate heir of his great uncle, Fray Joachín de Hinojosa, who had been granted a tract of land in Coahuila and Texas, situated upon both sides of the Rio del Norte, and upon which the Pueblos of Ysleta, Socorro and Senecú were located. Continuing, he stated that the grant contained forty leagues of land, located equally upon each side of the river, and had been given to his uncle pursuant to the laws of New Spain, in consideration of his having colonized such lands. He concluded with a prayer, requesting that he be placed in legal possession of said lands and given a *testimonio* evidencing his ownership thereof.[6]

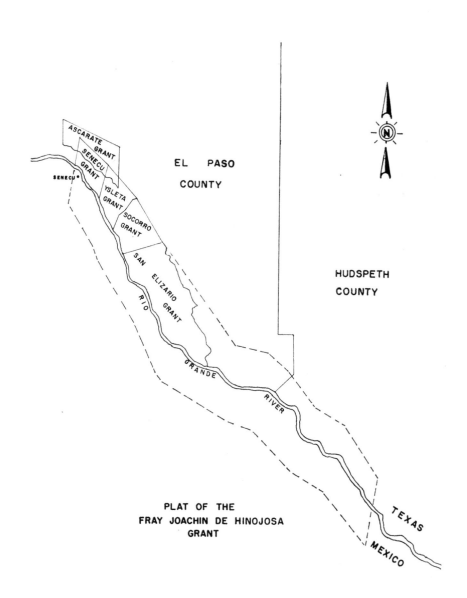

PLAT OF THE
FRAY JOACHIN DE HINOJOSA
GRANT

Judge Ballí referred the petition to Bruno Díaz de Salcedo, Intendente of San Luis Potosí, who in turn sent it to the Viceroy for his consideration and further action. On October 7, 1796 Miguel de la Grua Talamanca y Branciforte, Viceroy of New Spain and President of the Audiencia, found Juan José de Ynojosa Ballí to be Hinojosa's heir and the legal owner of the forty leagues of land referred to in the petition. However, since the description contained in the petition was vague and uncertain, the Viceroy directed the Intendente to re-survey the grant and furnish him with a copy of the field notes. Pursuant to such instructions, a survey was run, and the following field notes[7] were returned to the Viceroy:

Commencing at a point upon the west bank of the Rio del Norte 22 cordeladas[8] north of the Church of Senecú; from this point extend the cord and measure one hundred cordeladas in a straight line in the direction of the west, and at the end of the last cordelada of the hundred, extend the cord anew and measure two thousand cordeladas in the direction of the southeast in a straight line parallel with the course of the Rio del Norte; from this point extend the cord in a straight line to the west bank of the Rio del Norte. Arriving at this point, cross to the east bank of the river, and commence to measure at a point directly opposite to the last mentioned; and from this point extend the cord and measure one hundred cordeladas in direction of the east. Arriving at the point where this measure ends, extend the cord and measure two thousand cordeladas in the direction of the northwest in a straight line parallel with the margin of the river; from this place extend the cord in a straight line to the east bank of the river at a point opposite the beginning point.

On November 18, 1796 the Viceroy issued a decree, formally recognizing and conforming Juan José de Ynojosa Ballí's title to the land set forth in the re-survey of the grant. This decree recited that such confirmation was made in accordance with the provisions of Law 11, Title 12, in Book 4 of the *Recopilación de las Leyes de los Reynos de las Indias*.[9] The Viceroy concluded his decree by ordering Salcedo to place the applicant in legal possession of the grant.[10]

There was no further mention of the Fray Joachín de Hinojosa Grant for more than a century. Interest in the grant was revived when Richard F. Burges and Lamar Davis, two prominent El Paso lawyers, advertised for information pertaining to the grant, with the view of purchasing the inchoate claim, in order to clear certain land titles in the El Paso Valley in which they were interested.[11]

The intestate death of the successive generations of descendants of Juan José de Ynojosa Ballí had fragmented the title to the grant. By a warranty deed dated January 19, 1911, Ygnacio Ballí acquired the interests of the thirty remote descendants of Fray Joachín de Hinojosa.[12] Ballí, in turn, conveyed the entire grant to Elizabeth C. Hendrix, a *feme sole* of Chicago, Illinois, by a special warranty deed dated January 29, 1915.[13] It was asserted in this instrument that the grant covered nine *haciendas* and six labors, or a total of 205,000 acres of land, adjacent to the Pueblos of Ysleta, Socorro and Senecú, which had been:

granted to Joachín de Hinojosa under Royal Cédula of the King of Spain made and published May 17, 1631, being Law 15, Title 12, in Book 4, of the *Recopilación de las Leyes de los Reynos de las Indias,* which land the said Joachín de Hinojosa took possession of, occupied, used and improved, and colonized according to the terms and conditions of said cédula, which occupation and possession was proved and title thereto ratified and confirmed by the Governor and Captain General in compliance with Law 16, Title 12, in Book 4, of the *Recopilación de las Leyes de los Reynos de las Indias.*[14]

The deed to Elizabeth C. Hendrix was field in the El Paso County Clerk's Office on March 25, 1915,[15] but for some unknown reason the deed to Ynacio Ballí was not recorded in El Paso County until October 8, 1917.[16] A copy of the grant to Fray Joachín de Hinojosa, which was certified to be a true copy of the original by Pilar de Laso, Judge of the Second Civil Court of the First Instance of the Canton de Bravos, was filed for record in El Paso County two days later.[17] A certificate dated August 28, 1852 was attached to this document, wherein David R. Diffenderfer, United States Consul to the City of El Paso del Norte, Mexico, certified that Pilar de Laso was the Judge of the First Instance and sole legal custodian of the archives and land titles of the Canton of Bravos. A certified copy of the confirmation grant, which had been prepared for Ygnacio Ballí by Agustín Alvarado, third constitutional judge of San Luis Potosí, pursuant to a decree issued by the judge of the First Instance of the Judicial District of San Luis Potosí on January 1, 1906, was recorded in the Records of the El Paso County Clerk's Office on December 24, 1917.[18]

The recording of the certified copies of the original and confirmation grants and the two deeds created a great deal of excitement in El Paso County, since such action cast a cloud upon most agricultural land in the El Paso valley. Apprehension was further heightened when it was rumored that Mrs. Hendrix planned to take immediate steps to dispossess everyone occupying lands embraced within the grant. In an effort to alleviate tension, Mrs. Hendrix published a letter in the El Paso *Herald,* stating that she was holding title to the grant in trust for Ygnacio Ballí, who was then dying in poverty in McAllen, Texas. She alleged that Ballí did not wish to "make trouble" for any person occupying land within the grant, and that he had authorized her to execute deeds to all such persons, free of cost except for notary fees. Continuing, she explained that Ballí believed that the grant had been given to Joachín Hinojosa for the purpose of educating and uplifting the Mexican people, and that if the grant should be recognized, one-half of the proceeds realized from the sale of the grant would be used to establish private schools for Mexicans in the El Paso Valley.[19]

Following the recommendation of her attorney, Mrs. Hendrix attempted to fence the grant and render it for ad valorem taxes. Her offer to render the grant for state and county taxes was summarily refused by Tax Assessor John T. Cain upon the advice of County Attorney William F. Fryer. The men she employed to erect a fence were promptly stopped by the parties in possession of the land under titles which had been recognized and patented by the State of Texas.[20]

Daisy Hoffman, one of the landowners whose title had been clouded by the Hendrix claim, filed a trespass to try title suit against Elizabeth C. Hendrix on August 19, 1918.[21] Mrs. Hendrix realized that it would be very difficult to prove the validity of the original and confirmation grants, due to their extreme age.[22] It became obvious that the claim could never be defended when a search of the Mexican archives failed to reveal the existence of either the original grant or the confirmation grant. The Texas Supreme Court, in passing upon the validity of the San Salvador del Tule Grant, which had been granted to Juan José de Ygnacio Ballí, held that:

A copy of a copy is not admissible in evidence, nor is a copy made and fully authenticated by an alcalde . . . of a title of land exhibited to him and not forming part of the archives of his office, entitled to any standing as evidence.[23]

The certified copy of the original grant was apparently only a copy of a copy, since it did not appear that the original document was in the archives of El Paso del Norte in 1852. The certificate affixed to the confirmation grant likewise did not affirmatively state that it was a true copy of the original instrument.

In addition to the lack of adequate documentary evidence, several other impediments to the recognition of Mrs. Hendrix' title existed. Most serious was the fact that even if it could be proved that the Fray Joachín de Hinojosa Grant was valid, the numerous inhabitants of Ysleta, Socorro, and San Elizario had occupied and adversely claimed most of the land covered by the grant for a period sufficient to have acquired title thereto by limitation. Also, it could be argued that since it was not the policy of church fathers to accept land for their personal benefit, the original grant must have been given to Hinojosa in his figuciary capacity as Pastor of the El Paso del Norte District, for the benefit of the inhabitants of the Pueblos of Ysleta, Socorro, and Senecú.

It is also noted that there was a discrepancy in the amount of land described in the deed to Mrs. Hendrix. It will be recalled that the confirmation grant affirmed Juan José de Ynojosa Ballí's title to forty leagues of land, or approximately 177,136 acres, while said deed purported to cover nine *haciendas* and six labors, or a total of 205,000 acres.

Confronted with these virtually insurmountable obstacles, Mrs. Hendrix decided not to contest Daisy Hoffman's action. On October 22, 1922 a default judgment was entered in favor of the plaintiff.[24] Since that date, no further steps have been taken to secure recognition of what might have been the earliest land grant issued covering lands now lying within the State of Texas.

R E F E R E N C E S

1 Fray Joachín de Hinojosa was Father Pastor of El Paso del Norte, Reverend Father Vice-Custodian, and Lieutenant Governor and Captain General of New Mexico. Carlos E. Castañeda, *Our Catholic Heritage in Texas* 1519-1936. (7 Vols.) 251. In the grant papers filed in El Paso County his name is spelled "Ynojosa."

2 Vina Walz. *History of the El Paso Area,* 1680-1692 (Mss., Doctoral Dissertation, University of New Mexico, 1951), 301-304.

3 *Deed Records* (Records of the El Paso County Clerk's Office, El Paso, Texas), CCLXXXVII, 298-305; and Legajo 139 (Mss., Records of the Audiencia de Guadalajara).

4 Vina Walz, *History of the El Paso Area,* 1680-1692 (Mss., Doctoral Dissertation, University of New Mexico, 1951), 304-318.

5 The Ballí (sometimes spelled "Vallí") and Ynojosa (frequently spelled "Hinojosa") families were closely interrelated. During the latter part of the eighteenth century, they were the wealthiest and most influential inhabitants of the lower Rio Grande Valley. These two families were also the largest land holders in that area. At the turn of the nineteenth century, they owned most of the land adjacent to the north bank of the Rio Grande between Weslaco, Texas and the Gulf of Mexico. As a matter of fact, on the same day upon which Juan José de Ygnacio Ballí requested confirmation of the Fray Joachín Hinojosa Grant, he applied for a grant covering seventy-two square leagues, and known as San Salvador del Tule. The San Salvador del Tule Grant is situated in Hidalgo County, Texas. This grant, and its famous salt lake, El Sal del Rey, have played an important role in the land history of Texas.

Juan José Ballí was the son of José María de Ballí and Rosa María Hinojosa de Ballí. He succeeded his maternal grandfather, Juan José Hinojosa, as Chief Justice of the Town of Reynosa. He also held the rank of Captain in the Royal Army of Spain. He died in prison in 1804, after having been arrested for smuggling. Texas v. Cardenas, 47 Tex. 250 (1877); and Florence Johnson Scott, *Historical Heritage of the Lower Rio Grande Valley* (San Antonio, 1937), 104-106, 159; and Florence Johnson Scott, *Royal Land Grants North of the Rio Grande* (Rio Grande City, 1969), 71-74.

6 *Deed Records* (Records of the El Paso County Clerk's Office, El Paso, Texas), CCCXVI, 362.

7 *Ibid.*

8 A cordelada was defined in the decree as a cord of well twisted istle which was fifty varas in length.

9 This law requires all settlers and housekeepers who receive allotments of land to take possession thereof within three months, and plant willows or other trees along their boundaries, in order to separate them from adjoining lands. The grants were to be forfeited in the event the recipients failed to comply with such conditions. *Recopilación de Leyes de los Reynos de las Indias* (Madrid, 1943), II, 41.

10 *Deed Records* (Records of the El Paso County Clerk's Office, El Paso, Texas), CCCXVI, 362.

11 *El Paso Herald*, March 20, 1918.

12 *Deed Records* (Records of the El Paso County Clerk's Office, El Paso, Texas), CCCXIII, 347.

13 *Ibid.*, CCLV, 510.

14 Law 15, Title 12, in Book 4, of the *Recopilación de las Leyes de los Reynos de las Indias*, among other things, directs the Viceroys to recognize the land grants made by their predecessors. The 16th Law of said Title and Book instructs the attorneys for the Royal Audiencias to carefully examine applications for land grants, in order to insure that issuance of such grants would not prejudice any Indian rights. However, should the Viceroy make such a grant, then such officials were instructed not to interfere therewith. *Recopilación de las Leyes de los Reynos de las Indias* (Madrid, 1943), II, 42-43.

15 *Deed Records* (Records of the El Paso County Clerk's Office, El Paso, Texas), CCLV, 510.

16 *Ibid.*, CCCXIII, 347.

17 *Ibid.*, CCCLXXXVII, 299. This instrument contains a certificate over the signature of T. I. Miller, County Clerk of El Paso County, that the "Church Grant" was filed for record on August 28, 1852, and was "filed" on September 13, 1852 by Jno M. Carty, Deputy Clerk. However, the Deed Records for this period do not contain this document.

18 *Ibid.*, CCCXVI, 362.

19 *El Paso Herald*, March 21, 1918.

20 *Ibid.*

21 Hoffman v. Hendrix (Mss., Records of the El Paso District Clerk's Office, El Paso, Texas), No. 16,320.

22 *El Paso Herald*, March 21, 1918.

23 Texas v. Cardenas, 47 Tex. 250 (1877). *Caveat:* Subsequent historical research has located a copy of the "Church Grant" in *Legajo* 139 of *Archivo General de Indias* (Mss., Records of the Audiencia de Guadalajara, Mexico).

24 *Minute Book of the 65th Judicial District Court* (Mss., Records of the El Paso District Clerk's Office, El Paso, Texas), V, 184.

CHAPTER 23

The Rancho de Ysleta Grant ❦

● THE HISTORY of the Rancho de Ysleta Grant commences on July 9, 1828, when the inhabitants of the Pueblo of San Antonio de Ysleta petitioned José Antonio Arce, Governor of Chihuahua, for a grant covering the lands located in the vicinity of Sierra Alta, which they had utilized for a number of years as community pasture. The petitioners directed the Governor's attention to the fact that the original town grant given to their pueblo in 1751, and confirmed in 1825, had become insufficient, since all of those lands had been appropriated and placed under cultivation. They further alleged that much of the grazing land in the area had already been appropriated, and that unless they were given these additional lands, they would not have sufficient pasturage for the livestock owned by the families residing in or near the pueblo.

Governor Arce, with the consent of the Second Constitutional Congress of the State of Chihuahua, approved the request on August 13, 1828, and granted the pueblo a community pasture grant not to exceed an aggregate of one league of land for each family. The Governor ordered the Constitutional Alcalde of El Paso del Norte, Agapito Albo, to survey the grant and place the interested parties in lawful possession of such lands.

Alcalde Albo called a public meeting in Ysleta on September 5, 1828, and appointed two chain carriers and a tally keeper to assist him in making the survey in accordance with the Governor's decree. The Alcalde furnished the chain carriers with a cord measuring one hundred ten varas in length, and administered the oath requiring the surveying party to faithfully and legally survey the lands. The surveying party commenced the survey at a monument on the west side of a hill known as La Loma del Tigua, which marked the northwest corner of the original Ysleta Town Grant. The survey ran north 55,000 varas to a monument of earth in the desert; thence in a southeasterly direction 52,000 varas to a monument of earth and stone located on the highest peak of Sierra Alta, to the west of which was Hueco Tanks; thence in an easterly direction 38,000 varas to a monument on a hill just northeast of Alamo Springs; thence in a southeasterly direction 55,000 varas to a monument of dirt and stone on Sierra Blanca Peak; thence in a westerly direction 80,000 varas to a monument on the hill known as Loma de San Juan de Cruz, which also marked the northeast corner of the original Ysleta Town Grant; and thence in a northwesterly direction to the place of beginning.

After the survey was completed, Alcalde Albo placed the citizens of Ysleta in legal possession of the one hundred eighty-six leagues, or 823,608 acres of land, embraced within the boundaries of the Rancho de Ysleta Grant. He also delivered a *testimonio* to the town officials, evidencing its ownership of the grant. The grant was confirmed and ratified by the Constitutional Congress of the State of Chihuahua on September 24, 1834.[1]

All of the acreage embraced in the Rancho de Ysleta Grant was originally located within the State of Chihuahua, but after the Texas Revolution, Texas asserted its claim to all lands located east of the Rio Grande, which included all of the grant. When Texas accepted the Texas Boundary Act of 1850, which established the Texas-New Mexico boundary along the 32nd degree North Latitude, jurisdiction over approximately 65,000 acres of land covered by the grant was transferred to New Mexico.

The earliest attempt to secure recognition of the Rancho de Ysleta Grant occurred in July, 1855, when the inhabitants of Ysleta allegedly presented their *testimonios* for their town and pasture grants to the Rio Grande Commission for its investigation. The claimants of the Rancho de Ysleta Grant asserted that the Commission conducted a full and complete investigation into the validity of their claims in accordance with the provisions of Section 5 of the Act of February 11, 1858,[2] but did not recommend its confirmation. They contended that the sole reason for the Rio Grande Commission's failure to recommend confirmation of their grant was that its size exceeded the eleven league limitation contained in the first section of the Act.[3]

The claim to the Rancho de Ysleta Grant was dormant until 1887. Early in the summer of that year John P. Randolph, a surveyor from El Paso, heard the tradition that the City of Ysleta owned a vast unrecognized Mexican grant. Upon investigating the rumor, Randolph learned that the original *testimonio* had been destroyed when the State Capitol had burned, but fortunately the claimants had secured a certified copy of the *expediente* on July 15, 1855, from Judge Pilar de Laso, custodian of the archives of El Paso del Norte.

Concluding that the grant constituted a valid claim which was fully guaranteed by the Treaty of Guadalupe Hidalgo, Randolph entered into an agreement with the duly authorized officials of the City of Ysleta, the corporate successor to the Pueblo of San Antonio de Ysleta, on July 15, 1887. This agreement appointed Randolph attorney in fact for the city, and provided that if he prosecuted the city's claim to final judgment, the city would convey an undivided one-half interest in the grant to him as consideration for such services.[4]

One of Randolph's first acts as attorney in fact for the Town of Ysleta was the recording of the certified copy of the grant papers in El Paso County on September 1, 1888.[5]

Next, he caused a trespass to try title suit to be filed on February 28, 1889 in the 34th Judicial District Court of El Paso County, Texas, against the Trustees of the Texas Pacific Land Trust.[6] Charles J. Canda, Simeon J. Drake and William Strauss, as Trustees of the Texas Pacific Land Trust, claimed one hundred ninety-three sections of patented land which conflicted with the grant. These lands had been located by the Texas and Pacific Railway Company between December 20, 1878 and January 20, 1879 by virtue of certain land certificates which had been donated to the railroad by the State of Texas in return for its having built a railroad from Texarkana to Fort Worth. When the railroad went in to receivership in 1885, these lands were conveyed to the Trustees of the Texas Pacific Land Trust for the benefit of the holders of the railroad's Income and Land Grant Bonds.

About nine months after filing of the suit, the Pueblo of Ysleta revoked its agreement with John P. Randolph on the grounds that he had failed to perform diligently the provisions of the contract.[7] The Ysleta officials then tried, without success, to compromise the controversy directly with the Texas Pacific Land Trust. After their negotiations ended in failure, the city entered into a new agreement with Randolph on January 11, 1890. Randolph again agreed to prosecute the claim to final judgment for one-half of all the lands recovered.[8]

Ludwig Heldt was employed by Randolph to survey and plat the grant. His survey was completed on June 10, 1890, and disclosed that the grant embraced approximately 716,510 acres of land.[9]

After the Court of Private Land Claims was established in 1891, John P. Randolph caused a suit to be instituted in that court in an effort to secure recognition of the city's claim to the grant insofar as it covered the 65,628 acres of land contained in two triangular tracts located in Otero County, New Mexico.[10]

At this point, the attorneys for the Texas Pacific Land Trust announced that the grant papers had been forged. For some unexplained reason, someone had changed the year in the date of Judge Laso's certificate on the certified copy of the *testimonio* from 1855 to 1853. Randolph could not explain this alteration, and thereafter took no further steps to secure recognition of the grant.

Meanwhile, it was realized that if a dependable and adequate water supply could be obtained that agriculture in the Mesilla and El Paso Valleys could be greatly expanded. In order to insure such a water supply, three separate reclamation and irrigation projects were advanced. Ernest Dale Owen, the Chicago attorney and land speculator who was interested in the Ronquillo and La Prieta Grants, advocated construction of a dam across the Rio Grande at the northern end of the Mesilla Valley near Fort Selden, New Mexico. He proposed to transport the water conserved by such a dam to a mesa by means of a canal which ran through a tunnel in the Organ Mountains. He believed that if the dam and canal system were constructed he would be able to place 200,000 acres of land located in the western portion of the Rancho de Ysleta Grant under cultivation.

In connection with this scheme, Owen entered into a contract with the City of Ysleta, wherein he agreed to perfect the city's title to the grant and to protect it against all adverse claims asserted by John P. Randolph or his assigns. In consideration for such professional services, the city granted Owen an option to purchase the entire grant for ten cents an acre.[11]

Pursuant to this agreement, Owen revived the city's suit in the Court of Private Land Claims. He elected to prosecute the claim against the United States involving the New Mexican portion of the grant first, because a favorable judgment would clear title to all of the grant lands located within New Mexico, for there were no patented tracts located within the boundaries of that portion of the grant. Should the Court of Private Land Claims recognize the validity of the New Mexican portion of the grant, it would give Owen a decided advantage in his anticipated suits for recognition of the larger and more valuable portion of the grant which was located in Texas.

The United States, in its Answer, denied the city's allegations that a valid grant had been made to the Pueblo of Ysleta. The government further alleged that the *testimonio* offered by the plaintiff had been manufactured and anti-dated. In support of its Answer, the government offered affidavits by the custodians of the Mexican Archives at El Paso del Norte and Chihuahua. These affidavits stated that each custodian had diligently searched the archives under his jurisdiction, and was unable to find any document, note, memorandum or entry refering to or pertaining to the Rancho de Ysleta Grant. No explanation was submitted to the court by the plaintiff as to why the original copy of the *expediente* of the grant, which allegedly was in existence in the year 1855, when the certified copy had been made by Judge Pilar de Laso, could not be found in the archives of El Paso del Norte.

The Court of Private Land Claims, in a unanimous decision dated September 27, 1894, held that the claim should be rejected. The court commented on the fact that the plaintiff had not presented sufficient evidence to prove existence of a valid grant, but it actually based its opinion dismissing the plaintiff's petition on the grounds that the court did not have jurisdiction over a claim which was clearly located within the boundaries of the State of Texas at the time of the signing of the Treaty of Guadalupe Hidalgo.[12] This adverse decision by the Court of Private Land Claims practically ruined the claimants' chances of securing recognition of the Texas portion of the grant.

Subject to and apparently in anticipation of a favorable decision by the Court of Private Land Claims, on September 13, 1894 Owen caused a trespass to try title suit to be filed in the City of Ysleta's name in the 34th Judicial District Court of El Paso County, Texas against the trustees of the Texas Pacific Land Trust, in an effort to secure recognition of the claim insofar as it covered the lands in conflict with the trust's lands.[13] The State of Texas, which owned a majority of the balance of the acreage which conflicted with the grant, was not joined, because the State could not be sued without legislative consent. The State held these lands for the benefit of the permanent school and University funds.

The defendants requested that the case be transferred to the United States Circuit Court for the Western District of Texas on the grounds that there was a diversity of citizenship between the parties. The plaintiffs protested the defendants' application by arguing that a municipal corporation was not a citizen of any state, and therefore, there was no diversity of citizenship between the parties. The Texas courts ordered the case removed to the Federal Court on October 1, 1894.[14]

The Judge of the United States Circuit Court for the Western District of Texas, T. S. Maxey, in his decision of April 16, 1895, upheld the validity of the removal by holding that a municipal corporation was a citizen of the State which created it.[15]

The removal of the case to the Federal Court amounted to a major set-back for the proponents of the grant, for Judge Maxey was the jurist who had presided over the trial of the José Lerma Grant.[16] In his decision rejecting the validity of that grant, Judge Maxey had held that a certified copy of the *expediente* of an alleged Mexican land grant would not be sufficient evidence to establish the validity of such a claim when no evidence of the grant could be found in the proper archives of Mexico. The United States Fifth Circuit Court of Appeals had confirmed this decision.[17]

Confronted with the adverse precedents established by decisions of the Court of Private Land Claims and the United States Circuit Court of Appeals, which, when taken together, presented an insurmountable barrier against recognition of the Texas portion of the Rancho de Ysleta Grant, Ernest Dale Owen decided it was impractical, if not futile, to further prosecute the claim. The suit was formally dismissed on October 21, 1899, when the court called the case, and the plaintiff failed to appear.[18]

The dismissal of the City of Ysleta's suit ended the high hopes of its claimants to secure judicial recognition of the Rancho de Ysleta Grant. Likewise, all of Owen's dreams of building the Fort Selden dam, and his related schemes of promoting agricultural development of the mesa lands east of El Paso, Texas, were abruptly cancelled.

R E F E R E N C E S

1 *Deed Records* (Mss., Records of the El Paso County Clerk's Office, El Paso, Texas), XXVI, 19.

2 Gammel, *The Laws of Texas*, III, 1533.

3 City of Ysleta v. United States (Mss., Court of Private Land Claims, Records of the Bureau of Land Management, Santa Fe, New Mexico), No. 33.

The claimants of the Rancho de Ysleta Grant attempted to explain their failure to present any evidence supporting this contention by stating that all of the original title papers collected by the commission, together with its records, abstracts of claims and final report, had been destroyed when the State Capitol Building burned on November 9, 1881. Part of their allegations were false, since it is now known that this data was lost sometime prior to January 27, 1858. *Journal of the House of Representatives, State of Texas, 7th Legislature* (Austin, 1858), 705.

It should be noted that an alternate reason for the failure of the Rio Grande Commission to recommend confirmation of the Rancho de Ysleta Grant may be that it considered the concession evidenced by the *testimonio* to be merely a license, instead of the conveyance of a fee simple title. The *testimonio* did not grant the land for cultivation and pasturage, as was customary in Mexican grants to pueblos. Actually, there is nothing in said *testimonio* which would indicate that the inhabitants of the Pueblo de Ysleta desired, or that Governor Arce, in granting their request, or that the Constitutional Congress in conforming said concession, intended to convey any right to the inhabitants of the Pueblo de Ysleta beyond a commons upon which the residents of such village could pasture their livestock in conformity with their ancient usage. If this were true, then the Rancho de Ysleta Grant was merely a license, which would have been revoked by the Treaty of Guadalupe Hidalgo. Pueblo of Zia v. United States, 168 U.S. 198 (1897).

4 *Deed Records* (Mss., Records of the El Paso County Clerk's Office, El Paso, Texas), XXVI, 19.

5 *Ibid.*, XIV, 313.

6 Town of Ysleta v. Canda (Mss., Records of the El Paso District Clerk's Office, El Paso, Texas), No. 1140. This suit was dismissed by the Court on May 18, 1897 for lack of prosecution. *Minute Book* (Mss., Records of the El Paso District Clerk's Office, El Paso, Texas), IX, 324.

7 *Deed Records* (Mss., Records of the El Paso County Clerk's Office, El Paso, Texas), XX, 104.

8 *Ibid.*, VIII, 332.

9 *Book* (Mss., Records of the El Paso County Surveyor's Office, El Paso, Texas), I, 392.

10 City of Ysleta v. United States (Mss., Court of Private Land Claims, Records of the Bureau of Land Management, Santa Fe, New Mexico), No. 33.

11 *Deed Records* (Mss., Records of the El Paso County Clerk's Office, El Paso, Texas), XXXVI, 250; also *El Paso Herald*, August 23, 1894.

12 *Journal* (Mss., Court of Private Land Claims, Records of the Bureau of Land Management, Santa Fe, New Mexico), II, 219. It is very difficult to reconcile the court's decision in this case with its discussions which recognize the validity of numerous other land grants located east of the Rio Grande.

13 City of Ysleta v. Canda (Mss., Records of the El Paso District Clerk's Office, El Paso, Texas), No. 2000.

14 City of Ysleta v. Canda (Mss., Records of the United States Circuit Court for the Western District of Texas, El Paso, Texas), No. 190.

15 City of Ysleta v. Canda, 67 F. 6 (1895).

16 Morris v. Canda (Mss., Records of the United States Circuit Court for the Western District of Texas, El Paso, Texas), No. 67.

17 Morris v. Canda, 80 F. 739 (1897).

18 *Minute Book* (Mss., Records of the United States Circuit Court for the Western District of Texas, El Paso, Texas), II, 62.

CHAPTER 24

The La Prieta Grant ੩↔

● THE MOST NOTORIOUS LAND GRANT in the El Paso area is a three hundred twenty-five square league tract known as the La Prieta Grant. By Royal Decree dated March 13, 1751, the frontier villages of Ysleta, Socorro, and San Elizario each received a town grant from the King of Spain. Through the years, as the population of each of these villages gradually multiplied, the lands which had formerly been utilized as a common pasturage, were allotted and distributed among new residents and placed under cultivation. By 1825, the citizens of each of these villages commenced pasturing their cattle and sheep upon the vacant public lands north of their respective grants. After the citizens of Ysleta received the Rancho de Ysleta Grant on August 13, 1828 as a pasturage for their livestock, serious disputes arose between the residents of Ysleta and those of Socorro and San Elizario. These conflicts developed when the citizens of Ysleta attempted to prohibit inhabitants of the other two towns from grazing their cattle upon the lands within the Rancho de Ysleta Grant.

In order to settle these local conflicts and dispel all doubts concerning the respective rights of each of the three towns, the Governor of Chihuahua, José V. Madero, on May 18, 1832 acknowledged the petition of the citizens of Socorro and San Elizario by granting them all of the lands lying between the Rancho de Ysleta and the José Lerma Grants as a pasture for their livestock. This concession was surveyed by Julián Bernal, the constitutional alcalde of El Paso del Norte, between June 21 and July 4, 1832. The survey commenced at Loma San Juan de la Cruz, which was the northwest corner of the Socorro Grant; and ran thence in an easterly direction thirty leagues to El Capitán de Guadalupe Peak; thence in a southerly direction a distance of twenty leagues to Sierra la Mesa; thence in a westerly direction thirteen leagues to the top of Sierra Blanca and the northeast corner of the José Lerma Grant; thence westerly along the north line of the José Lerma Grant eight leagues to the Rio Bravo del Norte; and thence up the river to the place of beginning. The grant stipulated that the lands were to be used jointly by the residents of the two towns for a period of fifty years, after which time the grant was to be distributed among the inhabitants of the two towns for their use, without any restrictions on alienation. Upon the partitioning of the lands, the inhabitants of Socorro were to receive one hundred eighty leagues, and the residents of San Elizario were to receive one hundred forty-five leagues.[1]

The La Prieta and the Rancho de Ysleta Grants were both ratified and confirmed by the Constitutional Congress of the State of Chihuahua on September 24, 1834. Governor José J. Calvo issued Decree Number 17 on September 24, 1834, giving official notice of congressional confirmation.[2]

The La Prieta Grant — which contained three hundred twenty-five leagues, or 1,439,100 acres of land — was occupied and claimed by the inhabitants of the two pueblos after Texas acquired its independence, but no steps were taken prior to 1889 to secure recognition of their claim by the State. Meanwhile without any knowledge of the grant, Texas and Pacific Railway Company located numerous land certificates on the lands embraced within the grant. By 1889 the railroad had secured patents on approximately four hundred sixty-eight alternate odd sections of land in the Texas and Pacific Railway Company blocks which conflicted with the La Prieta Grant. In addition to the even numbered school land sections in the Texas and Pacific Railway Company blocks, there were numerous Public School Land and University Land Blocks of land which also conflicted with the claim.

On September 28, 1889 the town of San Elizario conveyed an undivided one-half of its interest in the La Prieta Grant to John P. Randolph, who was a Deputy Surveyor for El Paso County, in consideration of his agreeing to institute a suit for recognition of that town's interest in the grant. The town also appointed Randolph as its attorney in fact, with authority to represent the town in all matters concerning its remaining interest in such lands.[3] The town of Socorro also retained Randolph to represent its interests. By deed dated April 12, 1890, Socorro conveyed an undivided one-half of its interest in the grant to Randolph. The conveyance was te be void if Randolph failed to discharge his obligations.[4] Randolph recorded the *testimonio* of the grant in El Paso County, but for some unexplained reason he never attempted to file a copy of the grant papers in the General Land Office.

Randolph hired Ludwig Heldt, County Surveyor for El Paso County, to survey the grant. Heldt allegedly surveyed the grant and made a crude sketch of it in November, 1890. Next, Randolph subdivided the grant into three hundred twenty-five consecutively numbered lots which contained one league, or 4,428 acres, each.

Randolph sold a substantial number of these lots, together with some undivided interests in the entire grant to a group of eastern speculators.[5]

In order to further justify the claim, Randolph secured a title opinion from A. J. Evans, an attorney from San Antonio, Texas which found title to the grant to be valid, and stated it would undoubtedly be upheld and recognized by the courts of Texas. In an effort to fulfill his contractual obligation, Randolph retained Attorney O. A. Lorrazolo to institute suit to secure recognition of the grant. In consideration for his legal services, Lorrazola was to receive an undivided one-eight interest in the entire grant.[6] Lorrazola filed a trespass to try title suit on March 4, 1891, in the name of the towns of San Elizario and Socorro against Charles J. Canda, Simeon J. Drake, and Fredric P. Olcott.[7] The plaintiffs sought to secure recognition of the grant insofar as it conflicted with the lands which had been patented to the Texas and Pacific Railway Company and subsequently conveyed to the defendants as Trustees of the Texas Pacific Land Trust.[8] The balance of the land which conflicted with the grant was held by the State of Texas for the University or Public School Fund. The State was not joined in this suit, for it could not be sued without special legislative permission and consent.

After the plaintiffs had filed their suit, Randolph made a diligent search of the principal archives of Mexico in an effort to find some evidence supporting the validity of the grant. However, his search failed to produce the *expediente* of the grant, the Decree of Confirmation, or any evidence mentioning or refering to the grant.

The decision of the United States Court of Appeals, rejecting the Ronquillo Grant,[9] established the rule that in order to sustain the validity of a

Mexican land grant, some documentary evidence must be found in the Archives of Mexico. The adverse decree of the Court of Private Land Claims concerning the Rancho de Ysleta Grant,[10] which was a companion to the La Prieta Grant, further weakened the claim. Confronted with these adverse decisions, Randolph saw that he would be unable to prove adequately the genuineness of the grant. When the case came up for trial on October 2, 1894, the plaintiffs failed to appear, and the court dismissed the cause for want of prosecution.[11]

The dismissal of the suit materially weakened the prospects for the future recognition of the grant, and the eastern speculators realized that it probably would never be confirmed. They promptly began unloading their interests by peddling small tracts of land within the grant to innocent purchasers throughout the United States.

The La Prieta land promoters would approach a prospective purchaser with an astounding "get rich quick" scheme. They presented the desert and surrounding worthless lands within the grant as being rich agricultural lands. The eastern dupe would immediately become interested in purchasing such lands at the bargain prices offered by the swindlers. The scheme then proceeded with an explanation that there would be a slight delay in their obtaining a perfect title to the land, for the State of Texas had not officially recognized title to the grant. At this point, a copy of a plat of the grant would be produced, together with an abstract made by the Empire Title Insurance Company and the Lone Star Abstract Company. The plat contained a notation that Judges Willie West,[12] and McGowan of Austin, and Judge A. J. Evans of San Antonio had pronounced the grant good in any court of justice. The abstract contained Evans' title opinion and a complete chain of instruments conveying title into the seller. The promoters would then explain that they were selling the land at such a ridiculously low price in order to raise money to finance a suit for confirmation of the grant. The suckers usually took the bait, with visions and high hopes of realizing a fantastic return on their investment. The victims could have easily determined that the peddlers had no valid title to the lands. However, they relied upon fraudulent representations, and received only the proverbial gold brick in return for their hard earned cash.

The earlier deeds described the property conveyed as being either an undivided portion of the grant or lot in Randolph's subdivision. In order to simplify their traffic in these fraudulent conveyances and to lend authenticity to their transactions, the speculators superimposed the boundaries of the La Prieta Grant on a copy of the official General Land Office map of El Paso County, and their later deeds described the property being conveyed as a particular section in a certain railroad block, as shown by the official map of El Paso County on file in the State Land Office.[13]

In 1907 a second group of La Prieta land speculators entered upon the scene. It appears that after Randolph's death, his wife, Minnie H. Randolph, retained John T. Selman, of Dallas, Texas, to sell the remainder of Randolph's one-half interest in the grant. Selman offered to sell the interest to James O. Wiley, a Dallas attorney. After Wiley had examined the title to Randolph's interest, he advised Selman that he did not believe Randolph's estate had a valid claim to any part of the grant. He apparently felt that Randolph's failure to secure recognition of the grant within the seventeen years which had elapsed since execution of the agreements and deeds between Randolph and the Towns of Socorro and San Elizario amounted to a fatal breach of contract. Wiley advised Selman to secure a new title directly from the cities of Socorro and San Elizario. Pursuant to Wiley's recommendation, Selman and an associate, W. H. Marsh, of Tyler, Texas, petitioned the town council of each city, requesting that the original contracts and deeds made in favor of John P. Randolph be rescinded and annulled. They also requested the councils to deed an undivided one-half interest in the grant to them in consideration of their agreeing to prosecute the La Prieta claim to a final judgment. Acting upon the petition, the town council of Socorro passed an ordinance on August 30, 1907, which repealed and cancelled the contract and deed which it had given to Randolph on the grounds that he had failed to comply with their terms and conditions.[14] The town council of San Elizario passed a similar ordinance on September 7, 1907.[15] Each town then deeded Selman and Marsh an undivided one-fourth interest in their respective claims to cover the expenses of the recovery proceedings. The towns also agreed that they were to receive an additional one-fourth interest upon final judgment.[16]

Shortly after he completed his transaction with the towns of Socorro and San Elizario, Selman sold his entire interest in the grant to James O. Wiley for $1,000.[17] Wiley subsequently traded his interest to W. H. Yoakum. At the time of the trade, he notified Yoakum that he had no faith in the legality of the grant, and that he was trading him nothing but wind.[18] Yoakum, in turn, sold the interest to C. T. Gregory for an alleged consideration of $460,000.[19]

As the commerce in fraudulent conveyances pertaining to the La Prieta Grant began to snowball, the El Paso County Judge, the El Paso County Clerk, the Commissioner of the General Land Office, the Attorney General of Texas, and the Governor of Texas became increasingly interested in putting a stop to the La Prieta Land Grant swindle. During the twenty-year period since Randolph first asserted the claim, more than three hundred deeds were placed on record in El Paso County. All of these deeds described lands which had previously been appropriated by the Public School Fund, the University of Texas Fund, or the Texas and Pacific Railway Company.

Commissioner of the General Land Office J. T. Robinson made a trip to Mexico in order to search the archives at Juarez, Chihuahua, Zacatecas, Durango, Guadalajara and Mexico City for evidence pertaining to the grant. After a diligent search and inquiry, he failed to find any information relating to the grant.[20] He then advised the El Paso county clerk that even if the grant had been legally made, he did not believe it would ever be confirmed.[21] The Secretary of State also reported that his records revealed that the Empire Title Insurance Company had never been granted a charter by the State of Texas, and that the Lone Star Abstract Company could not be located.[22]

On December 28, 1909 the commissioner's court of El Paso County, Texas passed a resolution directing its county clerk not to record any more La Prieta deeds. The court contended that by recording such deeds, the clerk was assisting the speculators in perpetration of a fraud by giving apparent sanction to the deeds, and thereby creating an invalid chain of title to such property. After passage of this resolution, the clerk gave each person attempting to file a deed pertaining to the grant a copy of the resolution, and advised each that the grant was considered fraudulent and had never been recognized by the State.

As a result of the persistent efforts of Commissioner Robinson both W. H. Yoakum and C. T. Gregory, the last parties actively engaged in the scheme, were indicted in Dallas, Texas for selling or offering to sell land under the fraudulent La Prieta Grant. Gregory skipped the country in order to avoid arrest. Yoakum as convicted, fined $100, and given six months in jail for his part in the fraud.[23]

The State, through its Attorney General, J. P. Lightfoot, filed a trespass to try title suit in the 53rd Judicial District Court against James O. Wiley, W. H. Yoakum, and C. T. Gregory, in order to clear the State's title to the Public School and University lands which conflicted with the La Prieta Grant. However, this suit was dismissed on November 25, 1913, at the request of Governor Calquitt. The Governor explained his actions by pointing out that a suit instituted by the State would permit La Prieta land swindlers to get their claim against the Public School and University lands into court, when they could not do so otherwise without Legislative sanction.[24]

With Yoakum's conviction and the dismissal of the State's suit, further traffic in the La Prieta land deeds ceased. The extensive publicity scared off the remaining promoters or forewarned any more victims.

R E F E R E N C E S

[1] *Deed Records* (Mss., Records of the El Paso County Clerk's Office, El Paso, Texas), XX, 107 and 108.

[2] *Ibid.*, XX, 109. Nothing in the La Prieta Grant indicates that the inhabitants of the Pueblos de Socorro and San Elizario desired or that the Mexican officials intended to grant or confirm anything beyond a commons whereupon the residents of such villages could pasture their livestock. The United States held a similar concession to a pueblo

to be a mere license, which was revoked by the Treaty of Guadalupe Hidalgo. Pueblo of Zia v. United States, 168 U.S. 198 (1897).

3 *Ibid.*, XX, 18.

4 *Ibid.*, XX, 111.

5 *Ibid.*, XIX, 304, 480; XX, 138; XXIV, 370; and XXV, 374, 375.

6 *Ibid.*, XXXV, 359.

7 Towns of San Elizario and Socorro v. Canda (Mss., Records of the United States Circuit Court for the Western District of Texas, El Paso, Texas), No. 131.

8 *The Daily Herald* (El Paso, Texas), March 5, 1891. The original court papers in Cause No. 131 have been lost, but a copy of the petition is set out verbatim in this issue of *The Daily Herald*. A copy of this petition is also contained in the Records of the Texas Pacific Land Trust, Dallas, Texas.

9 Owen v. Presidio Mining Co., 61 F. 6 (1893).

10 City of Ysleta v. United States (Mss., Court of Private Land Claims, Records of the Bureau of Land Management, Santa Fe, New Mexico), No. 33.

11 *Minute Book* (Mss., Records of the United States Circuit Court for the Western District of Texas, El Paso, Texas), I, 499.

12 Judge Robert G. West, of Austin, Texas, wrote a scholarly title opinion covering the validity of the grant in connection with his endorsement of the plat. In this opinion, West reviewed the law relative to Spanish land grants in the disputed territory between the Rio Grande and Nueces. He concluded that the towns of Socorro and San Elizario had acquired perfect title to the three hundred twenty-five leagues of land in controversy; that the town, by proper action of their respective town councils, could dispose of the grant; and that title to the grant was not affected by the subsequent locations made by the Texas and Pacific Railway Company. Robert G. West, "Validity of Certain Spanish Land Grants in Texas," *Texas Law Review* (1924), II, 435-444.

13 John J. Terrell, *Biennial Report of the Commissioners of the General Land Office* (Austin, 1908), 7-8.

14 *Deed Records* (Mss., Records of the El Paso County Clerk's Office, El Paso, Texas), CLXVI, 500.

15 *Ibid.*, CLXVI, 489.

16 *Ibid.*, CLXVI, 489-511.

17 *Ibid.*, CLXXXV, 60.

18 Letter by Paul CcComb to W. H. Abrams, March 4, 1911. (Mss., Records of the Texas Pacific Land Trust, Dallas, Texas).

19 *Deed Records* (Mss., Records of the El Paso County Clerk's Office, El Paso, Texas), CLXXV, 153.

20 Letter from Commissioner J. T. Robinson to the El Paso Chamber of Commerce, October 9, 1911. (Mss., Records of the El Paso County Clerk's Office, El Paso, Texas).

21 Letter from Commissioner J. T. Robinson to Park Pittman, March 20, 1907. (Mss., Records of the El Paso County Clerk's Office, El Paso, Texas).

22 *Ibid.*, October 16, 1907.

23 *Ibid.*, March 7, 1912.

24 *Report of the Commissioner of the General Land Office*, 1910-1912, 5.

CHAPTER 25

The José Lerma Grant 🙢

● ON AUGUST 15, 1823, Don José Lerma,[1] a retired Army Lieutenant
and prominent citizen of El Paso del Norte, requested the Ayuntamiento
of that town, to grant him a fifty-league tract of vacant land pursuant to
the National Colonization Law of January 3, 1823. Lerma's petition embraced all of the lands located on the left bank of the Rio Grande lying
between the spring known as Ojo del Toro and the mountain called Sierra
Blanca. He recited that he intended to settle the lands with families who
wished to accompany him, cultivate the river bottoms and *ancones*, and
ranch the adjoining hills. He specifically requested that the grant include
all water holes and minerals contained within the tract.

The Ayuntamiento granted the land to Lerma on August 23, 1823, subject
to approval of the Provincial Deputation of Chihuahua. The matter was
transmitted to the Provincial Deputation, which approved the concession
on October 10, 1823, after finding the formation of the proposed settlement
would be beneficial to the public welfare. The Provincial Deputation then
directed the Ayuntamiento to appoint a commission to survey the grant
and deliver possession of the lands to Lerma.

In compliance with the Provincial Deputation's Decree, the Ayuntamiento, on October 30, 1823, appointed a commission consisting of José
Ignacio Rascón, the President of the Ayuntamiento, Councilmen José
María Velarde, José Morales, José Manuel García, and José Francisco
Carbajal, Town Attorney Juan J. Gil, and Juan María Ponce de León,
Secretary of the Ayuntamiento. The commission was given authority to
survey and delineate the boundaries of the grant and place Lerma in possession of such lands. The survey was begun on November 10, 1823, and
was completed twenty days later. The survey commenced at a point on
the left bank of the river opposite Sierra de Todos Santos and Ojo del Toro;
and ran thence in an easterly direction 35,000 varas to the highest peak of
the Sierra Blanca; thence southeasterly 55,000 varas to the Sierra del Agui-
la; thence southweesterly 22,000 varas to some hot springs on the left bank
of the river; and thence up the river with its meanders to the place of beginning. The directions taken by the surveying party were estimated, due
to the fact that no members of the commission had sufficient mathematical
experience to determine the exact courses taken with any degree of oc-
curacy. The distances traversed, however, were accurately measured by
José Manuel García and José Francisco Carbajal, who served as chain

carriers. Upon completing the survey, the commission placed Lerma in legal possession of the grant, and requested him to exert himself in the prompt settlement and development of such lands. The commission concluded its duties by filing a formal report of its actions with the Ayuntamiento, which approved the commission's report on December 12, 1823, and ordered the original copy of the proceedings to be filed in its archives and a copy thereof to be delivered to Lerma for his protection.[2]

Shortly after Lerma acquired the grant, he was temporarily recalled to active duty and was appointed Commander of a military company stationed at Presidio del Norte. One of his sons, Juan Lerma, and his brother-in-law, Fermín Leiva, managed the grant while he was away. When José Lerma returned, he granted a number of persons[3] from El Paso del Norte and San Elizario permission to pasture their cattle and horses upon the grant. Lerma also permitted his tenants to cultivate a number of fields of corn and beans along the banks of the river. His tenants built a few jacales, corrals, and fences upon the grant. Most of the valley land between Ojo del Toro and Ojo Caliente was eventually occupied by Lerma's tenants.

In 1828 the Ayuntamiento of El Paso del Norte refused to acknowledge Lerma's title, and attempted to issue three new land grants of one league each within the boundaries of the José Lerma Grant. When Lerma learned of the Ayuntamiento's actions, he petitioned the Governor of Chihuahua, requesting the ratification and confirmation of the concession. In response to Lerma's petition, Governor José Antonio Arce presented the request to the Second Constitutional Congress of the State of Chihuahua for its consideration. The Congress passed the following Act:

CIRCULAR No. 23

The Citizen José Antonio Arce, Retired Lieutenant and Colonel of the Active Army, and Constitutional Governor of the State of Chihuahua,

To All of Its Inhabitants, Greeting:

Know ye, That the Second Constitutional Congress of the State of Chihuahua, has decreed the following:

The Second Constitutional Congress of the State of Chihuahua Hereby Ratifies and Confirms the Decree of the Supreme Provincial Deputation, made on the 10th day of October, 1823, and the acts in conformity therewith had, By the Ayuntamiento of Paso del Norte, granting to Don José Lerma, Retired Lieutenant of the Active Army, for Distinguished Military Services, Rendered for the Republic, Fifty Leagues of Land.

For the Observance of the Governor of the State, and for exact Publication and Circulation.[4]

Boniface Rojos	Palace of Congress
José de Jesús Muñóz	June 30, 1828
Deputy Secretaries	Esteban Aguirre, *President*

In compliance with the provisions of this act, Governor Arce addressed the following communication[5] to the president of the Ayuntamiento of El Paso del Norte, on June 30, 1828:

The decree or title of possession ordered to be given by the Provincial Deputation and the Council of El Paso del Norte, in the year 1823, whereby fifty leagues of land on the left side of the Rio Bravo were granted to Don José Lerma, has been ratified and confirmed by the Second Constitutional Congress of this State, in consideration of distinguished military service rendered to the Republic by the retired Lieutenant José Lerma. Therefore, this government considers the land transferred by the granted bounty as an exclusive property of said José Lerma, ratifying it in all its parts. The Council of El Paso del Norte will act accordingly.

After confirmation of the grant, Lerma, through his tenants, continued to use and occupy the grant until they were forced to abandon the land in 1833 or 1834 due to the increased hostility of the Indians. Lerma sold the grant to his two sons, Juan and Félix, on December 15, 1840, for a consideration of $4,000.[6]

The grant was not re-occupied until 1846, when First Lieutenant Félix Lerma and his troops from El Paso del Norte defeated the Indians and drove them into the Carrizo Mountains. Juan Lerma managed the grant between 1846 and 1850. He also allowed a number of persons from El Paso del Norte and San Elizario to use the grant as a pasturage for their cattle.

From time to time, Félix loaned his brother various sums of money. Finally, in 1850, Félix verbally agreed to cancel this indebtedness, which he believed amounted to approximately $700, in exchange for Juan's share of the grant. Félix never received a formal deed covering Juan's undivided one-half interest in the grant, but relied upon the Mexican law, which permitted the conveyance of real estate by oral agreement.[7]

Félix Lerma never resided on the grant after he had acquired Juan's interest, but he had a number of tenants on the land until 1861. When the United States troops abandoned Fort Quitman in 1861, Félix Lerma's tenants were forced to vacate the lands due to the renewal of Indian hostilities, but he continued to permit a number of persons living south of the river in the vicinity of the grant to graze their cattle and cut wood off his lands.[8]

After José Lerma's death, Félix Lerma could not find his father's papers, which contained the *testimonio* of the grant and a copy of the 1828 Act of Confirmation. In order to protect his interest, Félix obtained a certified copy of the grant, and the approval by the Provincial Deputation. At the same time, but under separate cover, he obtained a certified copy of the governor's letter advising the Ayuntamiento of confirmation of the grant by the Second Constitutional Congress of Chihuahua. These copies were both certified to by Pilar de Laso, Second Alcalde of the town of El Paso del Norte, as being true copies of the originals, on December 20, 1852. Pilar de Laso was custodian of the archives of the Ayuntamiento of El Paso del Norte.

Nothing further was heard of the grant until 1887. On September 29, 1887, Félix Lerma entered into an irrevocable Power of Attorney and Agreement with John P. Randolph, of El Paso, Texas, whereby Randolph was authorized to make sales, to receive monies, to make compromises, and to institute suits for recovery and recognition of the José Lerma Grant. In consideration of such services and $1,000 cash, Félix Lerma conveyed an undivided one-half interest in the grant to John P. Randolph.[9]

The Mexican certified copy of the grant and approval by the Provincial Deputation was recorded in the Deed Records of El Paso County by Randolph on October 4, 1887.[10] He then obtained a certified copy of these two instruments from the El Paso County Clerk. Using this certified copy as his authority, Randolph, in his capacity as a Deputy Surveyor for El Paso County, proceeded to survey the José Lerma Grant. The survey showed that the grant contained approximately 370,000 acres of land.[11]

Randolph filed a certified copy of the grant, the approval by the Provincial Deputation, and the survey, in the General Land Office on November 28, 1887.[12] For some unexplained reason, Randolph did not record the Mexican certified copy of the Governor's Circular Letter in El Paso County until January 25, 1888, nor file it in the General Land Office until March 13, 1888.[13]

The confusion resulting from the inability of the owners of Texas land certificates to determine whether the lands upon which they planned to locate their certificates had previously been appropriated by secret and unrecorded Spanish or Mexican grants, prompted the members of the Constitutional Convention to include the following provision[14] in the Constitution of 1876:

No claim of title or right to land, which issued prior to the 13th day of November, 1835, which has not been duly recorded in the county where the land was situated at the time of such record, or which has not been duly archived in the General Land Office, shall ever hereafter be deposited in the General Land Office, or recorded in this State, or delineated on the maps or used as evidence in any of the courts of this State, and the same are stale claims; but this shall not affect such rights or presumptions as arise from actual possession.

In compliance with the prohibition contained in Section 4 or Article XIII of the Texas Constitution of 1876, R. M. Hall, Commissioner of the General Land Office, refused to recognize the José Lerma Grant, and declared that the grant papers were not to be regarded as an archive or a part of the records of the General Land Office. The lands embraced within said grant were never delineated upon the official county maps of the General Land Office.[15]

On December 15, 1887, W. H. Stevenson located Survey 126 as a 160-acre pre-emption claim. This survey commenced at a southeast corner of Section 48, Block 72, Township 7, Texas & Pacific Railway Company, El Paso County, Texas (now located in Hudspeth County, Texas), and ran south 950 varas; thence west 950 varas; thence north 950 varas; and thence east 950 varas to the point of beginning.[16]

Félix Lerma filed a friendly suit against W. H. Stevenson in the United States Circuit Court for the Western District of Texas, on August 9, 1888[17] Lerma alleged in his petition that he was the sole owner of the José Lerma Grant. He further alleged that the defendant's survey had been illegally made and cast a cloud upon his title. The case was submitted to the court upon an agreed statement of facts, wherein the defendant conceded that a valid grant had been made by the Ayuntamiento of El Paso del Norte in 1823, that the grant had been approved by the Provincial Deputation of Chihuahua in 1823, and that the grant had been confirmed by the Second Constitutional Congress of Chihuahua in 1828.

The court recognized that this was a friendly suit brought for the sole purpose of bolstering a stale claim and circumventing the prohibition contained in Section 4 of Article 13 of the Texas Constitution of 1876. In his opinion dated October 7, 1889, Judge Thomas S. Maxey stated that it was questionable whether the papers introduced by the plaintiff evidenced the issuance of a valid grant. He also found that the act of filing the title documents in El Paso County and the General Land Office was a nullity, and that the fact the plaintiff and his predecessors had cattle wandering over this immense tract of land afforded no presumption that he owned or claimed it. Despite these findings, the Judge held that, because the defendant had admitted and conceded that the plaintiff's title was valid, to reject it without judicial inquiry or to prohibit its use as evidence would impair the obligations of a contract and infringe upon property rights guaranteed by the Treaty of Guadalupe Hidalgo. Therefore, the court, in rendering its judgment in favor of Félix Lerma, expressly limited the decision to the facts of the case as agreed upon by the parties.[18]

During the years 1887 and 1888 Randolph, individually and as Attorney in Fact for Félix Lerma, had made numerous sales of various undivided interests under the José Lerma Grant. On October 24, 1890 Félix Lerma confirmed Randolph's acts by delivering a Warranty Deed[19] to the following persons for the following undivided interests in the grant: H. R. Hilderbrand (4|32), Rosina Sealey (4|32), Joseph Eubank (1|32), Joseph Eikel (5|64), William Brenstedt (5|64), Eugene Williams (5|32), E. J. Gurley (5|32), John A. Morris (8|32).

Fortified with the tacit recognition of the grant by the Federal Circuit Court, the new owners of the José Lerma Grant were in a position to make a bona fide effort to assert their claim against the Trustees of the Texas

Pacific Land Trust for the one hundred and twenty sections of land which they owned within the boundaries of the grant.

On March 28, 1889 John A. Morris and the other owners of the José Lerma Grant filed a trespass to try title suit in the United States Circuit Court for the Western District of Texas against Charles J. Canda and the other Trustees, lessees and assignees of the Texas Pacific Land Trust.[20] The plaintiffs alleged in their petition that they were the legal owners of the lands covered by the José Lerma Grant, but that the State of Texas, in violation of the Treaty of Guadalupe Hidalgo and the Constitution of the United States, had sought to divest them of their property rights by illegally issuing patents covering lands located within the grant. The plaintiffs closed by requesting the court to recognize their title to the lands embraced within the boundaries of the grant. The trustees denied the plaintiff's allegations, and also filed a cross bill, in which they asserted their claim to the alternate one hundred twenty sections of land which had been patented by the State of Texas to the Texas & Pacific Railway and subsequently purchased by them for a valuable consideration without notice of plaintiffs' claim.[21]

The case came up for trial on October 8, 1894. During the trial, the plaintiffs asserted that a valid grant had been issued to José Lerma under the Colonization Law of January 4, 1823, and confirmed in 1828. In support of this contention, they introduced the Mexican certified copies of the grant, the approval by the Provincial Deputation, and the Governor's Circular Letter. The plaintiffs then attempted to substantiate the validity of such grant with testimony by Félix Lerma. He testified that he knew the grant was valid, because:

his father had told him so, and he had read it many times. He also stated that after his father's copy of the *testimonio* had been lost he had secured a certified copy of all of the papers pertaining to the grant which were then filed in the archives of the Ayuntamiento of El Paso del Norte. He stated that he saw the original *expediente* in such archives on December 20, 1852, when he obtained the certified copies; that he compared the certified copies with the originals, and that the certified copies were true copies of the originals. Lerma stated that the last time he saw the original *expediente* of the grant was in 1862 in the Office of the Judge of Letters, who was the Custodian of the Archives of the Ayuntamiento. He presumed that the grant papers had been lost or destroyed during the Mexican Revolution, which occurred later in 1862. It is commonly known that during the Revolution of 1862 El Paso del Norte had been occupied by predatory bands, and that these forces confiscated a portion of the Public Archives in order to make cartridges. Lerma concluded his testimony by describing the facts pertaining to his acquisition, use, and sale of the grant.

When the plaintiffs rested their case, the defendants proceeded with the presentation of their views by attacking the validity of the grant on the

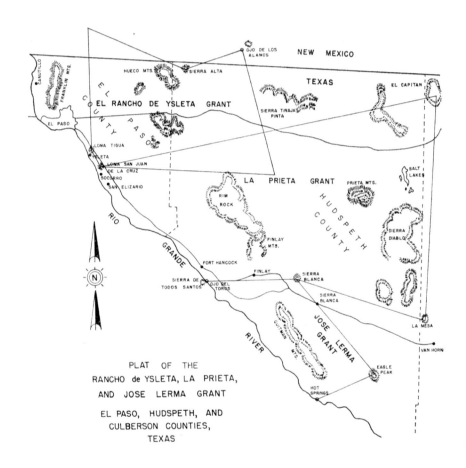

PLAT OF THE
RANCHO de YSLETA, LA PRIETA,
AND JOSE LERMA GRANT

EL PASO, HUDSPETH, AND
CULBERSON COUNTIES,
TEXAS

grounds that the Ayuntamiento lacked jurisdiction to issue a colonization grant to José Lerma under the National Colonization Law of 1823. They argued that the only authority an Ayuntamiento had over land matters was the allotment and distribution of lands contained within its particular town grant. Their contentions were based upon the decision of the Court of Private Land Claims rejecting the Heath Grant.²² In rebuttal, the plaintiffs argued that there was a long line of court decisions which held that it would be presumed that offiicials making a grant knew the law and acted accordingly. In opposing this argument, the defendants pointed out that such a presumption would arise only when there was long, peaceful possession of the grant, and that the occasional occupancy and small tillage was not sufficient to create a presumption that a valid grant had been issued in this case.

Continuing their jurisdictional attack on the grant, the defendants asserted that the Ayuntamiento had no power to issue a colonization grant on August 23, 1823, because the Mexican Constituent Congress had repealed the National Colonization Law on April 11, 1823. The plaintiffs attempted to controvert this attack by claiming that the Constituent Congress was not a duly elected body, and therefore it could not legally repeal the Colonization Law. Next, they claimed that the alleged repealing act was in fact only a resolution denouncing the National Colonization Law. Finally, the plaintiffs asserted that if the alleged act, which purportedly repealed the National Colonization Law, had been enacted by a legally constituted body, the act would not become effective in El Paso del Norte until actual notice of the suspension had been circulated in that town. They noted that the defendants had submitted no affirmative evidence of such promulgation. The defendants effectively trumped this contention by calling the court's attention to the fact that this same argument had been rejected by the Court of Private Land Claims in the Cessna Case.²³

The defendants next attacked the validity of the José Lerma Grant by pointing out that the title papers offered by the plaintiffs clearly showed on their faces that they were merely copies of documents which were allegedly located in the archives of the Ayuntamiento of El Paso del Norte in 1852, but which could not be found there in 1896. Continuing this line of argument, the defendants noted that the plaintiffs' claim was primarily based upon the Congressional Ratification of the grant in 1828, but that the instrument offered by the plaintiffs was merely a circular letter by the governor, announcing such ratification. The defendants asserted that the original decree should be in the archives at Chihuahua, but a diligent search of those archives failed to produce any evidence that such a decree had been enacted on June 30, 1828. This search further disclosed that while the Second Constitutional Congress of Chihuahua had been installed on June 30, 1828, it had not opened its session until July 1, 1828. The defendants contended that these facts strongly indicated that the purported decree had not been enacted, as alleged, but was probably supurious or forged. The defendants next cited a number of cases holding that adequate record evidence of a grant must be found in the archives of Mexico, in order to establish its validity. They argued that, in view of the fact that since none of the original title papers pertaining to the grant or any mention thereof could be found in the archives of Mexico, the plaintiffs' claim should be rejected. The plaintiffs attempted to answer this attack by pointing out that the National Colonization Law of 1823 did not specifically require the recording of the *expediente* in the archives of Mexico. They also contended that, in view of the fact that all lands now located within the State of Texas had formerly belonged to Mexico, all persons desiring to acquire title to land from Texas were required by the doctrine of constructive notice to conduct a diligent investigation, in order to determine whether or not such land had previously been granted by Mexico.

When the plaintiffs attempted to assert that their title had been previously recognized in the case of Lerma v. Stevenson, the defendants promptly pointed out to the court that the Judge had been bound by the stipulations filed in the case, and therefore was obligated to recognize Lerma's claim. They stated that the Judge apparently suspected a collusion because he expressly limited his decision to the particular facts involved in that case.

The defendants' next argument was that, in view of the fact that the plaintiffs were claiming the mineral rights under the grant had been conveyed to them by virtue of the grant to José Lerma and its subsequent confirmation, a copy of the original Decree of Confirmation of 1828 must be produced, in order to verify that the rights to such minerals had actually been confirmed. They pointed out that under Mexican law all mineral rights under a colonization grant would have been automatically reserved by the government, unless they were expressly conveyed.[24]

The court, in its decree[25] dated October 8, 1894, ordered the plaintiffs recover nothing by their suit against the defendants, and gave the Trustees a writ of possession for the one hundred twenty sections of land described in their cross-action. The plaintiffs appealed the case to the United States Circuit Court of Appeals, 5th Circuit, New Orleans, Louisiana. The Appellate Court affirmed[26] the lower court's judgment on May 4, 1897. The Appellate Court's decision finally removed the cloud which the plaintiffs' questionable claim had cast upon 370,000 acres of Texas soil, and indeed all hope of securing the recognition of the José Lerma Grant.

REFERENCES

1 José Lerma was born in Valle del San Darlolo in the State of Chihuahua, Mexico. He was married to Bartola Leiva, and they had four children: Juan, Félix, María de Jesús and Lázaro. José Lerma died at Chihuahua, Mexico in 1842. *Deposition of Félix Lerma in the Case John A. Morris et al v. Charles J. Canda et al*, (Mss., Records of the United States Circuit Court for the Western District of Texas, El Paso, Texas), No. 67.

2 *Deed Records* (Mss., Records of the El Paso County Clerk's Office, El Paso, Texas), XII, 550-556.

3 Galisto Leiva, Domisio Hidalgo, Antonio Arroyo, Juan Arroyo, José Barrios, Lorenzo Barrios, Lázaro Archuleta, José María García, José María Montes, Francisco García, Juan Romero, and Carlisto Olguin.

4 This act was embodied in Félix Lerma's petition in his suit against W. H. Stevenson. This act was apparently never offered into evidence, and was never recorded in El Paso County, Texas, nor filed in the General Land Office. No further reference to this document is made in the subsequent litigation concerning the José Lerma Grant. Lerma v. Stevenson, (Mss., Records of the United States Circuit Court for the Western District of Texas, El Paso, Texas), No. 51. All of the original papers filed in this suit have been lost, but a copy of plaintiff's petition is contained in the Records of the Texas Pacific Land Trust, Dallas, Texas.

5 *Brief for Plaintiffs in Error in the Case John A. Morris et al v. Charles J. Canda et al, Cause No. 368* (Mss., Records of the United States Circuit Court of Appeals, New Orleans, Louisiana), 10.

6 *Deed Records* (Mss., Records of the El Paso County Clerk's Office, El Paso, Texas), XIV, 220-223. In his suit against W. H. Stevenson, Félix Lerma claimed to have derived his interest in the grant by inheritance from his father, instead of by purchase. Lerma v. Stevenson (Mss., Records of the United States Circuit Court for the Western District of Texas, El Paso, Texas), No. 51.

7 *Deposition of Félix Lerma in the Case John A. Morris et al v. Charles J. Canda et al*, (Mss. Records of the United States Circuit Court for the Western District of Texas, El Paso, Texas), No. 67.

8 *Ibid.*

9 *Deed Records* (Mss., Records of the El Paso County Clerk's Office, El Paso, Texas), XXXVI, 29.

10 *Ibid.*, XII, 550-556.

11 *Book of Field Notes* (Mss., Records of the El Paso County Surveyor's Office, El Paso, Texas), I, 380.

12 *File No. Bexar 1-2693* (Mss., Records of the General Land Office, Austin, Texas).

13 *Ibid.*; and *Deed Records* (Mss., Records of the El Paso County Clerk's Office, El Paso, Texas), XIV, 48-50.

14 Gammel, *The Laws of Texas*, VIII, 822. The Texas Supreme Court, in interpreting this provision, which was a portion of Section 4 of Article XIII, held, in 1889, that the State had the power to declare what evidence could be archived in the General Land Office, recorded in the several counties, or delineated on public maps, but that the provision, insofar as it prevented persons from establishing their ownership of land in the courts of justice, was invalid because it was repugnant to, and conflicted with, Article I, Section 10, of the Fourteenth Amendment of the Constitution of the United States. Trans-Mexican Railway Co. v. Locke, 74 Tex. 370 (1889).

[15] *File No. Bexar 1-2693* (Mss., Records of the General Land Office, Austin, Texas).

[16] *File No. Bexar Pre-emption 6688* (Mss., Records of the General Land Office, Austin, Texas).

[17] Lerma v. Stevenson (Mss., Records of the United States Circuit Court for the Western District of Texas, El Paso, Texas), No. 51.

[18] Lerma v. Stevenson, 40 F. 356 (1889).

[19] *Deed Records* (Mss., Records of the El Paso County Clerk's Office, El Paso, Texas), XX, 233.

[20] Morris v. Canda, (Mss., Records of the United States Circuit Court for the Western District of Texas, El Paso, Texas), No. 67.

[21] *Ibid.*

[22] Cessna v. United States (Mss., Court of Private Land Claims, Records of the Bureau of Land Management, Santa Fe, New Mexico), No. 59.

[23] *Ibid.*

[24] *Defendants' Brief in the Case John A. Morris et al v. Charles J. Canda et al,* No. 368 (Mss., Records of the United States Circuit Court of Appeals, 5th Circuit, New Orleans, Louisiana).

[25] *Minute Book* (Mss., Records of the United States Circuit Court for the Western District of Texas), I, 458.

[26] Morris v. Canda, 80 F. 739.

CHAPTER 2 6

The José Ygnacio Ronquillo Grant ᷒

● Taking advantage of his official position to advance his personal interests, the officer in command of the frontier forces on the upper Rio Grande, Lieutenant Colonel José Ynacio Ronquillo, petitioned the Alcalde of Presidio del Norte, on January 15, 1832, for a grant of two hundred twenty-five square leagues of land located on the north bank of the Rio Grande opposite that town. The lands requested by Ronquillo embraced all of the lands lying between the mouth of Cibolo Creek, Ancón Grande, Los Alamos de San Juan, and Sierrita del Alamo. In response to this petition, the Constitutional Alcalde of Presidio del Norte, Cesario Herrera, granted the lands to Ronquillo on January 16, 1832, in accordance with the provisions of Title 12, Book 4, of the *Recopilación de las Leyes de los Reynos de las Indias.* The grant was issued subject to the conditions that he reside upon the grant for a period of four years, improve it within a period of three years, and agree to station a sufficient force of men, arms and horses on the grant to defend the area from Indian attack. Ronquillo was also expressly prohibited from alienating or encumbering the grant for a period of four years.[1]

On January 21, 1832, Herrera appointed as a commission Tomás García, José Valdes, and Dolores Parros to survey the grant. The survey was commenced on January 25, 1832, at the mouth of Cibolo Creek opposite Sierrita de San Cristóbal and ran up the east bank of the Rio Grande in a northwesterly direction, a distance of approximately fifteen leagues, to Ancón Grande; thence in a northeasterly direction, a distance of approximately fifteen leagues, to Los Alamos de San Juan; thence in a southeasterly direction, a distance of approximately fifteen leagues, to Sierrita del Alamo; and thence in a southwesterly direction, a distance of approximately fifteen leagues, to the place of beginning. After the survey had been completed, Herrera placed Ronquillo in possession of the lands embraced within the survey.[2]

Immediately after Ronquillo received the concession, he moved his family to the grant and established his headquarters at the place known as El Cibolo, located on Cibolo Creek approximately three miles north of Presidio del Norte. The settlement consisted of Ronquillo's stone house and a number of small huts for his peons and soldiers. Ronquillo and his family continuously lived on the grant between January 15, 1832 and November 27, 1832, except for several short periods when he sent his family to Presidio del Norte for protection while he was away with his troops on military expeditions. Several small fields were cultivated and some livestock was pastured on the grant. Ronquillo rented portions of the grant to a number of persons from Presidio del Norte. He also owned and operated a silver mine located on the grant which subsequently was known as the José Ruedas Mine.

As a result of Indian hostilities in the latter part of 1832, Ronquillo was transferred from Presio del Norte to Ojos Calientes. Upon receiving notice of his transfer, Ronquillo petitioned Herrera, requesting that he be excused from performance of the conditions specified in the grant on the grounds that he would be unable to fulfill them because of his conflicting military duties. Herrera issued a certificate on November 27, 1832, waiving performance of the conditions and restrictions contained in the grant. Ronquillo realized that he could not safely leave his family on the grant and that the premises could not be operated profitably without personal supervision. Therefore, on November 27, 1832, he sold the grant to his former *major-domo*, Hypólito Acosta, and moved his family to Presidio del Norte.[3]

After Ronquillo and his troops left the area, the Indian menace increased. The grant lands, which were mostly desolate and dry, soon became practically worthless without military protection. Confronted with these depressing conditions, Acosta, on May 10, 1833, accepted an offer by Señorita Juana Pedrasa to purchase the grant for 5,000 *pesos*.[4] The Indian situation caused Pedrasa to postpone indefinitely her plans of occupying the grant. Sometime within the next few years, she moved to Chihuahua, Mexico, where she married Ben Leaton.[5]

After the Treaty of Guadalupe Hidalgo transferred *de jure* jurisdiction over the land lying north of the Rio Grande to the United States, Leaton realized that if the Connelly Trail developed into a major line of communication between the United States and Mexico, a port of entry would be established north of the river, and the grant would become very valuable. In 1848 the Leatons settled at and occupied the old San José Mission, which was located upon the only tract of land north of the river suitable for agriculture. Ben Leaton purchased the mission and its lands on August 19, 1848 from Juan Bustillos, who allegedly had received a grant covering the mission from Lucas Aguilar, Alcalde of Presidio del Norte, on December 21, 1832.[6] However, it appears that Leaton paid Cesario Herrera $500 to manufacture a fraudulent title, which formed the basis of the alleged Juan Bustillos Grant. When Leaton attempted to dispossess a number of Mexican who were living on the alleged grant, they notified the Governor of Chihuahua of the conspiracy. Herrera was arrested and taken to Chihuahua in 1849 for trial. However, he was acquitted by the Mexican court when it was shown that the complainants had no title to the land, and jurisdiction over the land in question had passed to the United States. Thereafter, the Juan Bustillos Grant was considered to be completely void.[7]

Leaton's first effort to secure recognition of the José Ygnacio Ronquillo Grant occurred in 1850, when he retained R. A. Howard, Deputy Surveyor for the Bexar Land District, to survey the grant. Howard completed his survey on July 24, 1850, and filed it in the records of the Bexar Land District on February 27, 1851. The survey disclosed that the grant covered 2,345½ square miles of land, or approximately 1,500,000 acres.[8] The grant also was delineated on the 1855 General Land Office map of El Paso and Presidio Counties as the Ben Leaton Claim. Leaton recorded[9] a copy of the *testimonio* of the grant and the conveyance to Acosta and Juana Pedrasa in the Deed Records of Bexar County, Texas on July 16, 1851.

After having the grant surveyed and the title papers recorded, Leaton consulted an attorney about securing passage of an act confirming the grant. However, the attorney pointed out a glaring and fatal defect in Juana's title. He stated that although the conditions requiring Ronquillo to occupy and improve the grant probably could be waived due to their conflict with his military duties, he doubted that an alcalde had authority to waive the condition prohibiting the sale of the grant for a period of four years after its issuance. If Herrera did not have authority to waive this condition, the conveyance to Acosta was void. This defect apparently caused Leaton to abandon further efforts to secure recognition of the grant.

Years later, the Texas & Pacific Railway Company, the Galveston, Harrisburg & San Antonio Railway Company, the Houston & Texas Central Railway Company, the Mexican Central Railway Company, and the Gulf, Colorado & Santa Fe Railway Company received numerous land certificates pursuant to various Acts by the Texas Legislature, which had been passed in order to encourage construction of railroads in Texas. These certificates provided that they could be located anywhere upon the vacant unappropriated public domain of the State. Each of these companies located a large number of certificates upon the lands embraced within the boundaries of the grant between 1877 and April 22, 1882. Most of the alternate odd-numbered sections located within these conflicting railroad blocks had been patented to these powerful corporations. The even-numbered sections were set aside for the benefit of the Public School Fund of the State of Texas. By 1882, when the Big Bend area of Texas became relatively safe from the Indian menace, the grant was entirely covered by conflicting junior surveys.

While on a trip to Fort Davis in 1880, John W. Spencer, a pioneer resident of Presidio County, noticed a peculiar ledge of rock. He broke off a few samples and showed them to Colonel W. R. Shafter, who was then the commanding officer of Fort Davis. Any assay of the samples proved them to be very rich in silver ore. This valuable mineral deposit was located in Section 8, Block 8, H&TC Ry. Co. Survey, Presidio County, Texas. Shafter, Spencer, Lieutenant John L. Bullis, and Lieutenant Louis Wilhelmi jointly agreed to acquire and develop the deposit. On October 12, 1880 Bullis' wife, Alice, purchased Section 8 from the State of Texas. Thereafter, she conveyed an undivided one-fourth interest in Section 8 to each of her husband's partners. The land was patented to Alice Bullis, John W. Spencer, Wm. R. Shafter, and Louis Wilhelmi on November 16, 1885. Thereafter, they conveyed their interests to the Presidio Mining Company, which had been organized on October 20, 1883. The company commenced actual mining operations in 1884.[10] The town of Shafter sprang up near the Presidio Mining Company's mine.

The Cibolo Creek Mill and Mining Company was organized on February 8, 1884 to mill and process the ore which was mined in the Shafter area. This company erected a small stamp mill on two tracts of land located in Section 327, which it had purchased from Milton Favor. It also opened a mine on Section 5, Block 8, H&TC Railway company Survey, Presidio County, Texas, which it had purchased from the Houston & Texas Central Railway Company. The Cibolo Creek Mill and Mining Company also opened a mine on Section 1, Block 8, H&TC Railway Company Survey. The company had taken a mineral lease on this land from Frederick P. Olcott, successor in interest of the Houston & Texas Central Railway Company's lands.[11]

The interest created by the widespread reports that the Presidio Mining Company and the Cibolo Creek Mill and Mining Company were reaping fabulous profits from their silver mines caused Victor Ochoa, a grandson of Ben and Juana Leaton, to revive his ancestor's dormant claim to the

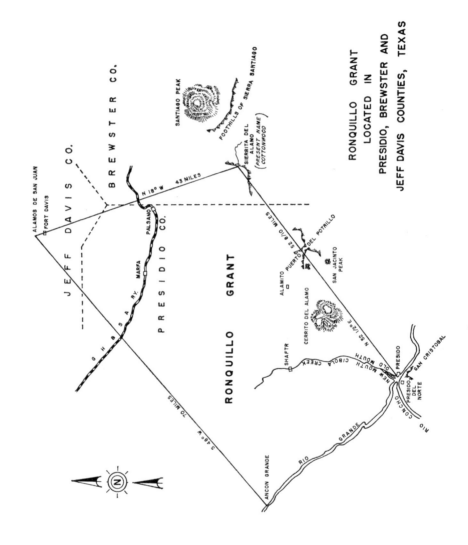

RONQUILLO GRANT
LOCATED IN
PRESIDIO, BREWSTER AND
JEFF DAVIS COUNTIES, TEXAS

José Ygnacio Ronquillo Grant. In 1885 Ochoa interested John R. Randolph in the speculative possibilities offered by this immense unrecognized land claim. Randolph contacted T. T. Teel, a prominent attorney of San Antonio, Texas, and requested him to represent the Leaton heirs in their efforts to secure confirmation of the grant. After locating the title papers to the grant in the County records at San Antonio, Teel notified Ochoa that he believed the grant was valid, but that he doubted that the Alcalde's certificate would be sufficient to overcome the legal obstacle which arose as a result of Ronquillo's having violated the condition which prohibited the conveyance of the land for a period of four years.

Sometime during the month of March, 1887, Teel made a special trip to Juárez, Mexico, to find additional evidence pertaining to the grant. While searching the archives there, Teel discovered a decree dated January 25, 1832, by the Constitutional Congress of the State of Chihuahua concerning the José Ygnacio Ronquillo Grant. Teel, who had only a slight knowledge of the Spanish language, realized that the decree was some type of confirmation of the grant. He secured a certified copy of the decree, but did not immediately attempt to have it translated. Before Teel was able to have the certified copy closely examined, it was lost.[12]

When Teel discovered the loss of the certified copy of the "Juárez Decree," he requested Victor Ochoa to secure another copy for him. Realizing that only a few people knew of Teel's startling discovery, Ochoa decided to remedy the defect in his ancestor's title by spiriting the original decree from the Juárez archives and substituting in its place a forged or spurious decree which was identical to the original in all respects, except it confirmed the action taken by the Alcalde of Presidio del Norte on November 27, 1832, instead of confirming the original grant.[13] Ochoa undoubtedly believed that if he could make it appear that the Chihuahuan Congress had confirmed the waiver of the conditions contained in the grant that the impediment to the title of the Leaton Heirs would be satisfactorily overcome. Once the forged decree had been slipped into the Juárez archives, Ochoa obtained a certified copy of the fraudulent instrument. He delivered this copy to Teel, who, believing the document was trustworthy, had it translated. He relied strongly upon the forged decree in reaching his decision that the grant was valid.

On May 10, 1887 Teel secured a Power of Attorney and Agreement from Isabella Shirley, the sole living child of Ben and Juana Leaton, and her husband, Frank Shirley. This instrument conveyed an undivided one-half interest in the grant to Teel in exchange for his agreement to secure the confirmation and recognition of the José Ygnacio Ronquillo Grant.[14] He also secured similar instruments from all the heirs of William and Joseph Leaton, the deceased sons of Ben and Juana Leaton.[15] Teel conveyed an undivided one-fourth interest in the grant to J. S. Dougherty and W. O.

Ellis on June 13, 1888. Teel also conveyed an undivided one-eighth interest in the grant to John P. Randolph on May 4, 1888, in consideration for Randolph's having referred the matter to him. Randolph obtained an additional undivided one-eighth interest in the grant on July 7, 1889 from Victor Ochoa, who had also acquired a Power of Attorney for the Leaton Heirs, covering the remaining one-half interest. Ochoa gave this interest to Randolph in consideration for the services he had rendered and monies he had expended in collecting information and evidence to be used in perfecting title to the José Ygnacio Ronquillo Grant. Randolph, in turn, sold an undivided one-eighth interest in the grant to H. R. Hilderbrand and Rosina Sealey, on December 3, 1889, for a consideration of $5,000.[16]

Teel obtained a certified copy of the grant, the Howard field notes, and the deeds to Acosta and Pedrasa from the Bexar County Clerk. He filed these instruments in the General Land Office on July 24, 1887, together with a formal protest against the issuance of patents to any individual or corporation on any survey located upon or within the limits of the grant.[17] Complying with the terms and provisions of his agreement with the Leaton Heirs, Teel also field a trespass to try title suit in the United States Circuit Court for the Western District of Texas on June 27, 1889, against the Cibolo Creek Mill and Mining Company and the Presidio Mining Company. In his petition, Teel claimed that the Leaton Heirs were the owners of the lands covered by the José Ygnacio Ronquillo grant. He further asserted that Texas, in violation of the specific guarantees contained in the Treaty of Guadalupe Hidalgo and Article XIII of the United States Constitution, had sought to divest the Leaton heirs of their just and legal title to the grant by issuing patents to the defendants. In addition to the recovery and judicial recognition of the grant, the complainants sought to recover the sum of one million dollars as damages, and six thousand dollars per month as rentals from the defendants.[18]

A similar suit was filed in the same court on July 5, 1889 by Teel for the Leaton heirs against the Texas & Pacific Railway Company, the Houston & Texas Central Railway Company, the St. Louis & Texas Railway Company, and the Galveston, Harrisburg & San Antonio Railway Company.[19] By this suit, Teel hoped to secure judicial recognition of the grant insofar as it conflicted with the large number of railroad land blocks which were located within its boundaries.

In the meantime, an interloper by the name of E. N. Ronquillo[20] brazenly proclaimed that he was the sole owner of the José Ygnacio Ronquillo Grant by virtue of purchase and inheritance. Having deduced that the deeds from José Ygnacio Ronquillo to Hypolito Acosta and Hypolito Acosta to Juana Pedrasa were invalid because they had been executed in direct violation of the express condition prohibiting such conveyances, he contended that the property rightfully belonged to the Heirs of José Ygnacio Ronquillo, who died at San Elizario, Texas in 1860. Relying upon this premise, he had systematically acquired quitclaim deeds from all of his other heirs.[21] E. N. Ronquillo promptly sold the grant to James J. Fitzgerrell, of Las Vegas, New Mexico, for an alleged consideration of $100,000,[22] who in turn transferred an undivided two-thirds interest in the property to Seth Crews, of Chicago, Illinois, for $150,000.[23] Fitzgerrell and Crews jointly conveyed all of their interest in the grant to Ernest Dale Owen, Trustee[24] for the stockholders of the Chicago & Texas Land & Cattle Company, on August 28, 1889, for four and one-half million dollars.[25]

Upon learning of E. N. Ronquillo's adverse claim, Teel had him arrested on a charge of asserting a fraudulent land claim.[26] Ronquillo promptly applied for a writ of habeas corpus. At the hearing on Ronquillo's writ, Teel showed that the José Ygnacio Ronquillo, who had received the grant, had been a soldier at Presidio del Norte in 1832, and had died at Ojos Calientes in 1834 or 1835. Teel was also able to prove that the José Ygnacio Ronquillo, who was E. N. Ronquillo's father, was never a soldier, had never lived at Presidio del Norte, and had died in 1860 at San Elizario, Texas. It appeared that E. N. Ronquillo based his claim to the José Ygnacio Ronquillo Grant solely upon the principle of *idem sonans*.[27] Despite the evidence introduced by Teel, Judge Allen Falvey released Ronquillo.

In April, 1889 the Leaton Heirs revoked the Powers of Attorney they had given Teel, on the grounds that he had failed to secure recognition of the José Ygnacio Ronquillo Grant, and had thereby permitted certain adverse claimants, who had settled upon portions of the lands embraced within the grant, to perfect their titles under the statutes of limitation.[28] Having been discharged by the Leaton heirs, Teel dismissed each of the suits he had filed.

In a determined effort to secure judicial recognition of E. N. Ronquillo's chain of title to the grant by the Federal Courts, Ernest Dale Owen filed seven trespass to try title suits in the United States Circuit Court for the Western District of Texas between January 29th and April 17, 1890.[29] Five of these suits were against the railroad companies and mining companies which claimed under junior conflicting surveys. One suit was against José Félix Gomerez and the other heirs of José Ygnacio Ronquillo, who had died in 1834 or 1835 at Ojos Calientes. The last suit was against Isabela Shirley and the other heirs of Ben and Juana Leaton.

Owen alleged in each case that he was the owner of the land by virtue of the grant issued to Ronquillo by the Alcalde of Presidio del Norte on November 27, 1832, and confirmed by the Constitutional Congress of Chihuahua on September 24, 1834. He further asserted that the patents under which each of the defendants claimed were invalid, and constituted a cloud upon his title. The State of Texas, which claimed a major portion of the land within the grant, was not made a party to any of these suits, because the State could not be sued without Legislative consent.

In their answer, the Leaton Heirs recognized the validity of the grant, but denied that Owen was the owner of the grant. They contended that the deeds into Juana Pedrasa had conveyed all of José Ygnacio Ronquillo's interest to them. José Félix Gomerez and his co-defendants also recognized the validity of the grant, but disputed Owen's allegation that he had acquired the land by mesne conveyances from the heirs of José Ygnacio Ronquillo. They stated that they were the true heirs of the original grantee. The defendants in each of the other cases denied the validity of the grant and its subsequent confirmation. They based their title to certain portions of the lands covered by the José Ygnacio Ronquillo Grant upon valid patents issued by the State of Texas.

In order to substantiate their allegation that the grant had never been confirmed, the defendants in Causes Numbered 12 through 16, inclusive, each filed an affidavit, stating that the alleged Confirmation Decree dated September 24, 1834, which was located in the Juárez archives, was a forgery. Depositions taken by these defendants tended to prove that Victor Ochoa had secured the printing of the alleged decree in El Paso, Texas, had forged the rubrics, and then placed the spurious instrument in the Juárez archives. It was obvious that the instrument was a forgery, as the paper and ink were unquestionably of recent date, and the rubrics thereon were so crudely executed that their falsification could be seen immediately.[30]

Confronted with this evidence, Owen had no alternative but to admit that the Juárez Decree was a forgery. In an effort to explain this spurious instrument. Owen contended that there had been an original decree dated September 24, 1834 in the Juárez archives which confirmed the José Ignacio Ronquillo Grant, but it had been subreptitiously removed from the archives by Ochoa and a forgery substituted in its place, in an attempt to bolster the Leaton heirs' claim.

Since several reliable persons had advised Owen that they had seen the original decree in the Juárez archives and believed it was genuine, he concluded that another copy of the decree was probably in the State archives at Chihuahua, Mexico. Therefore, Owen employed E. N. Ronquillo, who knew the Spanish language and would be of invaluable assistance in searching the old Mexican archives, and A. G. Foster, a reputable El Paso attorney, to locate another copy of the decree. Ronquillo and Foster went to Chihuahua, only to find that the archives for the month of September, 1834 had been lost or destroyed. Mr. J. Melchor de la Garza, who had been manager of the State's printing office in 1834, advised them that they might be able to locate a copy of the decree in El Valle or one of the other districts of the State of Chihuahua. The archives at El Valle, Mexico were incomplete, and they failed to find a copy of the decree there. Next, they went to Parral, Mexico, but were also unable to find the decree in the archives of that city. The Mayor of Parral advised them that the most complete set of archives in the State were located at Santa Bárbara, Mexico, a small out-of-the-way mining town whose records had not been ransacked during any of the frequent Mexican revolutions. Ronquillo and Foster went to Santa Bárbara in October, 1890 and requested permission to search its archives in an effort to find a copy of the Decree of Confirmation of September 23, 1834. After some difficulty, the Secretary of the Ayuntamiento of Santa Bárbara agreed to personally conduct a search of the archives in an effort to locate the decree. As a result of this search, the decree was found in duplicate in the proper bundle for the year 1834. The Santa Bárbara copy of the alleged Decree of Confirmation of September 23, 1834 was identical to, and a facsimile of, the copy allegedly found by Teel in the archives of Juárez, Mexico, except that the Santa Bárbara Decree did not have Governor José J. Calvo's rubric affixed thereto. Ronquillo was able to procure one of the copies of this decree, which he delivered to Owen.[31]

Notwithstanding the fortuitous finding of the Santa Bárbara Decree, Owen realized that it would be virtually impossible to secure recognition of his claim as long as the other proponents of the grant continued their disconcerting flanking attacks. In order to eliminate all further confusion over the identity of the original grantee, Owen purchased the interests owned by the Heirs of José Ygnacio Ronquillo, who died in 1834 or 1835 at Ojos Calientes.[32] Despite his earlier position that the deeds to Hypolito Acosta and Juana Pedrasa did not constitute a legal conveyance of the grant, Owen deemed it prudent to also purchase the claims of the Acosta and Leaton heirs.[33] By joining all of the adverse interests asserted by the various proponents of the grant, Owen was in a position to devote all of his attention to the attack upon the junior claimants of the lands covered by the José Ygnacio Ronquillo Grant.

After Ernest Dale Owen, trustee, had bought his peace with all of the other possible claimants of the grant, he entered into agreed judgments, on April 23, 1891, with the heirs of José Ygnacio Ronquillo and the heirs of Ben and Juana Leaton, whereby Owen's title to the grant, as between such heirs, was forever quieted and confirmed. The court, however, limited the decrees to the parties involved in the Shirley and Gomerez cases, and otherwise refused to pass upon the validity of the grant.[34]

In July, 1891 Ernest Dale Owen, Trustee, amended his Bills of Complaint in each of the remaining suits, alleging in said Amended Bills that he claimed the José Ygnacio Ronquillo Grant by virtue of a concession made by the Alcalde of Presidio del Norte on January 25, 1832, and subsequently confirmed by the Constitutional Congress of the State of Chihuahua on September 24, 1834, as evidenced by a decree found in the archives of Santa Bárbara, Mexico.

Due to the immense potential value of the silver mine located in Section 8, Block 8, H&TC Ry. Co. Survey, Presidio County, Texas, Owen elected to have his suit against the Presidio Mining Company tried first. The cause came up for hearing before Judge T. S. Maxey on March 21, 1892. At the trial, Owen introduced a certified copy of the *testimonio* and the duplicate printed copy of the Santa Bárbara Decree in support of the grant. The defendants raised four principal defenses in the case.

First, they asserted that the original grant was a forgery. In support of this contention, they introduced numerous depositions, showing many of the oldest and more reputable citizens of Presidio del Norte, Mexico had never known nor heard of the José Ygnacio Ronquillo Grant prior to 1848. They also offered depositions showing that Ben Leaton and Cesario Herrera had entered into a conspiracy to forge and pre-date the necessary grant papers to convey the tract of land upon which Fort Leaton was located to Ben Leaton, and that Herrera had been subsequently arrested by the Mexican authorities for manufacturing fraudulent land titles. Arguing that this circumstantial evidence, when coupled with the fact that the complainant had failed to produce or account for the loss of the *testimonio* and had been unable to locate the *expediente* in the Mexican archives, raised an insurmountable presumption against the authenticity of the grant. Owen attempted to rebut this argument by showing that the original grant papers had been recorded in San Antonio, Texas shortly after the end of the Mexican War, and no one had questioned the validity of the grant at that time. He also offered depositions by a number of witnesses, showing that the land had been granted to Ronquillo by Alcalde Herrera in 1832. He asserted that it would be unreasonable to presume that the name of José Ygnacio Ronquillo, who had been one of the most prominent and influential men in the State of Chihuahua, could be linked with a fraudulent grant of land of this magnitude without arousing an immediate protest by his heirs. Such a fraudulent grant would undoubtedly have brought forth ardent protest from the citizens of Presidio del Norte similar to the one which led to the original arrest of Alcalde Herrera in 1848. In an effort to account for his having been unable to find the *expediente* of the grant in the archives of Mexico, Owen pointed out that it was commonly known that a large portion of the archives of the northern frontier states had been plundered and destroyed during numerous revolutions which plagued Mexico.

Second, they alleged that even if the grant had not been forged and pre-dated, the concession was invalid, since the Alcalde of Presidio del Norte did not have authority to issue a grant to José Ygnacio Ronquillo in 1832 covering one and a half million acres of land. They pointed out that, under the Colonization Law of the State of Chihuahua of May 25, 1825, which had been passed in conformity with the National Colonization Law of 1824, only the governor had authority to make grants of land, and even he had no authority to grant more than eleven leagues of land. Owen answered this contention by arguing that the grant was not a colonization grant. He argued that it was a military grant, and therefore, not subject to the limitation contained in the various colonization laws. Continuing this line of argument, he pointed out that under Spanish law, sub-delegates[35] unquestionably had authority to issue grants to an individual. He then called the court's attention to Decree No. 65, which had been passed by the Congress of Chihuahua on August 5, 1825, abolishing the position of Sub-Delegate, and transferring the duties and authority formerly exercised by the Sub-Delegates to the Constitutional Alcaldes. Next, Owen argued that the court was bound by the decisions of the United States Supreme Court, which established the rule that it would be presumed that public officials of former sovereigns knew the local law and had lawfully performed their duties.[36] Concluding his logistical feat of legal gymnastics, Owen contended that Cesario Herrera, the Constitutional Alcalde of Presidio del Norte, unquestionably had authority to issue an individual military land grant to José Ygnacio Ronquillo.

The third point raised by the defendants was that the Decree of Confirmation found at Santa Bárbara was a forgery. They offered a considerable amount of testimony by expert witnesses which tended to substantiate their allegation, but they did not offer any evidence concerning the method by which the forgery was made, or the person or persons who made it. The defendants' expert testimony was based partly on an examination of the instrument itself and partly on a comparison of the decree with certain companion printed decrees found in the archives of Santa Bárbara. The defendants' expert printing witnesses testified that the ink of the decree appeared to be very fresh, and the style of type used in the printing of the decree and the paper upon which it was printed were not in existence in 1834. The defendants also presented a number of expert witnesses who were familiar with Spanish and Mexican legal documents. They testified that the decree contained numerous errors in accentuation, orthography, and typography, and these errors indicated that the instrument was a forgery. These witnesses further stated that only the national government had authority to grant mineral rights, and the fact that the alleged decree by the State of Chihuahua purported to confirm the grant, together with its minerals, indicated that the decree was a forgery. Next, the defendants' witnesses testified that Article 46 of the Constitution of the State of Chihuahua of 1825 required all the State laws to be signed or authenticated by the Secretary of State, and that the Santa Bárbara decree did not comply with that article. The defendants concluded their argument on this point by unexpectedly announcing that they had found all of the original decrees passed by the Legislature of the State of Chihuahua during the month of September, 1834 in the Secretary of State's office in Chihuahua, Mexico, and that these archives did not contain a copy of the alleged Decree of Confirmation, which was allegedly No. 16, but instead they had found an insignificant decree bearing the same number and date which pertained to the administration of local justice.

In rebuttal, Owen offered a number of depositions tracing the history of the discovery of the Santa Bárbara Decree. These depositions disclosed that the decree had been found in the proper place, in the proper bundle of decrees, and in the proper order. The officials at Santa Bárbara testified that in their opinion the decree was genuine. Next, the complainant offered depositions by two eminent Chicago microscopists, Henry L. Toleman and Marshall D. Ewell, who both testified that the paper upon which the Santa Bárbara decree was printed was old hand-made foreign or Spanish paper, which was in common use in Mexico in 1834; that the style of type used in printing the decree was in common use between 1810 and 1834; that the decree had been printed on an old style hand press, and that, although there was no test to determine the age of the printer's ink, the ink on the decree was brown or rusty with age. In conclusion, these experts stated that there was nothing about the decree which would lead them to believe that it was not actually printed in 1834.

Next, Owen introduced a deposition by Frederic Hall, the famous and scholarly author of Hall's Mexican Law. Hall stated that he was very familiar with Mexican legal documents, having been legal advisor to Emperor Maximillian in 1867 and a counsel for the Mexican Central Railroad in 1882. After conducting a thorough examination of the duplicate copy of the Santa Bárbara decree, Hall stated that he believed the instrument was genuine.

Owen also introduced depositions by James Alexander Forves, the keeper of the Archives of the United States Surveyor General in San Francisco, California; and Xavier Blanchard De Bray, the Spanish Clerk and Translator for the General Land Office of Texas. Both of these persons stated that it was a well known fact that Mexican decrees of the period around 1834 generally contained numerous errors in typography, spelling and grammar. They believed that if a decree did not contain such errors that it would tend to indicate that such a perfect decree was a forgery.

Owen answered the defendants' attack upon the Santa Bárbara decree on the grounds that it had not been authenticated by the Secretary of State by showing that the act of August 2, 1830 amended the former law by providing that only the decrees which required general statewide observance had to be authenticated by the Secretary of State. However, Owen could not offer any explanation as to why the archives of the Secretary of State's office did not contain a copy of their decree of confirmation, nor could he explain the existence of the second decree, No. 16.

The defendants' final defensive arguments were that they were innocent purchasers of the lands for value, without actual notice of the complainant's claim, or in the alternative, they had acquired title to the lands by adverse possession. Owen answered the first of these contentions by showing that the grant has lawfully been duly recorded in Bexar County, and that the constructive notice resulting therefrom prevented the defendants from becoming innocent purchasers. Turning to the second contention, he argued that the defendants had acquired no rights under the three-year statute of limitation, because the State's patents had not conveyed a color of title, which was a requisite to acquiring title under that statute, since the State could not lawfully patent lands which had previously been appropriated under a valid Mexican land grant. He also pointed out that a number of his predecessors in title were married women, and that their disabilities of coverture prevented the defendants from perfecting title under the five-year statute of limitation.[37]

After considering the pleadings, evidence and arguments, the court, in its decision dated April 12, 1892, held that a grant actually had been issued to José Ygnacio Ronquillo in 1832, but that the Alcalde of Presidio del Norte did not have authority, under the laws of Mexico, to make such a valid concession. The court further found that the grant had never been confirmed by the Congress of the State of Chihuahua. The court concluded its decree by dismissing the suit.[38]

Owen appealed the trial court's decision to the United States Circuit Court of Appeals.[39] The appellate court, after reviewing some 1,900 pages of printed record, 566 pages of printed briefs, and listening to three days of oral arguments, affirmed the judgment of the lower court. The court, in its decision dated March 13, 1893, held that Owen had not satisfactorily proved that the Alcalde of Presidio del Norte had actually made a grant to José Ygnacio Ronquillo on January 25, 1832. The court also held that in order to prove the execution of a valid grant, some documentary evidence thereof must be found in the archives of Mexico, and that a certified copy of an alleged *testimonio* obtained from the records of Bexar County, Texas was not sufficient evidence to prove the grant. The court further found that even if it assumed that the purported grant had actually been made by Herrera, such assumption would not raise a presumption that an alcalde had legal authority to issue a valid concession. On the contrary, the court specifically held that an alcalde did not have the authority to make a grant of the public lands after the adoption of the State Colonization Law of May 25, 1825.

Continuing, the court stated that the principal issue in the case was whether or not the grant had been confirmed by the Congress of Chihuahua in 1834. If the grant had to be confirmed, then the issues concerning the genuineness of the grant papers and an alcalde's authority were rendered moot. The court stated that it seriously doubted the genuineness of the decree of confirmation, since no duly authenticated copy of the decree had been found in any of the archives of Mexico, and because the decree violated both the State's and National Government's policy prohibiting the granting of more than eleven leagues of land to one individual. The court further stated it believed that the original papers had been forged and pre-dated; that the scheme had been abandoned shortly after the former public official (who purportedly made the grant) had been arrested on a charge of issuing fraudulent land titles; that the scheme had not been revived until after the defendants had discovered and expended large sums of money developing the mineral resources located within its boundaries, and that in order to obtain the minerals under the fraudulent claim, some interested party or parties concocted the alleged decree or decrees of confirmation. The court concluded its opinion by holding that the Santa Bárbara decree was also a forgery, but it expressly exonerated Owen from all knowledge of, or complicity in, the attempted fraud.[40] As a result of the decisive rejection of the grant by the federal courts, Owen decided to dismiss all of his other suits without prejudice to his rights.[41]

In a final desperate effort to secure recognition of the José Ygnacio Ronquillo Grant, Ernest Dale Owen, Trustee, invoked the jurisdiction of the Texas courts by filing a trespass to try title suit against the Cibolo Creek Mill & Mining Company in a District Court at Presidio, Texas, on June 9, 1896. In his petition, Owen alleged that he was the sole owner of the lands covered by the José Ygnacio Ronquillo Grant, and that the Cibolo Creek Mill & Mining Company had ejected him from Sections 1 and 5, Block 8, H&TC Ry. Co. Survey, and a portion of Survey 327, Presidio County, Texas. The case was transferred to El Paso County, Texas on a change of venue. The case was set for hearing on May 27, 1897. When the case came up for trial, the plaintiff dismissed his petition, but the case proceeded to trial on the defendant's plea in reconvention. After the defendant had presented its testimony proving its title to the lands in question, the court instructed a verdict in its favor.[42] Owen appealed the case to the Texas Court of Civil Appeals, which affirmed the decision on November 24, 1897.[43] The refusal of the Texas courts to recognize the validity of the title to the José Ygnacio Ronquillo Grant ended Owen's persistent efforts to secure its recognition, and finally cleared the title to an area approximately twice the size of the State of Rhode Island.

REFERENCES

1 *Deed Records* (Mss., Records of the Bexar County Clerk's Office, San Antonio, Texas), J-1, 48-52.

2 *Ibid.*   3 *Ibid.*   4 *Ibid.*

5 Ben Leaton, a native of Kentucky, was actively engaged in the Chihuahua trade in the latter part of the 1830's. It is not known when he first met Juana Pedrasa, but they were living together in Chihuahua, Mexico in 1839. Tradition has it that Leaton was a member of Colonel Alexander W. Doniphan's forces, but Josiah Gregg's reference to him on May 14, 1847, as being a desperado at Parras, Mexico, does not bear out that story. Leaton was unquestionably acquainted, if not actually associated, with Dr. Henry Connelly in the opening of the Connelly Trial in 1839-1840. Shortly after the close of the Mexican War, Leaton settled on the American side of the river a few miles east of Presidio del Norte at the old San José Mission, which had been built in 1715. He converted the mission into an almost impregnable stronghold. After Leaton remodeled the mission, it was called Fort Leaton. Leaton used the fort as his headquarters for a lucrative three-way trade with the Indians, Anglos, and Mexicans. He was kind and hospitable toward his friends, but brutal and ruthless in his dealings with his adversaries. He cold-bloodedly slaughtered and murdered a band of Indians, whom he had invited to the fort for a feast, because they had stolen some of his livestock. He was charged by the Mexican government with furnishing the Indians with arms, encouraging them to plunder south of the border, and then purchasing the property stolen from the Mexicans. On the other hand, Leaton was active and interposing in his assistance to American travelers who passed through the area. He died at Fort Leaton in 1852. Ralph P. Bieber, *Exploring Southwestern Trails* (Glendale, 1936), 284-289; Mrs. O. L. Shipman, *Taming of the Big Bend* (N.P., N.D.), 6, 10; Maurice Garland Fulton, *Diary and Letters of Josiah Gregg — Excursions in Mexico and California, 1847-1850* (Norman, 1944), 127; and *Senate Executive Documents*, 31st Cong., 1st Sess., No. 1 (1850).

6 *Deed Records* (Mss., Records of the Presidio County Clerk's Office, Presidio, Texas), XII, 23 and 29.

7 *Appellant's Brief in the Case Owen v. Presidio Mining Company et al, Cause No. 58* (Mss., Records of the United States Circuit Court of Appeals, 5th Circuit, New Orleans, Louisiana), 91.

8 *Book of Field Notes* (Mss., Records of the Bexar County Surveyor's Office, San Antonio, Texas), F-1, 54.

9 *Deed Records* (Mss., Records of the Bexar County Clerk's Office, San Antonio, Texas), J-1, 48-52.

10 *Appellee's Brief in the case of Owen v. Presidio Mining Company et al, Cause No. 58,* (Mss., Records of the United States Circuit Court of Appeals, 5th Circuit, New Orleans, Louisiana), 117-128.

11 *Statements of Fact in the case of Owen v. Cibolo Creek Mill and Mining Company et al, Cause No. 2662,* (Mss., Records of the El Paso District Clerk's Office, El Paso, Texas).

12 *Appellee's Brief in the case Owen v. Presidio Mining Company et al, Cause No. 58,* (Mss., Records of the United States Circuit Court of Appeals, 5th Circuit, New Orleans, Louisiana), 162.

13 *Ibid.,* 108, 109.

210   SPANISH AND MEXICAN LAND GRANTS

14 *Deed Records* (Mss., Records of the Presidio County Clerk's Office, Presidio, Texas), XIII, 76.

15 *Power of Attorney Records* (Mss., Records of the Presidio County Clerk's Office, Presidio County, Texas), I, 35, 39, and 42.

16 *Deed Records* (Mss., Records of the Presidio County Clerk's Office, Presidio, Texas), VII, 531; and XIII, 125, 190.

17 *Letter File No. 210482* (Mss., Records of the General Land Office, Austin, Texas).

18 Leaton v. The Cibolo Creek Mill and Mining Co. (Mss., Records of the United States Circuit Court for the Western District of Texas, El Paso, Texas), No. 73.

19 Shirley v. Texas & Pacific Railway Co. (Mss., Records of the United States Circuit Court for the Western District of Texas, El Paso, Texas), No. 74.

20 Estanislado N. Ronquillo was a well known attorney of Juárez, Mexico. When he mysteriously disappeared in 1891, it was generally believed that he had been murdered. His skeleton was dug up on Upson Avenue, El Paso, Texas, on November 26, 1918. El Paso *Herald*, November 26, 1919.

21 *Deed Records* (Mss., Records of the Presidio County Clerk's Office, Presidio, Texas), XIII, 91, 107, 116, and 117.

22 *Ibid.*, XIII, 97.

23 *Ibid.*, XIII, 109.

24 Ernest Dale Owen, a prominent Chicago attorney, was associated with Seth Crews in the general practice of law. He speculated heavily in western land ventures. Owen died in Chicago on May 14, 1914, at the age of sixty-four. He left no children, but was survived by his wife. *Chicago Legal News*, May 16 1914.

25 *Ibid.*, XIII, 134.

26 El Paso *Times*, January 29, 1890.

27 *Appellee's Brief in the case Owen v. Presidio Mining Company et al, No. 58* (Mss., Records of the United States Circuit Court of Appeals, 5th Circuit, New Orleans, Louisiana), 53.

28 *Deed Records* (Mss., Records of the Presidio County Clerk's Office, Presidio, Texas), XIII, 76, 79 and 83.

29 Owen v. Presidio Mining Co., No. 12; Owen v. Cibolo Creek Mill & Mining Co., No. 13; Owen v. Galveston, Harrisburg & San Antonio Railway Co., No. 14; Owen v. Texas & Pacific Railway Co., No. 15; Owen v. Houston, Texas Central Railway Co., No. 16; Owen v. Gomerez, No. 17; and Owen v. Shirley, No. 18; (Mss., Records of the United States Circuit Court for the Western District of Texas, El Paso, Texas).

30 *Appellant's Brief in the case Owen v. Presidio Mining Company et al, No. 58* (Mss., Records of the United States Circuit Court of Appeals, 5th Circuit, New Orleans, Louisiana), 108.

31 *Ibid.*, 109, 110, and 156.

32 *Deed Records* (Mss., Records of the Presidio County Clerk, Presidio, Texas), XIII, 471, 474, 476 and 505.

33 *Ibid.*, XIII, 281, 283, 287, 370, 416, 419-423, 482, 565 and 631.

34 *Minute Book* (Mss., Records of the United States Circuit Court for the Western District of Texas, El Paso, Texas), I, 247.

35 Among the outstanding reforms in colonial administration introduced by Charles III in the latter part of the eighteenth century were certain changes in local government. New Spain was divided into twelve *Intendencias*. The *Intendencia* was presided over

by a *Gobernador Intendente,* and was divided into districts, or *Partidos.* Each *Partido* was in charge of a *Subdelegado,* or Sub-Delegate, who was nominated by the *Gobernador Intendente,* but appointed by the Viceroy. C. H. Haring, *The Spanish Empire in America,* (New York, 1947), 144 & 145.

36 United States v. Peralta, 19 How. (60 U.S.) 343 (1857); and Gonzales v. Ross, 120 U.S. 605 (1887).

37 Owen v. Presidio Mining Co. (Mss., Records of the United States Circuit Court for the Western District of Texas, El Paso, Texas), No. 12.

38 *Minute Book* (Mss., Records of the United States Circuit Court for the Western District of Texas, El Paso, Texas), I, 327.

39 Owen v. Presidio Mining Co. (Mss., Records of the United States Circuit Court of Appeals, 5th Circuit, New Orleans, Louisiana), No. 58.

40 Owen v. Presidio Mining Co., 61 F. 6 (1893).

41 *Minute Book* (Mss., Records of the United States Circuit Court for the Western District of Texas, El Paso, Texas), I, 524.

42 Owen v. Cibolo Creek Mill & Mining Co., (Mss., Records of the El Paso District Clerk's Office, El Paso, Texas), No. 2662.

43 Owen v. Cibolo Creek Mill & Mining Co., 43 S.W. 297 (1897).

PART III

Bibliography

~~~~~~

PRIMARY SOURCES

A. Administrative Decisions, Journals, Laws, Reports and Statutes

Appendix to the Journals of the Senate of the Third Legislature, State of Texas, Second Session (Austin, 1850).

Biannual Report of Commissioner of the General Land Office (Austin, 1908).

Chamizal Arbitration — Appendix to the Case of the United States Before the International Boundary Commission, United States — Mexico (2 Vols., Washington, 1911).

Chamizal Arbitration — Counter Case of the United States of America Before the International Boundary Commissioner, United States — Mexico (Washington, 1911).

Decisions of the Department of the Interior and the General Land Office (Washington, 1908), I, XXVI, XXXVIII.

H. P. N. Gammel, *The Laws of Texas* (10 Vols., Austin, 1898).

Frederic Hall, *The Laws of Mexico* (San Francisco, 1885).

Journal of the House of Representatives of the State of Texas, Fourth Legislature, Extra Session (Austin, 1853).

Journal of the House of Representatives of the State of Texas, Fifth Legislature (Austin, 1854).

Journal of the House of Representatives of the State of Texas, Seventh Legislature (Austin, 1858).

Journal of the Senate of the State of Texas, Fifth Legislature (Austin, 1854).

Journal of the Senate of the State of Texas, Seventh Legislature (Austin, 1858).

Francisco F. de la Maza, *Código de Colonización y Terrenos Baldíos* (Mexico, 1893).

Hunter Miller, *Treaties and Other International Acts of the United States of America* (6 Vols., Washington, 1937).

Proceedings of the International (Water) Boundary Commission, United States and Mexico, Treaties of 1884 and 1889 (2 Vols., Washington, 1903).

Recopilación de Leyes de Los Reynos de las Indias (Madrid, 1943).

Report of the Boundary Commissioner, The State of New Mexico v. The State of Texas (Washington, D.C., 1930).

Report of Commissioner of General Land Office, 1910-1912 (Austin, 1912).

Report of the Special Master in the Case of the State of New Mexico v. The State of Texas (Washington, D.C., 1926).

Matthey G. Reynolds, *Spanish and Mexican Land Laws* (St. Louis, 1895).

United States Statutes at Large, IX, XVI, XXVI, XXXVI, XLV.

Vernon's Annotated Revised Civil Statutes of the State of Texas, Revision of 1925 (Kansas City, 1947).

B. Collections

Judge Josiah F. Crosby-Letters (Mss, Records of the Texas Archives, Austin, Texas).

Letters and Papers of Charles S. Taylor (Mss., Records of Stephen F. Austin State Teacher's College, Nacogdoches, Texas).

Records of the Executive Office, December 21, 1856 — December 21, 1857, E. M. Pease (Mss., Records of the Texas Archives, Austin, Texas).

C. Government Documents

1. *House Executive Documents*
   31st Cong., 1st Sess., Doc. 1 (1849); 33rd Cong., 1st Sess., Doc. 109 (1853; 34th Cong., 3rd Sess., Doc. 1 (1856); 45th Cong., 2nd Sess., Doc. 93 (1878); and 49th Cong., 1st Sess., Doc. 196 (1886).

2. *House Report*
   36th Cong., 1st Sess., Report 321 (1859).

3. *Senate Executive Documents*
   31st Cong., 1st Sess., Doc. 1 (1850); 32nd Cong., 1st Sess., Doc. 119 (1852); 43rd Cong., 1st Sess., Doc. 43 (1873); 43rd Cong., 1st Sess., Doc. 56 (1873); 47th Cong., 1st Sess., Doc. 70 (1882); 49th Cong., 2nd Sess., Doc. 113 (1887); 50th Cong., 1st Sess., Doc. 19 (1887).

D. Letters

W. J. Anderson to J. J. B., May 25, 1964; Myra Ellen Jenkins to J. J. B., July 25, 1963, September 7, 1970; Paul McComb to W. H. Abrams, March 4, 1911 (Mss., Records of Texas Pacific Land Trust, Dallas, Texas); José García Noblijas to J. J. B., June 15, 1959; J. T. Robinson to El Paso Chamber of Commerce, October 9, 1911 (Mss., Records of El Paso

County Clerk's Office, El Paso, Texas); J. T. Robinson to Park Pitman, March 20, 1907 (Mss., Records of El Paso County Clerk's Office, El Paso, Texas); J. T. Robinson to Park Pitman, March 7, 1912 (Mss., Records of El Paso County Clerk's Office, El Paso, Texas); J. T. Robinson to Park Pitman, October 16, 1907 (Mss., Records of El Paso County Clerk's Office, El Paso, Texas); J. T. Robinson to F. G. Turner, May 11, 1908 (Mss., Records of El Paso County Clerk's Office, El Paso, Texas); and James F. Smith to J. J. B., September 24, 1959.

E. Newspapers and Periodicals

Chicago *Legal News,* May 16, 1914.

The Daily Herald (El Paso, Texas), March 5, 1891.

El Paso *Daily Times,* (Mid-summer Trade Edition), August, 1887.

El Paso *Herald,* August 23, 1894; March 20, 1918; March 21, 1918; and November 26, 1919.

El Paso *Times,* January 29, 1890; July 3, 1949; and July 10, 1949.

Lone Star, February 7, 1883.

The San Antonio *Daily Express,* January 13, 1894.

State Gazette, August 27, 1853; and August 30, 1856.

F. Reported Court Decisions

Board of School Trustees of the City of San Antonio v. Galveston H&SA R. Co., 67 W. 147 (1902); Cartwright v. Public Service Company of New Mexico, 342 P. 2d 654 (1959); Cessna v. United States, 169 U.S. 165 (1898); City of Ysleta v. Canda, 67 F. 6 (1895); Crawford v. White, 25 S.W. 629 (1930); Crosby v. Di Palma, 141 S.W. 321 (1911); Dunn v. Wing, 128 S.W. 108 (1910); Gonzales v. Ross, 120 U.S. 605 (1887); Harris v. O'Connor, 185 S.W. 2d 993 (1944); Hamilton v. Texas, 152 S.W. 1117 (1913); Lerma v. Stevenson, 40 F. 356 (1889); McKinney v. Saviego, 18 How. (59 U.S.) 235 (1856); McMullen v. Hodges, 5 Tex. 33 (1849); Morris v. Canda, 80 F. 739 (1897); New York & Texas Land Co., Limited v. Thomson, 17 S.W. 920 (1891); New York & Texas Land Co., Limited v. Votaw, 150 U.S. 22 (1893); Owen v. Cibolo Mill and Mining Co., 43 S.W. 297 (1897); Owen v. Presidio Mining Co., 61 F. 6 (1893); Pence v. Cobb, 155 S.W. 608 (1913); Pueblo of Zia v. United States, 168 U.S. 198 (1897); San Francisco v. LeRoy, 138 U.S. 656 (1891); State of New Mexico v. State of Texas, 275 U.S. 279 (1927); State of Texas v. Cardenas, 47 Tex. 250 (1877); Stevens v. Crosby, 166 S.W. 62 (1914); Stevenson v. Bennett, 35 Cal. 424 (1868); Texas v. Indio Cattle Company, 154 S.W. 2d 308 (1941); Texas-Mexican Railway Company v. Locke, 74 Tex. 370 (1889); Town of Refugio v. Byrne, 25 Tex. 193

(1860); United States v. Chaves, 159 U.S. 452 (1895); United States v. Chaves, 175 U.S. 509 (1899); United States v. Crosby, 73 S.Ct.Rep. 915 (1926); United States v. Pendell, 185 U.S. 189 (1902); United States v. Peralta, 19 How. (60 U.S.) 343 (1857); United States v. Reymond, 166 U.S. 72 (1897); United States v. Santa Fe, 165 U.S. 675 (1897); and Wylie v. Wynne, 26 Tex. 43 (1861).

G. Records of the District Clerk's Office, Las Cruces, New Mexico Case

Pendell v. The Unknown Heirs, Executors and Administrators of George Baggs, Dec. No. 2741.

H. Records of the District Clerk's Office, El Paso, Texas

1. *Cases*
   Alexander v. Morehead, No. 1504; City of Ysleta v. Canda, No. 2000; The Corporation of the Town of Socorro v. The Corporation of the Town of San Elizario, No. 332; Crawford v. White, No. 29011; Crosby v. Cadwallader and Bros., No. 832; Hoffman v. Hendrix, No. 16,320; Magoffin v. Mills, No. 157; Owen v. Cibolo Creek Mill and Mining Co., No. 2662; Pueblo de Cenecú v. The Inhabitants of Ysleta, No. 46; Pueblo de Cenecú v. The Inhabitants of Ysleta, No. 99; and Town of Ysleta v. Canda, No. 1140.

2. *Minute Books*
   Minute Book, A, B, A-2, I, V, VII, VIII, IX, XIV, XX.

I. Records of the District Clerk's Office, Austin, Texas

1. *Case*
   Texas v. Meecham, No. 16,282.

2. *Minute Book*
   Minute Book, X.

J. Records of the Clerk of the Court of Civil Appeals, San Antonio, Texas

Brief
Appendices to the Brief of Appellants in Texas v. Valmont Plantations, No. 13,583.

K. Records of the Supreme Court's Clerk's Office, Austin, Texas

1. *Brief*
   Appellant's Brief in Clark v. Hills, No. 5534.

2. *Testimony*
   Testimony of Anson Mills in Clark v. Hills, No. 5534.

L. Records of the Court of Private Land Claims, Bureau of Land Management, Santa Fe, New Mexico

1. *Cases*

Alvarez v. United States, No. 280; Barela v. United States, No. 137; Barela v. United States, No. 281; Cessna v. United States, No. 59; City of Ysleta v. United States, No. 33; Colony of Refugio v. United States, No. 150; Corporation of the Grant of José Manuel Sánchez Baca v. United States, No. 138; Crosby v. United States, No. 139; Incorporation of Mesilla v. United States, No. 151; Ochoa v. United States, No. 193; Pendell v. United States, No. 168; and Reymond v. United States, No. 24.

2. *Journals*

Journal, I, II, III, and IV.

M. Records of the United States Circuit Court for the Western District of Texas, Austin, Texas

1. *Case*

Magoffin v. Campbell, No. 1290½.

2. *Deposition*

Deposition of Guadalupe Miranda in Magoffin v. Campbell, No. 1290½.

N. Records of the United States Circuit Court for the Western District of Texas, El Paso, Texas

1. *Cases*

Buchoz v. The El Paso Real Estate Company, No. 135; Buchoz v. Morehead, No. 101; City of Ysleta v. Canda, No. 190; Leaton v. The Cibolo Creek Mill and Mining Co. No. 73; Lerma v. Stevenson, No. 51; Morris v. Canda, No. 67; Owen v. The Cibolo Creek Mill and Mining Co., No. 13; Owen v. Galveston, Harrisburg & San Antonio Railway Co., No. 14; Owen v. Gomerez, No. 17; Owen v. Houston & Texas Central Railway Co., No. 16; Owen v. The Presidio Mining Co., No. 12; Owen v. Texas & Pacific Railway Co., No. 15; Owen v. Shirley, No. 18; Shirley v. Texas & Pacific Railway Co., No. 74; and Towns of San Elizario and Socorro v. Canda, No. 131.

2. *Depositions*

Deposition of Josiah F. Crosby in Warder v. The Campbell Real Estate Company, No. 277.

Deposition of Félix Lerma in Morris et al v. Canda, et al, No. 67.

3. *Minute Books*

Minute Book, I and II.

O. Records of the United States Circuit Court of Appeals, Fifth Circuit, New Orleans, Louisiana

1. *Cases*
   Owen v. The Presidio Mining Co., No. 58; and Morris v. Canda, No. 368.

2. *Briefs*
   Appellant's Brief in Ernest Dale Owen, Trustee, v. The Presidio Mining Company *et al*, No. 58.
   Appellee's Brief in Ernest Dale Owen, Trustee, v. The Presidio Mining Company *et al*, No. 58.
   Defendant's Brief in John A. Morris *et al* v. Charles J. Canda *et al*, No. 368.
   Brief for Plaintiffs in Error in John A. Morris *et al* v. Charles J. Canda *et al*, No. 368.

P. Records of the United States Supreme Clerk's Office, Washington, D.C.

Cases
Cessna v. United States, No. 78 of the October, 1896 Term; and United States v. Reymond, No. 706 in the October, 1896 Term.

Q. Records of the Dona Ana County Clerk's Office,

Las Cruces, New Mexico
Deed Records, B, IV, VI, XIV, XVII, XX, XXIX, XXXV, XXXVIII, XLIII, and XLVI.

R. Records of the El Paso County Clerk's Office, El Paso, Texas

1. *Deed Records*, A, B, C, D, E, F, G, I, V, B-3, IV, VIII, XI, XII, XIV, XIX, XX, XXIV, XXV, XXVI, XXXV, XXXVI, CLXVI, CLXXV, CLXXXV, CCLV, CCLXXXVII, CCCXIII, CCCXVI, and CCCLXXXVII.

2. *Minutes of the Commissioner's Court, Minute Book*, XIV.

S. Records of the Bexar County Clerk's Office, San Antonio, Texas

Deed Records, J-1.

T. Records of the Grant County Clerk's Office, Silver City, New Mexico

Deed Records, I and VII.

U. Records of Presidio County Clerk's Office, Presidio, Texas

1. *Deed Records*, VII, XII, and XIII.
2. *Power of Attorney Records*, I.

V. Records of the Bexar County Surveyor's Office, San Antonio, Texas

Book of Field Notes, F-1.

W. Records of the El Paso County Surveyor's Office, El Paso, Texas

Book of Field Notes, A-1, I.
Field Book, LXX, LXXIV.
Private Land Surveys.
Records, A (Transcribed); B (Transcribed).
Ysleta Grant Survey Book.

X. Records of the General Land Office, Austin, Texas

1. *County Maps*
   El Paso County, June, 1921.

2. *Land Files*

Bexar D-1034	Bexar B-1350	Bexar 1-1390
Bexar 1-1007	Bexar 1-1382	Bexar 1-2693
Bexar 1-1499	Bexar 1-2212	Bexar Pre-emption 6688.
Bexar 2-398	Bexar 1-1447	

3. *Letter Files*
   Letter Files 194,001½; 199,908; and 210,482.

Y. Records of the Archdiocese of Santa Fe, New Mexico

1. *Patentes,* IX.

2. *Accounts,* LXXXII.

Z. Records of the Audiencia de Guadalajara, Mexico

Archivo General de Indias, Legajo 139.

AA. Records of the Surveyor General's Office, Bureau of Land Management, Santa Fe, New Mexico

1. *Land Grant Reports*
   José Manuel Sánchez Baca Grant, Report No. 129; Bracito Grant, Report No. 6; Doña Ana Bend Colony Grant, Report No. 85; Mesilla Civil Colony Grant, Report No. 86; Refugio Civil Colony Grant, Report No. 90; Santa Teresa Grant, Report No. 111; Santa Rita del Cobre Grant, Reports Nos. 107 and 194; and Santo Tomás de Yturbide Colony Grant, Report No. 139.

2. *Land Claim Records*
   Land Claim Records, I, IV, V, VI, and VII.

BB. Records of the Cadastrial Engineer's Office, Santa Fe, New Mexico

José Manuel Sánchez Baca Grant, Map File 129; Bracito Grant, Map File 6; Doña Ana Bend Colony Grant, Map Files 24 and 85; Mesilla Civil Colony Grant, Map File 86; Refugio Civil Colony Grant, Map File 90; and Santa Teresa Grant, Map File 111.

CC. Records of the Museum of New Mexico, Santa Fe, New Mexico

Archives, 2, 128, 253, 410, and 1290.

DD. Records of the General Services Administrator, National Archives, Washington, D.C.

1. *Record Group 60, Year File 9865-92.*

Report of the United States Attorney, dated June 20, 1900, in the Corporation of the Grant of José Manuel Sánchez Baca v. United States.

Report of the United States Attorney, dated June 26, 1900, in Rafaela G. Barela and Ramón Gonzáles v. United States.

Report of the United States Attorney, dated June 21, 1900, in the Incorporation of Mesilla v. United States.

Report of the United States Attorney, dated August 29, 1900, in Pendell v. United States.

Report of the United States Attorney, dated July 29, 1901, in the Colony of Refugio and William Desauer v. United States.

Report of the United States Attorney, dated December 9, 1896, in Numa Reymond *et al* v. United States.

Supplemental Report of the United States Attorney, in Numa Reymond *et al* v. United States.

Report of the United States Attorney, dated August 4, 1903, in Blaza Alvarez de Sánchez *et al* v. United States.

2. *Record Group 76*

Petition in Pueblo de Cenecú v. United States, No. 120.

EE. Records of the Indian Claims Commission

Case

Lipan Apache Tribe v. United States, No. 22-C.

SECONDARY SOURCES

A. Books and Pamphlets

Eleanor B. Adams, *Bishop Tamaron's Visitation of New Mexico, 1760* (Albuquerque, 1954).

Francisco R. Almada, *Diccionario de Historia, Geografía, y Biografía Sonorenses* (Chihuahua, 1952).

Francisco R. Almada, *Resumen de Historia del Estado de Chihuahua* (Mexico, D. F., 1955).

Mrs. Edward E. Ayer, *The Memorial of Fray Alonso de Benevides, 1630* (Chicago, 1916).

Hubert Howe Bancroft, *History of Arizona and New Mexico* (San Francisco, 1889).

Hubert Howe Bancroft, *History of Mexico* (6 Vols., San Francisco, 1885).

Hubert Howe Bancroft, *History of the North Mexican States and Texas* (2 Vols., San Francisco, 1886).

F. C. Baker, *Irrigation in Mesilla Valley, New Mexico, Water Supply and Irrigation Paper No. 10* (Washington, 1898).

John Russell Bartlett, *Personal Narrative of Explorations and Incidents in Texas, New Mexico, California, Sonora, and Chihuahua* (2 Vols., New York, 1854).

Warren B. Beck, *New Mexico, A History of Four Centuries* (Norman, 1962).

Ralph P. Bieber, *Exploring Southwestern Trails* (Glendale, 1936).

William Campbell Binkley, *The Expansionist Movement in Texas* (Berkeley, 1925).

Frank W. Blackmar, *Spanish Institutions of the Southwest* (Baltimore, 1891).

Bernard E. Bobb, *The Viceregency of Antonio María Bucareli* (Austin, 1962).

Herbert O. Brayer, *Pueblo Indian Land Grants of the "Rio Abajo," New Mexico* (Albuquerque, 1938).

Ross Calvin, *Lieutenant Emory Reports* (Albuquerque, 1951).

H. Bailey Carroll and J. Villasana Haggard, *Three New Mexico Chronicles* (Albuquerque, 1942).

Carlos E. Castañeda, *Our Catholic Heritage in Texas* (7 Vols., Austin, 1926).

John C. Ceromony, *Life Among the Apaches* (San Francisco, 1868).

Fray Angelico Chavez, *Origins of New Mexico Families* (Santa Fe, 1954).

Charles F. Coan, *A History of New Mexico* (3 Vols., New York, 1925).

Roscoe P. and Margaret B. Conklin, *The Battlefield Overland Mail* (3 Vols., Glendale, 1947).

William Elsey Connelley, *Doniphan's Expedition* (Topeka, 1907).

Elliott Coues, *The Expedition of Zebulon Montgomery Pike* (3 Vols., New York, 1895).

J. A. de Excudero, *Noticias Estadisticas del Estado de Chihuahua* (Mexico, 1834).

J. Manuel Espinosa, *First Expedition of Vargas Into New Mexico, 1692* (Albuquerque, 1940).

Manrici Garland Fulton, *Diary and Letters of Josiah Gregg — Excursions in Mexico and California, 1847-1850* (Norman, 1944).

Paul Neff Garber, *The Gadsden Treaty* (Gloucester, 1959).

Rex E. Gerald, *Spanish Presidios of the Late Eighteenth Century in Northern New Spain* (Santa Fe, 1968).

William H. Goetzmann, *Army Exploration in the American West* (New Haven, 1959).

George Griggs, *History of Mesilla Valley or The Gadsden Purchase* (Mesilla, 1930).

Charles Wilson Hackett, *Historical Documents Relating to New Mexico, Nueva Vizcaya and Approaches Thereto, to 1773* (3 Vols., Washington, D.C., 1937).

Leroy R. Hafen, *Ruxton of the Rockies* (Norman, 1950).

George P. Hammond and Edward H. Howes, *Overland to California* (Berkeley, 1950).

C. H. Haring, *The Spanish Empire in America* (New York, 1947).

Wallace Hawkins, *El Sal del Rey* (Austin, 1947).

Frederick W. Hodge, *Handbook of American Indians North of Mexico* (2 Vols., New York, 1960).

Anne E. Hughes, *The Beginnings of Spanish Settlements in the El Paso District* (El Paso, 1935).

Lawrence Kinnaird, *The Frontiers of New Spain: Nicolas de Lafara's Description, 1766-1768* (Berkeley, 1958).

William Mack, *Corpus Juris* (76 Vols., New York, 1930).

William M. McKinney, *Texas Jurisprudence* (45 Vols., San Francisco, 1934).

Milo Milton Quaife, *The Personal Narrative of James O. Pattie* (Chicago, 1930).

Milo Milton Quaife, *The Southwestern Expedition of Zebulon Pike* (Chicago, 1925).

Irving Berdine Richman, *California Under Spain and Mexico* (New York, 1911).

George F. Ruxton, *Adventures in Mexico and the Rocky Mountains* (New York, 1848).

Florence Johnson Scott, *Historical Heritage of the Lower Rio Grande Valley* (San Antonio, 1937).

Florence Johnson Scott, *Royal Land Grants North of the Rio Grande, 1777-1821* (Rio Grande City, 1969).

Mrs. O. L. Shipman, *Taming of the Big Bend* (N.P., N.D.).

A. C. Spencer and Sidney Paige, *Geology of the Santa Rita Mining Area, New Mexico* (Washington, D.C., 1935).

Rex Strickland, *W. W. Mills: Forty Years at El Paso* (El Paso, 1962).

Alfred Barnaby Thomas, *Teodoro de Croix and the Northern Frontier of New Spain* (Norman, 1941).

Alfred Barnaby Thomas, *Forgotten Frontier* (Norman, 1932).

Turney, Burges, Culwell & Pollard, *The Texas and New Mexico Boundary Along the Rio Grande Valley Between the 32nd Parallel of North Latitude and the Parallel 31° 47' North Latitude (Latter Parallel Being the International Boundary Line Between the United States and Mexico)* (El Paso, 1930).

Ralph Emerson Twitchell, *The Spanish Archives of New Mexico* (2 Vols., Cedar Rapids, 1914).

Walter Prescott Webb and H. Bailey Carroll, *The Handbook of Texas* (2 Vols., Austin, 1952).

Paul I. Wellman, *The Indian Wars of the West* (Garden City, 1954).

A. Wislizenus, *Memoir of a Tour to Northern Mexico* (Washington, 1848).

B. Articles

Wm. H. H. Allison, "John G. Heath," *New Mexico Historical Review* (1931), VI, 360-375.

Wm. G. B. Carson, "William Carr Lane, Diary," *New Mexico Historical Review* (1964), XXXIX, 181-234.

William A. Duffin, "Overland Via Jackass Mail," *Arizona and the West* (1960), II, 35-53; 147-164; 279-292; 353-370.

John Ernest Grigg, "The History of Presidio County," *Voice of the Mexican Border, Centennial Edition, 1936,* 16 ff.

Henry W. Kelly, "Franciscan Missions of New Mexico, 1740-1760," *New Mexico Historical Review* (1940), XV, 345-368.

J. Charles Kelly, "The Historic Indian Pueblos of La Junta de Los Rios," *New Mexico Historical Review* (1953) XXVIII, 21-51.

Mario Lozano, "Commentary on Ordinances Related to Spanish and Mexican Grants," *Report of the Eighth Annual Texas Surveyor's Association Short Course* (1959), 61-73.

Fidelia Miller Puckett, "Ramon Ortiz: Priest and Patriot," *New Mexico Historical Review* (1950), XXV, 265-295.

John M. Sully, "The Story of the Santa Rita Mine," *Old Santa Fe* (1916), III, 138-150.

M. H. Thomlinson, "Forgotten Fort," *The New Mexico Magazine* (1943), XXIII, 39-41.

Robert G. West, "Validity of Certain Spanish Land Grants in Texas," *Texas Law Review* (1924), II, 435-444.

C. Thesis and Seminar Papers

Dale Collins, *Frontier Mining Days in Southwestern New Mexico* (Mss., Master's Thesis, Texas Western College, El Paso, Texas).

Queen M. Gary, *Brief History of the Lone Star School* (Mss., History Seminar Paper, Texas Western College, El Paso, Texas).

Nancy Lee Hammos, *A History of El Paso County, Texas, to 1900,* (Mss., Master's Thesis, Texas Western College, El Paso, Texas).

Grace Long, *The Anglo-American Occupation of the El Paso District* (Mss., Master's Thesis, University of Texas, Austin, Texas, 1931).

Mandi Elizabeth McFie, *A History of the Mesilla Valley* (Mss., Bachelor's Thesis, New Mexico A.&M. College, Las Cruces, New Mexico, 1903).

Vina Walz, *History of the El Paso Area, 1680-1692* (Mss., Doctoral Dissertation, University of New Mexico, 1951).

Katherine H. White, *The Pueblo de Socorro Grant* (Mss., Master's Thesis, Texas Western College, El Paso, Texas).

INDEX